D0977302

POEMS THAT LIVE FOREVER

Selected by Hazel Felleman

THE BEST LOVED POEMS OF THE AMERICAN PEOPLE

POEMS THAT LIVE FOREVER

POEMS
THAT LIVE
FOREVER

Selected by

HAZEL FELLEMAN

DOUBLEDAY
NEW YORK LONDON TORONTO SYDNEY AUCKLAND

PUBLISHED BY DOUBLEDAY
a division of Bantam Doubleday Dell Publishing
Group, Inc., 1540 Broadway, New York, New York 10036

DOUBLEDAY and the portrayal of an anchor with a dolphin
are trademarks of Doubleday, a division of Bantam Doubleday
Dell Publishing Group, Inc.

ISBN 0-385-00358-7
Library of Congress Catalog Card Number 65-13987
Copyright © 1965 by Doubleday, a division of
Bantam Doubleday Dell Publishing Group, Inc.
ALL RIGHTS RESERVED   PRINTED IN THE UNITED STATES OF AMERICA
40   39   38   37

ACKNOWLEDGMENTS: The editor wishes to express her thanks to the following publishers, authors, or authorized representatives, for their kind permission to reprint poems copyrighted or controlled by them:

APPLETON-CENTURY for "Around the Corner" from *Selected Poems of Charles Hanson Towne* (1925).

A. S. BARNES & COMPANY, INC., for "Alumnus Football" from *The Final Answer and Other Poems* by Grantland Rice, selected by John Kieran, copyright © 1955 by A. S. Barnes & Company, Inc.

THE BOBBS-MERRILL COMPANY, INC., for "The Kid Has Gone to the Colors" from the book of the same name by William Herschell, copyright 1917 by The Bobbs-Merrill Company, 1945 by Mrs. William Herschell; "A Life-Lesson" from *The Complete Poems of James Whitcomb Riley*; "When the Frost Is on the Punkin" from *Joyful Poems for Children* by James Whitcomb Riley.

BRANDT & BRANDT for "Jack Ellyat Heard the Guns" from *John Brown's Body* by Stephen Vincent Benét, copyright 1927, 1928 by Stephen Vincent Benét.

MARGARET E. BRUNER for "Epitaph for a Cat" from *Mysteries of Earth* (1934) by Margaret E. Bruner; "Whom the Gods Love" from *The Constant Heart* by Margaret E. Bruner.

GEORGE M. COHAN PUBLISHING Co., INC., for "Life's a Funny Proposition After All," words and music by George M. Cohan.

ROSICA COLIN LIMITED and MADAME CATHERINE GUILLAUME, nee Aldington, for "Lesbia" by Richard Aldington.

COWARD-McCANN, INC., for excerpts from *The White Cliffs* by Alice Duer Miller, copyright 1940 by Alice Duer Miller.

CURTIS BROWN, LTD., and J. M. DENT & SONS, LTD., for "Peekaboo, I Almost See You" from *The Private Dining Room and Other New Verses* by Ogden Nash, copyright 1949 by The Curtis Publishing Company.

J. M. DENT & SONS, LTD., for "A Little Dog-Angel" from *Spun-Yarn and Spindrift* by Norah Holland.

DODD, MEAD & COMPANY, McCLELLAND & STEWART, LTD., and SIDGWICK & JACKSON, LTD., for "Day that I Have Loved," "Sonnet V" (The Soldier) from *The Collected Poems of Rupert Brooke*, copyright 1915 by Dodd, Mead & Company, copyright 1943 by Edward Marsh.

DODD, MEAD & COMPANY for "Accountability," "Dawn," "A Death Song," "The Old Cabin," and "Howdy, Honey, Howdy!" from *The Complete Poems of Paul Laurence Dunbar*, copyright 1913 by Dodd, Mead &

Company; "Walking at Night" from *Tossed Coins* by Amory Hare, copyright 1920 by Dodd, Mead & Company; "For This Is Wisdom" from *India's Love Lyrics* by Laurence Hope, copyright 1902, 1929 by Dodd, Mead & Company; "Work: A Song of Triumph" from *The Hour Has Struck* by Angela Morgan, copyright 1914 by Angela Morgan.

DODD, MEAD & COMPANY, ERNEST BENN, LTD., and RYERSON PRESS for "The Cremation of Sam McGee" and "The Shooting of Dan McGrew" from *The Complete Poems of Robert Service.*

DOUBLEDAY & COMPANY, INC., for "Reverie" from *Noah an' Jonah an' Cap'n John Smith* by Don Marquis, copyright 1921 by D. Appleton & Company; "Noah an' Jonah an' Cap'n John Smith" from the book of the same name by Don Marquis, copyright 1913 by Sun Printing & Publishing Assn. and "Only Thy Dust" from *The Awakening and Other Poems* (1915) by Don Marquis; "Roofs" from *Joyce Kilmer: Poems, Essays and Letters, Volume I,* copyright 1915 by Current Literature Publishing Co.

DOUBLEDAY & COMPANY, INC., Mrs. George Bambridge, Methuen & Co., Ltd., and The Macmillan Company of Canada, Limited, for "Danny Deever" from *Barrack Room Ballads* by Rudyard Kipling.

E. P. DUTTON & Co., INC., for "Of Certain Irish Fairies" from *Lyric Laughter* by Arthur Guiterman, copyright 1939, by E. P. Dutton & Co., Inc.; "Soap, the Oppressor" from *Youngsters* by Burges Johnson, copyright 1921 by E. P. Dutton & Co., Inc., copyright renewed 1949 by Burges Johnson; "The Complacent Cliff-Dweller" and "Sitting Pretty" from *One to a Customer* by Margaret Fishback, copyright 1933 by E. P. Dutton & Co., Inc., copyright renewed © 1961 by Margaret Fishback Antolini.

E. P. DUTTON & Co., INC., and JOHN MURRAY, LTD., for "The Spires of Oxford" and "To Scott" from *The Spires of Oxford* by Winifred M. Letts, copyright 1917 by E. P. Dutton & Co., Inc., copyright renewed 1945 by Winifred M. Letts.

E. P. DUTTON & Co., INC., J. M. DENT & SONS, LTD., and the Estate of G. K. Chesterton for "The Donkey" from *The Wild Knight and Other Poems* by G. K. Chesterton.

MRS. NORMA MILLAY ELLIS for "And You As Well Must Die, Beloved Dust" and "First Fig" from *Collected Poems* by Edna St. Vincent Millay.

GOOD HOUSEKEEPING for "Understanding" by Pauline E. Soroka from *Good Housekeeping* (November 1938), copyright 1938 by The Hearst Corporation.

HARCOURT, BRACE & WORLD, INC., for "Threes" from *Smoke and Steel* by Carl Sandburg, copyright 1920 by Harcourt, Brace & World, Inc., copyright 1948 by Carl Sandburg; "Prayer for This House" by Louis Untermeyer, from *This Singing World,* by Louis Untermeyer, copyright 1923 by Harcourt, Brace & World, Inc., copyright by Louis Untermeyer.

HARCOURT, BRACE & WORLD, INC., and FABER & FABER, LTD., for "Exeunt" from *Things of This World,* copyright © 1956 by Richard Wilbur.

HARPER & ROW, PUBLISHERS, INCORPORATED, for "Whisperin' Bill" from *In Various Moods* by Irving Bacheller, copyright 1910, 1938 by Irving Bacheller; "Quiet Things" from *Songs of Hope* by Grace Noll Crowell, copyright by Harper & Brothers 1938; "Youth Sings a Song of Rosebuds" from *Copper Sun* by Countee Cullen, copyright 1927 by Harper & Brothers, copyright renewed © 1955 by Ida M. Cullen; "Fruit of the Flower" and "Judas Iscariot" from *Color* by Countee Cullen, copyright 1925 by Harper & Brothers, copyright renewed 1953 by Ida M. Cullen; "Epitaph" by Robert Richardson from *Mark Twain, A Biography* by Albert Bigelow Paine.

HARPER & ROW, PUBLISHERS, INCORPORATED, and BRANDT & BRANDT for "The Road to Vagabondia" from *Poems* by Dana Burnet, copyright 1915 by Harper & Brothers, copyright renewed 1943 by Dana Burnet.

HOLT, RINEHART AND WINSTON, INC., for "As in a Rose-Jar" from *Shadow of the Perfect Rose* by Thomas S. Jones, Jr., copyright 1937 by John L. Foley.

HOLT, RINEHART AND WINSTON, INC., Jonathan Cape, Limited and Laurence Pollinger, Limited, for "Acquainted with the Night," "Birches," "The Cow in Apple Time," "My November Guest," and "The Road Not Taken" from *Complete Poems of Robert Frost*, copyright 1916, 1921, 1928, 1934 by Holt, Rinehart and Winston, Inc., copyright renewed 1944, © 1956, © 1962 by Robert Frost; "Cool Tombs," "Grass," "Horses and Men in the Rain," from *Cornhuskers* by Carl Sandburg, copyright 1918 by Holt, Rinehart and Winston, Inc., copyright renewed 1946 by Carl Sandburg.

HOLT, RINEHART & WINSTON, INC., The Society of Authors, Literary Representative of the Estate of the late A. E. Housman, and Jonathan Cape, Ltd., for "Here Dead Lie We" from *Complete Poems* by A. E. Housman, copyright 1936 by Barclays Bank, Ltd., copyright renewed © 1964 by Robert E. Symons; "Loveliest of Trees," "Reveille," and "When I Was One-and-Twenty" from "A Shropshire Lad"—Authorized Edition —from *Complete Poems* by A. E. Housman, copyright © 1959 by Holt, Rinehart and Winston, Inc.

HOUGHTON MIFFLIN COMPANY for "A Charleston Garden" by Henry Bellaman; "Ballad of the Tempest" by James Thomas Fields; "Prelude" from *The New Day* by Richard Watson Gilder; "Her Letter" by Bret Harte; "The Deacon's Masterpiece, or the Wonderful 'One-Hoss Shay' " by Oliver Wendell Holmes; "To a Friend" by Amy Lowell; "Early Rising" and "Rhyme of the Rails" by John Godfrey Saxe; "The Fool's Prayer" by Edward Rowland; "Darius Green and His Flying-Machine" by John Townsend Trowbridge.

BRUCE HUMPHRIES, PUBLISHERS, for "The House of Falling Leaves We Entered in" from *The House of Falling Leaves* by William Stanley Braithwaite.

J. P. KENEDY & SONS for "A Builder's Lesson" by John Boyle O'Reilly from *Selected Poems* (1913).

JOHN G. KIDD & SON, INC., for "The Woman Who Understands" from *The Quiet Courage* by Everard Jack Appleton.

ALFRED A. KNOPF, INC., for "Do Not Weep, Maiden, for War Is Kind" from *Collected Poems of Stephen Crane* (1930); "Of Love" from *The Prophet* by Kahlil Gibran, copyright 1923 by Kahlil Gibran, copyright renewed 1951 by Administrators C. T. P. of Kahlil Gibran Estate, and Mary G. Gibran; "I, Too, Sing America," "Cross" from *Selected Poems* by Langston Hughes, copyright 1926 by Alfred A. Knopf, Inc., copy-

right renewed 1954 by Langston Hughes; "Epitaph in Sirmio" from
Poems by David Morton, copyright 1944 by David Morton.

J. B. LIPPINCOTT COMPANY for "To a Post-Office Inkwell" from *Poems* by
Christopher Morley, copyright 1919, 1947 by Christopher Morley;
"Washing the Dishes" from *Poems* by Christopher Morley, copyright
1917, 1945 by Christopher Morley.

J. B. LIPPINCOTT COMPANY and HUGH NOYES for "The Highwayman," "A
Victory Dance" (The Victory Ball) from *Collected Poems of Alfred
Noyes*, copyright 1906, 1934 by Alfred Noyes.

LITTLE, BROWN AND COMPANY and J. M. DENT & SONS, LTD., for "I Never
Even Suggested It" by Ogden Nash, copyright 1940 by The Curtis
Publishing Company; "So That's Who I Remind Me of" by Ogden
Nash, copyright 1942 by Ogden Nash, originally appeared the *The New
Yorker*; "Very Like a Whale" by Ogden Nash, copyright 1934 by The
Curtis Publishing Company.

LITTLE, BROWN AND COMPANY for "A Bird Came Down the Walk,"
"Chartless," "If I Can Stop One Heart from Breaking," "I've Seen a
Dying Eye," "The Morning after Death," "A Narrow Fellow in the
Grass," "No Time to Hate," and "There Is No Frigate Like a Book"
from *The Complete Poems of Emily Dickinson*.

LOTHROP, LEE & SHEPHARD COMPANY for "The Man from the Crowd,"
"The Calf-Path" by Sam Walter Foss.

THE MACMILLAN COMPANY for "A Net to Snare the Moonlight" from
Collected Poems by Vachel Lindsay, copyright 1913 by The Macmillan
Company.

THE MACMILLAN COMPANY, THE SOCIETY OF AUTHORS and DR. JOHN
MASEFIELD, O.M., for "On Growing Old" from *Collected Poems* by
John Masefield, copyright 1920, 1948 by John Masefield; "Sea Fever"
from *Collected Poems* by John Masefield, copyright 1912 by The Mac-
millan Company, copyright renewed 1940 by John Masefield.

THE MACMILLAN COMPANY, A. P. WATT & SON, and MRS. WILLIAM BUTLER
YEATS for "When You Are Old," copyright 1906 by The Macmillan
Company, copyright renewed 1934 by William Butler Yeats; and "A
Prayer for my Daughter," copyright 1924 by The Macmillan Company,
copyright renewed 1952 by Bertha Georgie Yeats; both from *Collected
Poems* by William Butler Yeats.

VIRGIL MARKHAM for "The Forgotten Man," "Victory in Defeat" by Edwin
Markham.

HUGH MEARNS for "Antigonish" by Hugh Mearns.

NEW DIRECTIONS, J. M. DENT & SONS, LTD., and Trustees of the Dylan
Thomas Estate for "Fern Hill" from *The Collected Poems of Dylan
Thomas*, copyright 1953 by Dylan Thomas, © 1957 by New Directions.

W. W. NORTON & COMPANY, INC., for "To My Dear and Loving Husband"
from *The American Tradition in Literature*, revised by Bradley, Beatty,
and Long, Editors, copyright © 1956, 1957, 1961 by W. W. Norton &
Company, Inc., New York, N.Y.

MISS THEO OXENHAM for "The Sacrament of Sleep" from *Selected Poems
of John Oxenham*.

A. D. PETERS for "They Say that in the Unchanging Place" from *Dedica-
tory Ode* by Hilaire Belloc.

G. P. PUTNAM'S SONS for "Dreamer of Dreams" by William Herbert Carruth
from *Each in His Own Tongue and Other Poems*, copyright 1909 by

William Herbert Carruth, copyright renewed 1936 by Katherine M. Carruth; "A Ballad in 'G'," and "Whist" from *The Rhymes of Ironquill* by Eugene F. Ware, copyright 1902, 1939 by G. P. Putnam's Sons.

RAND McNALLY & COMPANY for "My Ships" and "Solitude" by Ella Wheeler Wilcox.

THE REILLY & LEE COMPANY for "Becoming a Dad" and "Out Fishin'" from *Collected Verse* by Edgar A. Guest.

RUST CRAFT GREETING CARDS, INC., for "A Friend or Two" by Wilbur D. Nesbit.

CHARLES SCRIBNER'S SONS for "A Ballad of Trees and the Master" from *Poems* by Sidney Lanier; "Miniver Cheevy" and "Richard Cory" from *The Town Down the River and The Children of the Night* by Edwin Arlington Robinson; "Four Things" from *The Poems of Henry Van Dyke*.

CHARLES SCRIBNER'S SONS and WILLIAM HEINEMANN LTD., for "One, Two, Three!" from *Poems* by Henry Cuyler Bunner; "So Might It Be" and "Peace in the World" from *The Collected Poems of John Galsworthy*, copyright 1934 by Charles Scribner's Sons, copyright renewed © 1962.

ORA SEARLE for "I Heard a Bird Sing" by Oliver Herford.

THE VIKING PRESS, INC., for "On Being a Woman" from *The Portable Dorothy Parker*, copyright 1928, 1955 by Dorothy Parker.

THE VIKING PRESS, INC., and BRANDT & BRANDT for "Down the Glimmering Staircase" from *Collected Poems* by Siegfried Sassoon, copyright 1936 by Siegfried Sassoon.

THE VIKING PRESS, INC., and SIEGFRIED SASSOON for "Brevities" from *Collected Poems* by Siegfried Sassoon, copyright 1936 by Siegfried Sassoon.

A. P. WATT & SON and MISS D. E. COLLINS for "A Prayer in Darkness" by G. K. Chesterton.

MISS ANN WOLFE for "Autumn" from *Humoresque* by Humbert Wolfe.

INTRODUCTION

In compiling this book, I have chosen poems that have been like companions for many years. They are old friends to me though they range from the sublime to the most ridiculous.

Like my earlier volume, *The Best Loved Poems of the American People*, this anthology contains more favorite poems, both old and new, suitable for the enjoyment of the family.

There are poems of history, religion, love, sentiment, humor, friendship and others that serve to inspire, entertain, and, in time of need, to comfort. They bring back memories of childhood days and recreate scenes that have grown dim through the passing years.

In this potpourri of favorite poems (with a few prose selections) there should be something for the enjoyment of everyone.

HAZEL FELLEMAN
Editor, Queries & Answers page of The New York Times Book Review until 1950

CONTENTS

I. STORIES AND BALLADS

III. FRIENDSHIP

IX. REFLECTION AND CONTEMPLATION

XI. NATURE'S PEOPLE

Contents

XIV. FAMILIAR AND VARIED THEMES

I. Stories and Ballads

THE CALF-PATH

One day, through the primeval wood,
A calf walked home, as good calves should;
But made a trail all bent askew,
A crooked trail as all calves do.

Since then two hundred years have fled,
And, I infer, the calf is dead.
But still he left behind his trail,
And thereby hangs my moral tale.

The trail was taken up next day
By a lone dog that passed that way;
And then a wise bell-wether sheep
Pursued the trail o'er vale and steep,
And drew the flock behind him, too,
As good bell-wethers always do.

And from that day, o'er hill and glade,
Through those old woods a path was made;
And many men wound in and out,
And dodged, and turned, and bent about
And uttered words of righteous wrath
Because 'twas such a crooked path.
But still they followed—do not laugh—
The first migrations of that calf,
And through this winding wood-way stalked,
Because he wobbled when he walked.

This forest path became a lane,
That bent, and turned, and turned again;
This crooked lane became a road,
Where many a poor horse with his load
Toiled on beneath the burning sun,
And traveled some three miles in one.
And thus a century and a half
They trod the footsteps of that calf.

The years passed on in swiftness fleet,
The road became a village street;
And this, before men were aware,
A city's crowded thoroughfare;
And soon the central street was this
Of a renowned metropolis;
And men two centuries and a half
Trod in the footsteps of that calf.

Each day a hundred thousand rout
Followed the zigzag calf about;
And o'er his crooked journey went
The traffic of a continent.
A hundred thousand men were led
By one calf near three centuries dead.
They followed still his crooked way,
And lost one hundred years a day;
For thus such reverence is lent
To well-established precedent.

A moral lesson this might teach,
Were I ordained and called to preach;
For men are prone to go it blind
Along the calf-paths of the mind,
And work away from sun to sun
To do what other men have done.
They follow in the beaten track,
And out and in, and forth and back,
And still their devious course pursue,
To keep the path that others do.

But how the wise old wood-gods laugh,
Who saw the first primeval calf!
Ah! many things this tale might teach—
But I am not ordained to preach.

SAM WALTER FOSS

THE MAIN-TRUCK; OR A LEAP FOR LIFE

Old Ironsides at anchor lay,
  In the harbor of Mahon;
A dead calm rested on the bay—
  The waves to sleep had gone;
When little Jack, the captain's son,
  With gallant hardihood,
Climb'd shroud and spar—and then upon
  The main-truck rose and stood!

A shudder shot through every vein—
  All eyes were turn'd on high!
There stood the boy, with dizzy brain,
  Between the sea and sky!
No hold had he above—below.
  Alone he stood in air!
At that far height none dared to go—
  No aid could reach him there.

We gazed—but not a man could speak!—
  With horror all aghast
In groups, with pallid brow and cheek,
  We watch'd the quivering mast.
The atmosphere grew thick and hot,
  And of a lurid hue,
As, riveted unto the spot,
  Stood officers and crew.

THE FATHER CAME ON DECK!—He gasp'd,
  "O God, thy will be done!"
Then suddenly a rifle grasp'd,
  And aimed it at his son!
"Jump—far out, into the wave,
  Jump, or I fire," he said:
"That only chance your life can save!
  Jump—jump, boy!"—He obey'd.

He sunk—he rose—he lived—he moved—
  He for the ship struck out!

On board we hail'd the lad beloved,
   With many a manly shout,
His father drew, in silent joy,
   Those wet arms round his neck,
Then folded to his heart his boy,
   And fainted on the deck.

GEORGE P. MORRIS

THE CREMATION OF SAM MCGEE

There are strange things done in the midnight sun
By the men who moil for gold;
The Arctic trails have their secret tales
That would make your blood run cold;
The Northern Lights have seen queer sights,
But the queerest they ever did see
Was the night on the marge of Lake Lebarge
I cremated Sam McGee.

Now Sam McGee was from Tennessee, where the cotton blooms and blows,
Why he left his home in the South to roam 'round the Pole, God only knows.
He was always cold, but the land of gold seemed to hold him like a spell;
Though he'd often say in his homely way that "he'd sooner live in hell."

On a Christmas day we were mushing our way over the Dawson trail.
Talk of your cold! through the parka's fold it stabbed like a driven nail.
If our eyes we'd close, then the lashes froze till sometimes we couldn't see;
It wasn't much fun, but the only one to whimper was Sam McGee.

And that very night, as we lay packed tight in our robes beneath the snow,
And the dogs were fed, and the stars o'erhead were dancing heel and toe,

He turned to me, and "Cap," says he, "I'll cash in this trip, I guess;
And if I do, I'm asking that you won't refuse my last request."

Well, he seemed so low that I couldn't say no; then he says with a
   sort of moan:
"It's the cursed cold, and it's got right hold till I'm chilled clean
   through to the bone.
Yet 'tain't being dead—it's my awful dread of the icy grave that
   pains;
So I want you to swear that, foul or fair, you'll cremate my last
   remains."

A pal's last need is a thing to heed, so I swore I would not fail;
And we started on at the streak of dawn; but God! he looked ghastly
   pale.
He crouched on the sleigh, and he raved all day of his home in
   Tennessee;
And before nightfall a corpse was all that was left of Sam McGee.

There wasn't a breath in that land of death, and I hurried, horror-
   driven,
With a corpse half hid that I couldn't get rid, because of a promise
   given;
It was lashed to the sleigh, and it seemed to say: "You may tax
   your brawn and brains,
But you promised true, and it's up to you to cremate these last
   remains."

Now a promise made is a debt unpaid, and the trail has its own
   stern code.
In the days to come, though my lips were dumb, in my heart how
   I cursed that load.
In the long, long night, by the lone firelight, while the huskies,
   round in a ring,
Howled out their woes to the homeless snows—O God! how I
   loathed the thing.

And every day that quiet clay seemed to heavy and heavier grow;
And on I went, though the dogs were spent and the grub was getting
   low;
The trail was bad, and I felt half mad, but I swore I would not give
   in;

And I'd often sing to the hateful thing, and it hearkened with a grin.

Till I came to the marge of Lake Lebarge, and a derelict there lay;
It was jammed in the ice, but I saw in a trice it was called the "Alice May."
And I looked at it, and I thought a bit, and I looked at my frozen chum;
Then "Here," said I, with a sudden cry, "is my cre-ma-to-re-um."

Some planks I tore from the cabin floor, and I lit the boiler fire;
Some coal I found that was lying around, and I heaped the fuel higher;
The flames just soared, and the furnace roared—such a blaze you seldom see;
And I burrowed a hole in the glowing coal, and I stuffed in Sam McGee.

Then I made a hike, for I didn't like to hear him sizzle so;
And the heavens scowled, and the huskies howled, and the wind began to blow.
It was icy cold, but the hot sweat rolled down my cheeks, and I don't know why;
And the greasy smoke in an inky cloak went streaking down the sky.

I do not know how long in the snow I wrestled with grisly fear;
But the stars came out and they danced about ere again I ventured near;
I was sick with dread, but I bravely said: "I'll just take a peep inside.
I guess he's cooked, and it's time I looked," . . . then the door I opened wide.

And there sat Sam, looking cold and calm, in the heart of the furnace roar;
And he wore a smile you could see a mile, and he said: "Please close that door.
It's fine in here, but I greatly fear you'll let in the cold and storm—
Since I left Plumtree down in Tennessee, it's the first time I've been warm."

There are strange things done in the midnight sun
By the men who moil for gold;

The Arctic trails have their secret tales
That would make your blood run cold;
The Northern Lights have seen queer sights,
But the queerest they ever did see
Was that night on the marge of Lake Lebarge
I cremated Sam McGee!

ROBERT W. SERVICE

THE SHOOTING OF DAN MCGREW

A bunch of the boys were whooping it up in the Malamute saloon;
The kid that handles the music-box was hitting a jag-time tune;
Back of the bar, in a solo game, sat Dangerous Dan McGrew;
And watching his luck was his light-o'-love, the lady that's known
as Lou.

When out of the night, which was fifty below, and into the din
and the glare,
There stumbled a miner fresh from the creeks, dog-dirty, and loaded
for bear.
He looked like a man with a foot in the grave and scarcely the
strength of a louse,
Yet he tilted a poke of dust on the bar, and he called for drinks for
the house.
There was none could place the stranger's face, though we searched
ourselves for a clue;
But we drank his health, and the last to drink was Dangerous Dan
McGrew.

There's men that somehow just grip your eyes, and hold them hard
like a spell;
And such was he, and he looked to me like a man who had lived in
hell;
With a face most hair, and the dreary stare of a dog whose day is
done,
As he watered the green stuff in his glass, and the drops fell one by
one.
Then I got to figgering who he was, and wondering what he'd do,
And I turned my head—and there watching him was the lady that's
known as Lou.

His eyes went rubbering round the room, and he seemed in a kind
   of daze,
Till at last that old piano fell in the way of his wandering gaze.
The rag-time kid was having a drink; there was no one else on the
   stool,
So the stranger stumbles across the room, and flops down there like
   a fool.
In a buckskin shirt that was glazed with dirt he sat, and I saw him
   sway;
Then he clutched the keys with his talon hands—my God! but that
   man could play.

Were you ever out in the Great Alone, when the moon was awful
   clear,
And the icy mountains hemmed you in with a silence you most could
   hear;
With only the howl of a timber wolf, and you camped there in the
   cold,
A half-dead thing in a stark, dead world, clean mad for the muck
   called gold;
While high overhead, green, yellow and red, the North Lights swept
   in bars?—
Then you've a hunch what the music meant . . . hunger and night
   and the stars.

And hunger not of the belly kind, that's banished with bacon and
   beans,
But the gnawing hunger of lonely men for a home and all that it
   means;
For a fireside far from the cares that are, four walls and a roof above;
But oh! so cramful of cosy joy, and crowned with a woman's love—
A woman dearer than all the world, and true as Heaven is true—
(God! how ghastly she looks through her rouge—the lady that's
   known as Lou.)

Then on a sudden the music changed, so soft that you scarce could
   hear;
But you felt that your life had been looted clean of all that it once
   held dear;
That someone had stolen the woman you loved; that her love was a
   devil's lie;

That your guts were gone, and the best for you was to crawl away
and die.

'Twas the crowning cry of a heart's despair, and it thrilled you
through and through—

"I guess I'll make it a spread misère," said Dangerous Dan McGrew.

The music almost died away . . . then it burst like a pent-up flood;

And it seemed to say, "Repay, repay," and my eyes were blind with
blood.

The thought came back of an ancient wrong, and it stung like a
frozen lash,

And the lust awoke, to kill, to kill . . . then the music stopped with
a crash,

And the stranger turned, and his eyes they burned in a most peculiar
way;

In a buckskin shirt that was glazed with dirt he sat, and I saw him
sway;

Then his lips went in in a kind of grin, and he spoke, and his voice
was calm,

And "Boys," says he, "you don't know me, and none of you care a
damn;

But I want to state, and my words are straight, and I'll bet my poke
they're true,

That one of you is a hound in hell . . . and that one is Dan
McGrew."

Then I ducked my head, and the lights went out, and two guns
blazed in the dark,

And a woman screamed, and the lights went up, and two men lay
stiff and stark.

Pitched on his head, and pumped full of lead, was Dangerous Dan
McGrew,

While the man from the creeks lay clutched to the breast of the lady
that's known as Lou.

These are the simple facts of the case, and I guess I ought to know.

They say that the stranger was crazed with "hooch," and I'm not
denying it's so.

I'm not so wise as the lawyer guys, but strictly between us two—

The woman that kissed him and—pinched his poke—was the lady
that's known as Lou.

ROBERT W. SERVICE

ONE, TWO, THREE!

It was an old, old, old, old lady,
  And a boy that was half-past three;
And the way that they played together
  Was beautiful to see.

She couldn't go running and jumping,
  And the boy, no more could he;
For he was a thin little fellow,
  With a thin little twisted knee.

They sat in the yellow sunlight,
  Out under the maple tree;
And the game that they played I'll tell you,
  Just as it was told to me.

It was Hide-and-Go-Seek they were playing,
  Though you'd never have known it to be—
With an old, old, old, old lady,
  And a boy with a twisted knee.

The boy would bend his face down
  On his one little sound right knee,
And he'd guess where she was hiding,
  In guesses One, Two, Three!

"You are in the china-closet!"
  He would cry, and laugh with glee—
It wasn't the china closet,
  But he still had Two and Three.

"You are up in papa's big bedroom,
  In the chest with the queer old key!"
And she said: "You are *warm* and *warmer*;
  But you're not quite right," said she.

"It can't be the little cupboard
  Where mamma's things used to be—

So it must be the clothes-press, Gran'ma!"
And he found her with his Three.

Then she covered her face with her fingers,
    That were wrinkled and white and wee,
And she guessed where the boy was hiding,
    With a One and a Two and a Three.

And they never had stirred from their places,
    Right under the maple tree—
This old, old, old, old lady
    And the boy with the lame little knee—
This dear, dear, dear old lady,
    And the boy who was half-past three.

                          HENRY CUYLER BUNNER

GINEVRA

If thou shouldst ever come by choice or chance
To Modena, where still religiously
Among her ancient trophies is preserved
Bologna's bucket (in its chain it hangs
Within that reverend tower, the Guirlandine),
Stop at a palace near the Reggio gate,
Dwelt in of old by one of the Orsini.
Its noble gardens, terrace above terrace,
And rich in fountains, statues, cypresses,
Will long detain thee; through their arched walks,
Dim at noonday, discovering many a glimpse
Of knights and dames such as in old romance,
And lovers such as in heroic song—
Perhaps the two, for groves were their delight,
That in the spring-time, as alone they sat,
Venturing together on a tale of love,
Read only part that day.—A summer sun
Sets ere one-half is seen; but, ere thou go,
Enter the house—prithee, forget it not—
And look awhile upon a picture there.

'Tis of a lady in her earliest youth,
The very last of that illustrious race,
Done by Zampieri—but by whom I care not.
He who observes it, ere he passes on,
Gazes his fill, and comes and comes again,
That he may call it up when far away.

She sits, inclining forward as to speak,
Her lips half-open, and her finger up,
As though she said "Beware!" her vest of gold
Broidered with flowers, and clasped from head to foot,
An emerald stone in every golden clasp;
And on her brow, fairer than alabaster,
A coronet of pearls. But then her face,
So lovely, yet so arch, so full of mirth,
The overflowings of an innocent heart—
It haunts me still, though many a year has fled,
Like some wild melody!

Alone it hangs
Over a mouldering heirloom, its companion,
An oaken chest, half-eaten by the worm,
But richly carved by Antony of Trent
With scripture-stories from the life of Christ;
A chest that came from Venice, and had held
The ducal robes of some old ancestor.
That by the way—it may be true or false—
But don't forget the picture; and thou wilt not,
When thou hast heard the tale they told me there.

She was an only child; from infancy
The joy, the pride, of an indulgent sire.
Her mother dying of the gift she gave,
That precious gift, what else remained to him?
The young Ginevra was his all in life,
Still as she grew, forever in his sight;
And in her fifteenth year became a bride,
Marrying an only son, Francesco Doria,
Her playmate from her birth, and her first love.

Just as she looks there in her bridal dress,
She was all gentleness, all gayety,

Her pranks the favorite theme of every tongue.
But now the day was come, the day, the hour;
Now, frowning, smiling, for the hundredth time,
The nurse, that ancient lady, preached decorum;
And, in the lustre of her youth, she gave
Her hand, with her heart in it, to Francesco.

Great was the joy; but at the bridal feast,
When all sat down, the bride was wanting there.
Nor was she to be found! Her father cried,
" 'Tis but to make a trial of our love!"
And filled his glass to all; but his hand shook,
And soon from guest to guest the panic spread.
'Twas but that instant she had left Francesco,
Laughing and looking back and flying still,
Her ivory tooth imprinted on his finger.
But now, alas! she was not to be found;
Nor from that hour could anything be guessed
But that she was not!

Weary of his life,
Francesco flew to Venice, and forthwith
Flung it away in battle with the Turk.
Orsini lived; and long was to be seen
An old man wandering as in quest of something,
Something he could not find—he knew not what.
When he was gone, the house remained a while
Silent and tenantless—then went to strangers.

Full fifty years were past, and all forgot,
When on an idle day, a day of search
'Mid the old lumber in the gallery,
That mouldering chest was noticed; and 'twas said
By one as young, as thoughtless as Ginevra,
"Why not remove it from its lurking-place?"

'Twas done as soon as said; but on the way
It burst, it fell; and, lo! a skeleton,
With here and there a pearl, an emerald stone,
A golden clasp, clasping a shred of gold.
All else had perished—save a nuptial ring,
And a small seal, her mother's legacy,

Engraven with a name, the name of both,
"Ginevra."—There, then, had she found a grave!
Within that chest had she concealed herself,
Fluttering with joy, the happiest of the happy;
When a spring-lock, that lay in ambush there,
Fastened her down forever!

SAMUEL ROGERS

THE HIGHWAYMAN

PART I

The wind was a torrent of darkness among the gusty trees,
The moon was a ghostly galleon tossed upon cloudy seas,
The road was a ribbon of moonlight over the purple moor,
And the highwayman came riding—
    Riding—riding—
The highwayman came riding, up to the old inn-door.

He'd a French cocked-hat on his forehead, a bunch of lace at his
    chin,
A coat of the claret velvet, and breeches of brown doe-skin;
They fitted with never a wrinkle: his boots were up to the thigh!
And he rode with a jeweled twinkle,
    His pistol butts a-twinkle,
His rapier hilt a-twinkle, under the jeweled sky.

Over the cobbles he clattered and clashed in the dark inn-yard,
And he tapped with his whip on the shutters, but all was locked
    and barred;
He whistled a tune to the window, and who should be waiting
    there
But the landlord's black-eyed daughter,
    Bess, the landlord's daughter,
Plaiting a dark red love-knot into her long black hair.

And dark in the dark old inn-yard a stable-wicket creaked
Where Tim the ostler listened; his face was white and peaked;
His eyes were hollows of madness, his hair like moldy hay,
But he loved the landlord's daughter,
    The landlord's red-lipped daughter,
Dumb as a dog he listened, and he heard the robber say—

"One kiss, my bonny sweetheart, I'm after a prize to-night,
But I shall be back with the yellow gold before the morning light;
Yet, if they press me sharply, and harry me through the day,
Then look for me by moonlight,
    Watch for me by moonlight,
I'll come to thee by moonlight, though hell should bar the way."

He rose upright in the stirrups; he scarce could reach her hand,
But she loosened her hair i' the casement! His face burnt like a
    brand
As the black cascade of perfume came tumbling over his breast;
And he kissed its waves in the moonlight,
    (Oh, sweet black waves in the moonlight!)
Then he tugged at his rein in the moonlight, and galloped away to
    the West.

PART II

He did not come in the dawning; he did not come at noon;
And out o' the tawny sunset, before the rise o' the moon,
When the road was a gipsy's ribbon, looping the purple moor,
A red-coat troop came marching—
    Marching—Marching—
King George's men came marching, up to the old inn-door.

They said no word to the landlord, they drank his ale instead,
But they gagged his daughter and bound her to the foot of her nar-
    row bed;
Two of them knelt at her casement, with muskets at their side!
There was death at every window;
    And hell at one dark window;
For Bess could see, through her casement, the road that *he* would
    ride.

They had tied her up to attention, with many a sniggering jest;
They had bound a musket beside her, with the barrel beneath her
    breast!
"Now keep good watch!" and they kissed her. She heard the dead
    man say—
Look for me by moonlight;
    Watch for me by moonlight;
I'll come to thee by moonlight, though hell should bar the way!

She twisted her hands behind her; but all the knots held good!
She writhed her hands till her fingers were wet with sweat or blood!
They stretched and strained in the darkness, and the hours crawled
    by like years,
Till, now, on the stroke of midnight,
    Cold, on the stroke of midnight,
The tip of one finger touched it! The trigger at least was hers!

The tip of one finger touched it; she strove no more for the rest!
Up, she stood up to attention, with the barrel beneath her breast,
She would not risk their hearing: she would not strive again;
For the road lay bare in the moonlight;
    Blank and bare in the moonlight;
And the blood of her veins in the moonlight throbbed to her love's
    refrain.

Tlot-tlot; tlot-tlot! Had they heard it? The horse-hoofs ringing clear;
Tlot-tlot, tlot-tlot, in the distance? Were they deaf that they did
    not hear?
Down the ribbon of moonlight, over the brow of the hill,
The highwayman came riding,
    Riding, riding!
The red-coats looked to their priming! She stood up, straight and
    still!

Tlot-tlot, in the frosty silence! *Tlot-tlot,* in the echoing night!
Nearer he came and nearer! Her face was like a light!
Her eyes grew wide for a moment; she drew one last deep breath,
Then her finger moved in the moonlight,
    Her musket shattered the moonlight,
Shattered her breast in the moonlight and warned him—with her
    death.

He turned; he spurred to the Westward; he did not know who stood
Bowed, with her head o'er the musket, drenched with her own red
  blood!
Not till the dawn he heard it, his face grew gray to hear
How Bess, the landlord's daughter,
    The landlord's black-eyed daughter,
Had watched for her love in the moonlight, and died in the darkness
  there.

Back, he spurred like a madman, shrieking a curse to the sky,
With the white road smoking behind him, and his rapier brandished
  high!
Blood-red were his spurs in the golden noon; wine-red was his velvet
  coat,
When they shot him down on the highway,
    Down like a dog on the highway,
And he lay in his blood on the highway, with the bunch of lace at
  his throat.

. . . .

And still of a winter's night, they say, when the wind is in the trees,
When the moon is a ghostly galleon tossed upon cloudy seas,
When the road is a ribbon of moonlight over the purple moor,
A highwayman comes riding—
    Riding—riding—
A highwayman comes riding, up to the old inn-door.

Over the cobbles he clatters and clangs in the dark inn-yard;
And he taps with his whip on the shutters, but all is locked and
  barred;
He whistles a tune to the window, and who should be waiting
  there
But the landlord's black-eyed daughter,
    Bess, the landlord's daughter,
Plaiting a dark red love-knot into her long black hair.

                                                    ALFRED NOYES

HER LETTER

I'm sitting alone by the fire,
  Dressed just as I came from the dance,
In a robe even *you* would admire—
  It cost a cool thousand in France;
I'm be-diamonded out of all reason,
  My hair is done up in a cue:
In short, sir, "the belle of the season"
  Is wasting an hour upon you.

A dozen engagements I've broken;
  I left in the midst of a set;
Likewise a proposal, half spoken,
  That waits—on the stairs—for me yet.
They say he'll be rich—when he grows up—
  And then he adores me indeed;
And you, sir, are turning your nose up,
  Three thousand miles off, as you read.

"And how do I like my position?"
  "And what do I think of New York?"
"And now, in my higher ambition,
  With whom do I waltz, flirt, or talk?"
"And isn't it nice to have riches,
  And diamonds and silks, and all that?"
"And aren't they a change to the ditches
  And tunnels of Poverty Flat?"

Well, yes—if you saw us out driving
  Each day in the Park, four-in-hand,
If you saw poor dear mamma contriving
  To look supernaturally grand—
If you saw papa's picture, as taken
  By Brady, and tinted at that—
You'd never suspect he sold bacon
  And flour at Poverty Flat.

And yet, just this moment, when sitting
  In the glare of the grand chandelier—

In the bustle and glitter befitting
  The "finest *soirée* of the year"—
In the mists of a *gaze de Chambéry*,
  And the hum of the smallest of talk—
Somehow, Joe, I thought of the "Ferry,"
  And the dance that we had on "The Fork;"

Of Harrison's bar, with its muster
  Of flags festooned over the wall;
Of the candles that shed their soft lustre
  And tallow on head-dress and shawl;
Of the steps that we took to one fiddle,
  Of the dress of my queer *vis-à-vis;*
And how I once went down the middle
  With the man that shot Sandy McGee.

Of the moon that was quietly sleeping
  On the hill, when the time came to go;
Of the few baby peaks that were peeping
  From under their bedclothes of snow;
Of that ride—that to me was the rarest;
  Of—the something you said at the gate.
Ah! Joe, then I wasn't an heiress
  To "the best-paying lead in the State."

Well, well, it's all past; yet it's funny
  To think, as I stood in the glare
Of fashion and beauty and money,
  That I should be thinking, right there,
Of some one who breasted high water,
  And swam the North Fork, and all that,
Just to dance with old Folinsbee's daughter,
  The Lily of Poverty Flat.

But goodness! what nonsense I'm writing!
  (Mamma says my taste still is low),
Instead of my triumphs reciting,
  I'm spooning on Joseph—heigh-ho!
And I'm to be "finished" by travel—
  Whatever's the meaning of that.
Oh, why did papa strike pay gravel
  In drifting on Poverty Flat?

Good-night!—here's the end of my paper;
    Good-night!—if the longitude please—
For maybe, while wasting my taper,
    Your sun's climbing over the trees.
But know, if you haven't got riches,
    And are poor, dearest Joe, and all that,
That my heart's somewhere there in the ditches,
    And you've struck it—on Poverty Flat.

                                        BRET HARTE

THE PRISONER OF CHILLON

I

My hair is gray, but not with years,
        Nor grew it white
        In a single night,
As men's have grown from sudden fears.
My limbs are bowed, though not with toil,
    But rusted with a vile repose,
For they have been a dungeon's spoil,
    And mine has been the fate of those
To whom the goodly earth and air
Are banned and barred—forbidden fare.
But this was for my father's faith,
I suffered chains and courted death.
That father perished at the stake
For tenets he would not forsake;
And for the same his lineal race
In darkness found a dwelling-place.
We were seven—who now are one—
    Six in youth, and one in age,
Finished as they had begun,
    Proud of Persecution's rage:
One in fire, and two in field,
Their belief with blood have sealed—
Dying as their father died,

For the God their foes denied;
Three were in a dungeon cast,
Of whom this wreck is left the last.

II

There are seven pillars, of Gothic mold,
In Chillon's dungeons deep and old;
There are seven columns, massy and gray,
Dim with a dull imprisoned ray—
A sunbeam which hath lost its way,
And through the crevice and the cleft
Of the thick wall is fallen and left,
Creeping o'er the floor so damp,
Like a marsh's meteor-lamp.
And in each pillar there is a ring,
   And in each ring there is a chain:
That iron is a cankering thing,
   For in these limbs its teeth remain,
With marks that will not wear away
Till I have done with this new day,
Which now is painful to these eyes,
Which have not seen the sun so rise
For years—I cannot count them o'er;
I lost their long and heavy score
When my last brother drooped and died,
And I lay living by his side.

III

They chained us each to a column stone,
And we were three—yet, each alone;
We could not move a single pace;
We could not see each other's face,
But with that pale and livid light
That made us strangers in our sight;
And thus together, yet apart,
Fettered in hand, but joined in heart,

'Twas still some solace, in the dearth
Of the pure elements of earth,
To hearken to each other's speech,
And each turn comforter to each
With some new hope or legend old,
Or song heroically bold;
But even these at length grew cold.
Our voices took a dreary tone,
An echo of the dungeon-stone,
    A grating sound—not full and free,
    As they of yore were wont to be;
    It might be fancy—but to me
They never sounded like our own.

IV

I was the eldest of the three,
    And to uphold and cheer the rest
    I ought to do, and did, my best—
And each did well in his degree.
  The youngest, whom my father loved,
Because our mother's brow was given
To him, with eyes as blue as heaven—
  For him my soul was sorely moved;
And truly might it be distressed
To see such bird in such a nest;
For he was beautiful as day
    (When day was beautiful to me
    As to young eagles, being free)—
    A polar day, which will not see
A sunset till its summer's gone—
  Its sleepless summer of long light,
The snow-clad offspring of the sun:
  And thus he was as pure and bright,
And in his natural spirit gay,
With tears for naught but others' ills;
And then they flowed like mountain rills,
Unless he could assuage the woe
Which he abhorred to view below.

V

The other was as pure of mind,
But formed to combat with his kind;
Strong in his frame, and of a mood
Which 'gainst the world in war had stood,
And perished in the foremost rank
  With joy; but not in chains to pine.
His spirit withered with their clank;
  I saw it silently decline—
  And so, perchance, in sooth, did mine:
But yet I forced it on, to cheer
Those relics of a home so dear.
He was a hunter of the hills,
      Had followed there the deer and wolf;
      To him this dungeon was a gulf,
And fettered feet the worst of ills.

VI

  Lake Leman lies by Chillon's walls,
A thousand feet in depth below,
Its massy waters meet and flow;
Thus much the fathom-line was sent
From Chillon's snow-white battlement,
  Which round about the wave enthralls;
A double dungeon wall and wave
Have made—and like a living grave,
Below the surface of the lake
The dark vault lies wherein we lay;
We heard it ripple night and day;
  Sounding o'er our heads it knocked.
And I have felt the winter's spray
Wash through the bars when winds were high,
And wanton in the happy sky;
      And then the very rock hath rocked,
      And I have felt it shake, unshocked;
Because I could have smiled to see
The death that would have set me free.

VII

I said my nearer brother pined;
I said his mighty heart declined.
He loathed and put away his food;
It was not that 'twas coarse and rude,
For we were used to hunters' fare,
And for the like had little care.
The milk drawn from the mountain goat
Was changed for water from the moat;
Our bread was such as captives' tears
Have moistened many a thousand years,
Since man first pent his fellow-men,
Like brutes, within an iron den.
But what were these to us or him?
These wasted not his heart or limb;
My brother's soul was of that mold
Which in a palace had grown cold,
Had his free breathing been denied
The range of the steep mountain's side.
But why delay the truth?—he died.
I saw, and could not hold his head,
Nor reach his dying hand—nor dead—
Though hard I strove, but strove in vain,
To rend and gnash my bonds in twain.
He died—and they unlocked his chain,
And scooped for him a shallow grave
Even from the cold earth of our cave.
I begged them, as a boon, to lay
His corse in dust whereon the day
Might shine—it was a foolish thought;
But then within my brain it wrought,
That even in death his freeborn breast
In such a dungeon could not rest.
I might have spared my idle prayer—
They coldly laughed, and laid him there,
The flat and turfless earth above
The being we so much did love;
His empty chain above it leant—
Such murder's fitting monument!

VIII

But he, the favorite and the flower,
Most cherished since his natal hour,
His mother's image in fair face,
The infant love of all his race,
His martyred father's dearest thought,
My latest care, for whom I sought
To hoard my life, that his might be
Less wretched now, and one day free—
He too, who yet had held untired
A spirit natural or inspired—
He, too, was struck, and day by day
Was withered on the stalk away.
Oh, God! it is a fearful thing
To see the human soul take wing
In any shape, in any mood:
I've seen it rushing forth in blood;
I've seen it on the breaking ocean
Strive with a swoln, convulsive motion;
I've seen the sick and ghastly bed
Of Sin, delirious with its dread;
But these were horrors—this was woe
Unmixed with such—but sure and slow.
He faded, and so calm and meek,
So softly worn, so sweetly weak,
So tearless, yet so tender—kind,
And grieved for those he left behind;
With all the while a cheek whose bloom
Was as a mockery of the tomb,
Whose tints as gently sunk away
As a departing rainbow's ray;
An eye of most transparent light,
That almost made the dungeon bright;
And not a word of murmur, not
A groan o'er his untimely lot—
A little talk of better days,
A little hope my own to raise;
For I was sunk in silence, lost

In this last loss, of all the most.
And then the sighs he would suppress
Of fainting nature's feebleness,
More slowly drawn, grew less and less.
I listened, but I could not hear—
I called, for I was wild with fear;
I knew 'twas hopeless, but my dread
Would not be thus admonished;
I called, and thought I heard a sound—
I burst my chain with one strong bound,
And rushed to him:—I found him not.
I only stirred in this black spot;
I only lived—I only drew
The accursed breath of dungeon-dew;
The last, the sole, the dearest link
Between me and the eternal brink,
Which bound me to my failing race,
Was broken in this fatal place.
One on the earth, and one beneath—
My brothers—both had ceased to breathe.
I took that hand which lay so still—
Alas! my own was full as chill;
I had not strength to stir, or strive,
But felt that I was still alive—
A frantic feeling, when we know
That what we love shall ne'er be so.
    I know not why
    I could not die,
I had no earthly hope—but faith,
And that forbade a selfish death.

IX

What next befell me then and there
    I know not well—I never knew.
First came the loss of light and air,
    And then of darkness too.
I had no thought, no feeling—none:
Among the stones I stood a stone;
And was, scarce conscious what I wist,

As shrubless crags within the mist;
For all was blank, and bleak, and gray;
It was not night—it was not day;
It was not even the dungeon-light,
So hateful to my heavy sight;
But vacancy absorbing space,
And fixedness—without a place;
There were no stars, no earth, no time,
No check, no change, no good, no crime—
But silence, and a stirless breath
Which neither was of life nor death—
A sea of stagnant idleness,
Blind, boundless, mute and motionless!

x

A light broke in upon my brain—
  It was the carol of a bird;
It ceased, and then it came again—
  The sweetest song ear ever heard;
And mine was thankful till my eyes
Ran over with the glad surprise,
And they that moment could not see
I was the mate of misery;
But then, by dull degrees, came back
My senses to their wonted track:
I saw the dungeon walls and floor
Close slowly round me as before;
I saw the glimmer of the sun
Creeping as it before had done;
But through the crevice where it came
That bird was perched, as fond and tame,
  And tamer than upon the tree—
A lovely bird, with azure wings,
And song that said a thousand things,
  And seemed to say them all for me!
I never saw its like before—
I ne'er shall see its likeness more.
It seemed, like me, to want a mate,
But was not half so desolate;
And it was come to love me when

None lived to love me so again,
And, cheering from my dungeon's brink,
Had brought me back to feel and think.
I know not if it late were free,
   Or broke its cage to perch on mine;
But knowing well captivity,
   Sweet bird! I could not wish for thine!
Or if it were, in winged guise,
A visitant from Paradise;
For—Heaven forgive that thought, the while
Which made me both to weep and smile!—
I sometimes deemed that it might be
My brother's soul come down to me;
But then at last away it flew,
And then 'twas mortal—well I knew;
For he would never thus have flown,
And left me twice so doubly lone—
Lone—as the corse within its shroud,
Lone—as a solitary cloud,
   A single cloud on a sunny day,
While all the rest of heaven is clear,
A frown upon the atmosphere,
That hath no business to appear
   When skies are blue, and earth is gay.

XI

A kind of change came in my fate—
My keepers grew compassionate.
I know not what had made them so—
They were inured to sights of woe;
But so it was—my broken chain
With links unfastened did remain;
And it was liberty to stride
Along my cell from side to side,
And up and down, and then athwart,
And tread it over every part;
And round the pillars one by one,
Returning where my walk begun—
Avoiding only, as I trod,

My brothers' graves without a sod;
For if I thought with heedless tread
My step profaned their lowly bed,
My breath came gaspingly and thick,
And my crushed heart fell blind and sick.

XII

I made a footing in the wall:
    It was not therefrom to escape,
For I had buried one and all
    Who loved me in a human shape;
And the whole earth would henceforth be
A wider prison unto me;
No child, no sire, no kin had I,
No partner in my misery.
I thought of this, and I was glad,
For thought of them had made me mad;
But I was curious to ascend
To my barred windows, and to bend
Once more, upon the mountains high,
The quiet of a loving eye.

XIII

I saw them—and they were the same;
They were not changed, like me, in frame;
I saw their thousand years of snow
On high—their wide, long lake below,
And the blue Rhone in fullest flow;
I heard the torrents leap and gush
O'er channeled rock and broken bush;
I saw the white-walled distant town,
And whiter sails go skimming down;
And then there was a little isle,
Which in my very face did smile—
    The only one in view;
A small, green isle, it seemed no more,
Scarce broader than my dungeon floor;
But in it there were three tall trees,

And o'er it blew the mountain breeze,
And by it there were waters flowing,
And on it there were young flowers growing
  Of gentle breath and hue.
The fish swam by the castle wall,
And they seemed joyous, each and all;
The eagle rode the rising blast—
Methought he never flew so fast
As then to me he seemed to fly;
And then new tears came in my eye,
And I felt troubled, and would fain
I had not left my recent chain;
And when I did descend again,
The darkness of my dim abode
Fell on me as a heavy load;
It was as is a new-dug grave,
Closing o'er one we sought to save;
And yet my glance, too much oppressed,
Had almost need of such a rest.

XIV

It might be months, or years, or days—
  I kept no count, I took no note—
I had no hope my eyes to raise,
  And clear them of their dreary mote;
At last men came to set me free,
  I asked not why, and recked not where;
It was at length the same to me,
Fettered or fetterless to be;
  I learned to love despair.
And thus, when they appeared at last,
And all my bonds aside were cast,
These heavy walls to me had grown
A hermitage—and all my own!
And half I felt as they were come
To tear me from a second home.
With spiders I had friendship made,
And watched them in their sullen trade;
Had seen the mice by moonlight play—

And why should I feel less than they?
We were all inmates of one place,
And I, the monarch of each race,
Had power to kill; yet, strange to tell!
In quiet we had learned to dwell.
My very chains and I grew friends,
So much a long communion tends
To make us what we are:—even I
Regained my freedom with a sigh.

GEORGE GORDON BYRON

RICHARD CORY

Whenever Richard Cory went down town,
We people on the pavement looked at him:
He was a gentleman from sole to crown,
Clean favored, and imperially slim.

And he was always quietly arrayed,
And he was always human when he talked;
But still he fluttered pulses when he said,
"Good-morning," and he glittered when he walked.

And he was rich—yes, richer than a king—
And admirably schooled in every grace:
In fine, we thought that he was everything
To make us wish that we were in his place.

So on we worked, and waited for the light,
And went without the meat, and cursed the bread;
And Richard Cory, one calm summer night,
Went home and put a bullet through his head.

EDWIN ARLINGTON ROBINSON

MINIVER CHEEVY

Miniver Cheevy, child of scorn,
    Grew lean while he assailed the seasons;
He wept that he was ever born,
    And he had reasons.

Miniver loved the days of old
    When swords were bright and steeds were prancing;
The vision of a warrior bold
    Would set him dancing.

Miniver sighed for what was not,
    And dreamed, and rested from his labors;
He dreamed of Thebes and Camelot,
    And Priam's neighbors.

Miniver mourned the ripe renown
    That made so many a name so fragrant;
He mourned Romance, now on the town,
    And Art, a vagrant.

Miniver loved the Medici,
    Albeit he had never seen one;
He would have sinned incessantly
    Could he have been one.

Miniver cursed the commonplace,
    And eyed a khaki suit with loathing;
He missed the medieval grace
    Of iron clothing.

Miniver scorned the gold he sought,
    But sore annoyed was he without it;
Miniver thought, and thought, and thought,
    And thought about it.

Miniver Cheevy, born too late,
    Scratched his head and kept on thinking;
Miniver coughed, and called it fate,
    And kept on drinking.

EDWIN ARLINGTON ROBINSON

THE EVE OF ST. AGNES

St. Agnes' Eve—Ah, bitter chill it was!
The owl, for all his feathers, was a-cold;
The hare limped trembling through the frozen grass,
And silent was the flock in woolly fold:
Numb were the Beadsman's fingers, while he told
His rosary, and while his frosted breath,
Like pious incense from a censer old,
Seemed taking flight for heaven, without a death,
Past the sweet Virgin's picture, while his prayer he saith.

His prayer he saith, this patient, holy man;
Then takes his lamp, and riseth from his knees,
And back returneth, meager, barefoot, wan,
Along the chapel aisle by slow degrees:
The sculptured dead, on each side, seem to freeze,
Emprisoned in black, purgatorial rails:
Knights, ladies, praying in dumb orat'ries,
He passeth by; and his weak spirit fails
To think how they may ache in icy hoods and mails.

Northward he turneth through a little door,
And scarce three steps, ere Music's golden tongue
Flattered to tears this aged man and poor;
But no—already had his death-bell rung;
The joys of all his life were said and sung;
His was harsh penance on St. Agnes' Eve:
Another way he went, and soon among
Rough ashes sat he for his soul's reprieve,
And all night kept awake, for sinners' sake to grieve.

That ancient Beadsman heard the prelude soft;
And so it chanced, for many a door was wide,
From hurry to and fro. Soon, up aloft,
The silver, snarling trumpets 'gan to chide:
The level chambers, ready with their pride,
Were glowing to receive a thousand guests:
The carved angels, ever eager-eyed,
Stared, where upon their heads the cornice rests,
With hair blown back, and wings put cross-wise on their breasts.

At length burst in the argent revelry,
With plume, tiara, and all rich array,
Numerous as shadows haunting faerily
The brain, newstuffed in youth, with triumphs gay
Of old romance. These let us wish away,
And turn, sole-thoughted, to one Lady there,
Whose heart had brooded, all that wintry day,
On love, and winged St. Agnes' saintly care,
As she had heard old dames full many times declare.

They told her how, upon St. Agnes' eve,
Young virgins might have visions of delight,
And soft adorings from their loves receive
Upon the honeyed middle of the night,
If ceremonies due they did aright;
As, supperless to bed they must retire,
And couch supine their beauties, lily white;
Nor look behind, nor sideways, but require
Of Heaven with upward eyes for all that they desire.

Full of this whim was thoughtful Madeline:
The music, yearning like a God in pain,
She scarcely heard: her maiden eyes divine
Fixed on the floor, saw many a sweeping train
Pass by—she heeded not at all: in vain
Came many a tiptoe, amorous cavalier,
And back retired; not cooled by high disdain,
But she saw not: her heart was otherwhere:
She sighed for Agnes' dreams, the sweetest of the year.

She danced along with vague, regardless eyes,
Anxious her lips, her breathing quick and short:
The hallowed hour was near at hand: she sighs
Amid the timbrels, and the thronged resort
Of whisperers in anger, or in sport;
'Mid looks of love, defiance, hate, and scorn,
Hoodwinked with faery fancy; all amort,
Save to St. Agnes and her lambs unshorn,
And all the bliss to be before to-morrow morn.

So, purposing each moment to retire,
She lingered still. Meantime, across the moors,

Had come young Porphyro, with heart on fire
For Madeline. Beside the portal doors,
Buttressed from moonlight, stands he, and implores
All saints to give him sight of Madeline,
But for one moment in the tedious hours,
That he might gaze and worship all unseen;
Perchance speak, kneel, touch, kiss—in sooth such things have been.

He ventures in: let no buzzed whisper tell:
All eyes be muffled, or a hundred swords
Will storm his heart, Love's feverous citadel:
For him, those chambers held barbarian hordes,
Hyena foemen, and hot-blooded lords,
Whose very dogs would execrations howl
Against his lineage: not one breast affords
Him any mercy, in that mansion foul,
Save one old beldame, weak in body and in soul.

Ah, happy chance! the aged creature came,
Shuffling along with ivory-headed wand,
To where he stood, hid from the torch's flame,
Behind a broad hall-pillar, far beyond
The sound of merriment and chorus bland:
He startled her; but soon she knew his face,
And grasped his fingers in her palsied hand,
Saying, "Mercy, Porphyro! hie thee from this place;
They are all here to-night, the whole blood-thirsty race!

"Get hence! get hence! there's dwarfish Hildebrand:
He had a fever late, and in the fit
He cursed thee and thine, both house and land:
Then there's that old Lord Maurice, not a whit
More tame for his gray hairs—Alas me! flit!
Flit like a ghost away."—"Ah, Gossip, dear,
We're safe enough; here in this armchair sit,
And tell me how"—"Good Saints! not here, not here:
Follow me, child, or else these stones will be thy bier."

He followed through a lowly arched way,
Brushing the cobwebs with his lofty plume,
And as she muttered "Well-a-well-a-day!"
He found him in a little moonlight room,

Pale, latticed, chill, and silent as a tomb.
"Now tell me where is Madeline," said he,
"O tell me, Angela, by the holy loom,
Which none but secret sisterhood may see,
When they St. Agnes' wool are weaving piously."

"St. Agnes! Ah! it is St. Agnes' Eve—
Yet men will murder upon holy days:
Thou must hold water in a witch's sieve,
And be liege-lord of all the Elves and Fays,
To venture so: it fills me with amaze
To see thee, Porphyro!—St. Agnes' Eve!
God's help! my lady fair the conjurer plays
This very night: good angels her deceive!
But let me laugh awhile—I've mickle time to grieve."

Feebly she laugheth in the languid moon,
While Porphyro upon her face doth look,
Like puzzled urchin on an aged crone
Who keepeth closed a wondrous riddle-book,
As spectacled she sits in chimney nook.
But soon his eyes grew brilliant, when she told
His lady's purpose; and he scarce could brook
Tears, at the thought of those enchantments cold,
And Madeline asleep in lap of legends old.

Sudden a thought came like a full-blown rose,
Flushing his brow, and in his pained heart
Made purple riot: then doth he propose
A stratagem, that makes the beldame start:
"A cruel man and impious thou art:
Sweet lady! let her pray, and sleep, and dream
Alone with her good angels, far apart
From wicked men like thee. Go, go!—I deem
Thou canst not surely be the same that thou didst seem."

"I will not harm her, by all saints I swear,"
Quoth Porphyro: "O may I ne'er find grace
When my weak voice shall whisper its last prayer,
If one of her soft ringlets I displace,
Or look with ruffian passion in her face.
Good Angela, believe me, by these tears;

Or I will, even in a moment's space,
  Awake, with horrid shout, my foemen's ears,
And beard them, though they be more fanged than wolves and bears."

 "Ah! why wilt thou affright a feeble soul?
  A poor, weak, palsy-stricken, churchyard thing,
  Whose passing-bell may ere the midnight toll;
  Whose prayers for thee, each morn and evening,
  Were never missed."—Thus plaining, doth she bring
  A gentler speech from burning Porphyro;
  So woeful, and of such deep sorrowing,
  That Angela gives promise she will do
Whatever he shall wish, betide her weal or woe.

  Which was, to lead him, in close secrecy,
  Even to Madeline's chamber, and there hide
  Him in a closet, of such privacy
  That he might see her beauty unespied,
  And win perhaps that night a peerless bride,
  While legioned fairies paced the coverlet,
  And pale enchantment held her sleepy-eyed.
  Never on such a night have lovers met,
Since Merlin paid his Demon all the monstrous debt.

 "It shall be as thou wishest," said the Dame:
 "All cates and dainties shall be stored there
  Quickly on this feast-night: by the tambour frame
  Her own lute thou wilt see: no time to spare,
  For I am slow and feeble, and scarce dare
  On such a catering trust my dizzy head.
  Wait here, my child, with patience; kneel in prayer
  The while: Ah! thou must needs the lady wed,
Or may I never leave my grave among the dead."

  So saying, she hobbled off with busy fear.
  The lover's endless minutes slowly passed;
  The dame returned and whispered in his ear
  To follow her; with aged eyes aghast
  From fright of dim espial. Safe at last,
  Through many a dusky gallery, they gain
  The maiden's chamber, silken, hushed, and chaste;
  Where Porphyro took covert, pleased amain.
His poor guide hurried back with agues in her brain.

Her faltering hand upon the balustrade,
Old Angela was feeling for the stair,
When Madeline, St. Agnes' charmed maid,
Rose, like a missioned spirit, unaware:
With silver taper's light, and pious care,
She turned, and down the aged gossip led
To a safe level matting. Now prepare,
Young Porphyro, for gazing on that bed;
She comes, she comes again, like ring-dove frayed and fled.

Out went the taper as she hurried in;
Its little smoke, in pallid moonshine, died:
She closed the door, she panted, all akin
To spirits of the air, and visions wide:
No uttered syllable, or, woe betide!
But to her heart, her heart was voluble,
Paining with eloquence her balmy side;
As though a tongueless nightingale should swell
Her throat in vain, and die, heart-stifled, in her dell.

A casement high and triple-arched there was,
All garlanded with carven imageries
Of fruits, and flowers, and bunches of knot-grass,
And diamonded with panes of quaint device,
Innumerable of stains and splendid dyes,
As are the tiger-moth's deep-damasked wings;
And in the midst, 'mong thousand heraldries,
And twilight saints, and dim emblazonings,
A shielded scutcheon blushed with blood of queens and kings.

Full on this casement shone the wintry moon,
And threw warm gules on Madeline's fair breast,
As down she knelt for Heaven's grace and boon;
Rose-bloom fell on her hands, together pressed,
And on her silver cross soft amethyst,
And on her hair a glory, like a saint:
She seemed a splendid angel, newly dressed,
Save wings, for heaven:—Porphyro grew faint:
She knelt, so pure a thing, so free from mortal taint.

Anon his heart revives: her vespers done,
Of all its wreathed pearls her hair she frees;

Unclasps her warmed jewels one by one;
Loosens her fragrant bodice; by degrees
Her rich attire creeps rustling to her knees:
Half-hidden, like a mermaid in seaweed,
Pensive awhile she dreams awake, and sees,
In fancy, fair St. Agnes in her bed,
But dares not look behind, or all the charm is fled.

Soon, trembling in her soft and chilly nest,
In sort of wakeful swoon, perplexed she lay,
Until the poppied warmth of sleep oppressed
Her soothed limbs, and soul fatigued away;
Flown, like a thought, until the morrow-day;
Blissfully havened both from joy and pain;
Clasped like a missal where swart Paynims pray;
Blinded alike from sunshine and from rain,
As though a rose should shut, and be a bud again.

Stolen to this paradise, and so entranced,
Porphyro gazed upon her empty dress,
And listened to her breathing, if it chanced
To wake into a slumberous tenderness;
Which when he heard, that minute did he bless
And breathed himself: then from the closet crept
Noiseless as fear in a wide wilderness,
And over the hushed carpet, silent, stept,
And 'tween the curtains peeped, where, lo—how fast she slept.

Then by the bed-side, where the faded moon
Made a dim, silver twilight, soft he set
A table, and, half anguished, threw thereon
A cloth of woven crimson, gold, and jet:—
O for some drowsy Morphean amulet!
The boisterous, midnight, festive clarion,
The kettle-drum, and far-heard clarionet,
Affray his ears, though but in dying tone:—
The hall-door shuts again, and all the noise is gone.

And still she slept an azure-lidded sleep,
In blanched linen, smooth and lavendered,
While he forth from the closet brought a heap
Of candied apple, quince, and plum, and gourd;

With jellies soother than the creamy curd,
And lucent syrops, tinct with cinnamon;
Manna and dates, in argosy transferred
From Fez; and spiced dainties, every one,
From silken Samarcand to cedared Lebanon.

These delicates he heaped with glowing hand
On golden dishes and in baskets bright
Of wreathed silver: sumptuous they stand
In the retired quiet of the night,
Filling the chilly room with perfume light—
"And now, my love, my seraph fair, awake!
Thou art my heaven, and I thine eremite:
Open thine eyes, for meek St. Agnes' sake,
Or I shall drowse beside thee, so my soul doth ache."

Thus whispering, his warm, unnerved arm
Sank in her pillow. Shaded was her dream
By the dusk curtains:—'twas a midnight charm
Impossible to melt as iced stream:
The lustrous salvers in the moonlight gleam;
Broad golden fringe upon the carpet lies:
It seemed he never, never could redeem
From such a steadfast spell his lady's eyes;
So mused awhile, entoiled in woofed phantasies.

Awakening up, he took her hollow lute,—
Tumultuous—and, in chords that tenderest be,
He played an ancient ditty, long since mute,
In Provence called, "La belle dame sans merci":
Close to her ear touching the melody;—
Wherewith disturbed, she uttered a soft moan:
He ceased—she panted quick—and suddenly
Her blue affrayed eyes wide open shone:
Upon his knees he sank, pale as smooth-sculptured stone.

Her eyes were open, but she still beheld,
Now wide awake, the vision òf her sleep:
There was a painful change, that nigh expelled
The blisses of her dream so pure and deep:
At which fair Madeline began to weep,
And moan forth witless words with many a sigh,

While still her gaze on Porphyro would keep;
Who knelt, with joined hands and piteous eye,
Fearing to move or speak, she looked so dreamingly.

"Ah, Porphyro!" said she, "but even now
Thy voice was at sweet tremble in mine ear,
Made tuneable with every sweetest vow;
And those sad eyes were spiritual and clear;
How changed thou art! how pallid, chill, and drear!
Give me that voice again, my Porphyro,
Those looks immortal, those complainings dear!
Oh leave me not in this eternal woe,
For if thou diest, my Love, I know not where to go."

Beyond a mortal man impassioned far
At these voluptuous accents, he arose,
Ethereal, flushed, and like a throbbing star
Seen 'mid the sapphire heaven's deep repose;
Into her dream he melted, as the rose
Blendeth its odor with the violet,—
Solution sweet: meantime the frost-wind blows
Like Love's alarum, pattering the sharp sleet
Against the window-panes; St. Agnes' moon hath set.

'Tis dark, quick pattereth the flaw-blown sleet:
"This is no dream, my bride, my Madeline!"
'Tis dark: the iced gusts still rave and beat:
"No dream, alas! alas! and woe is mine!
Porphyro will leave me here to fade and pine.—
Cruel! what traitor could thee hither bring?
I curse not, for my heart is lost in thine,
Though thou forsakest a deceived thing;—
A dove forlorn and lost with sick unpruned wing."

"My Madeline! sweet dreamer! lovely bride!
Say, may I be for aye thy vassal blest?
Thy beauty's shield, heart-shaped and vermeil-dyed?
Ah, silver shrine, here will I take my rest
After so many hours of toil and quest,
A famished pilgrim,—saved by miracle.
Though I have found, I will not rob thy nest
Saving of thy sweet self; if thou thinkest well
To trust, fair Madeline, to no rude infidel.

"Hark! 'tis an elfin-storm from faery land,
  Of haggard seeming, but a boon indeed:
  Arise—arise! the morning is at hand;—
  The bloated wassailers will never heed:—
  Let us away, my love, with happy speed;
  There are no ears to hear, or eyes to see,—
  Drowned all in Rhenish and the sleepy mead:
  Awake! arise! my love, and fearless be,
For o'er the southern moors I have a home for thee."

She hurried at his words, beset with fears,
  For there were sleeping dragons all around,
  At glaring watch, perhaps, with ready spears.—
  Down the wide stairs a darkling way they found.—
  In all the house was heard no human sound.
  A chain-drooped lamp was flickering by each door;
  The arras, rich with horsemen, hawk, and hound,
  Fluttered in the besieging wind's uproar;
And the long carpets rose along the gusty floor.

They glide, like phantoms, into the wide hall;
  Like phantoms, to the iron porch, they glide;
  Where lay the Porter, in uneasy sprawl,
  With a huge empty flagon by his side:
  The wakeful bloodhound rose, and shook his hide,
  But his sagacious eye an inmate owns:
  By one, and one, the bolts full easy slide:—
  The chains lie silent on the footworn stones;—
The key turns, and the door upon its hinges groans.

And they are gone: ay, ages long ago
  These lovers fled away into the storm
  That night the Baron dreamt of many a woe,
  And all his warrior-guests, with shade and form
  Of witch, and demon, and large coffin-worm,
  Were long be-nightmared. Angela the old
  Died palsy-twitched, with meager face deform;
  The Beadsman, after thousand aves told,
For aye unsought-for slept amongst his ashes cold.

JOHN KEATS

SKIPPER IRESON'S RIDE

Of all the rides since the birth of time,
Told in story or sung in rhyme,—
On Apuleius's Golden Ass,
Or one-eyed Calender's horse of brass,
Witch astride of a human back,
Islam's prophet on Al-Borák,—
The strangest ride that ever was sped
Was Ireson's, out from Marblehead!
  Old Floyd Ireson, for his hard heart,
Tarred and feathered and carried in a cart
    By the women of Marblehead!

Body of turkey, head of fowl,
Wings a-droop like a rained-on fowl,
Feathered and ruffled in every part,
Skipper Ireson stood in the cart.
Scores of women, old and young,
Strong of muscle, and glib of tongue,
Pushed and pulled up the rocky lane,
Shouting and singing the shrill refrain:
  "Here's Flud Oirson, fur his horrd horrt,
   Torr'd an' futherr'd an' corr'd in a corrt
    By the women o' Morble'ead!"

Wrinkled scolds with hands on hips,
Girls in bloom of cheek and lips,
Wild-eyed, free-limbed, such as chase
Bacchus round some antique vase,
Brief of skirt, with ankles bare,
Loose of kerchief and loose of hair,
With conch-shells blowing and fish-horns' twang,
Over and over the Maenads sang:
  "Here's Flud Oirson, fur his horrd horrt,
   Torr'd an' futherr'd an' corr'd in a corrt
    By the women o' Morble'ead!"

Small pity for him!—He sailed away
From a leaking ship in Chaleur Bay,—

Sailed away from a sinking wreck,
With his own town's-people on her deck!
"Lay by! lay by!" they called to him.
Back he answered, "Sink or swim!
Brag of your catch of fish again!"
And off he sailed through the fog and rain!
　　Old Floyd Ireson, for his hard heart,
　　　Tarred and feathered and carried in a cart
　　　　By the women of Marblehead!

Fathoms deep in dark Chaleur
That wreck shall lie forevermore.
Mother and sister, wife and maid,
Looked from the rocks of Marblehead
Over the moaning and rainy sea,—
Looked for the coming that might not be!
What did the winds and the sea-birds say
Of the cruel captain who sailed away?—
　　Old Floyd Ireson, for his hard heart,
　　　Tarred and feathered and carried in a cart
　　　　By the women of Marblehead!

Through the street, on either side,
Up flew windows, doors swung wide;
Sharp-tongued spinsters, old wives gray,
Treble lent the fish-horn's bray.
Sea-worn grandsires, cripple-bound,
Hulks of old sailors run aground,
Shook head, and fist, and hat, and cane,
And cracked with curses the hoarse refrain:
　　"Here's Flud Oirson, fur his horrd horrt,
　　　Torr'd an' futherr'd an' corr'd in a corrt
　　　　By the women o' Morble'ead!"

Sweetly along the Salem road
Bloom of orchard and lilac showed.
Little the wicked skipper knew
Of the fields so green and the sky so blue.
Riding there in his sorry trim,
Like an Indian idol glum and grim,
Scarcely he seemed the sound to hear

Of voices shouting, far and near:
"Here's Flud Oirson, fur his horrd horrt,
Torr'd an' futherr'd an' corr'd in a corrt
By the women o' Morble'ead!"

"Hear me, neighbors!" at last he cried,—
"What to me is this noisy ride?
What is the shame that clothes the skin
To the nameless horror that lives within?
Waking or sleeping, I see a wreck,
And hear a cry from a reeling deck!
Hate me and curse me,—I only dread
The hand of God and the face of the dead!"
Said old Floyd Ireson, for his hard heart,
Tarred and feathered, and carried in a cart
By the women of Marblehead!

Then the wife of the skipper lost at sea
Said, "God has touched him! why should we!"
Said an old wife mourning her only son,
"Cut the rogue's tether and let him run!"
So with soft relentings and rude excuse,
Half scorn, half pity, they cut him loose,
And gave him a cloak to hide him in,
And left him alone with his shame and sin.
Poor Floyd Ireson, for his hard heart,
Tarred and feathered and carried in a cart
By the women of Marblehead!

JOHN GREENLEAF WHITTIER

MAUD MULLER

Maud Muller on a summer's day
Raked the meadow sweet with hay.

Beneath her torn hat glowed the wealth
Of simple beauty and rustic health.

Singing, she wrought, and her merry glee
The mock-bird echoed from his tree.

But when she glanced to the far-off town,
White from its hill-slope looking down,

The sweet song died, and a vague unrest
And a nameless longing filled her breast,—

A wish that she hardly dared to own,
For something better than she had known

The Judge rode slowly down the lane,
Smoothing his horse's chestnut mane.

He drew his bridle in the shade
Of the apple-trees, to greet the maid,

And asked a draught from the spring that flowed
Through the meadow across the road.

She stooped where the cool spring bubbled up,
And filled for him her small tin cup,

And blushed as she gave it, looking down
On her feet so bare, and her tattered gown.

"Thanks!" said the Judge; "a sweeter draught
From a fairer hand was never quaffed."

He spoke of the grass and flowers and trees,
Of the singing birds and the humming bees;

Then talked of the haying, and wondered whether
The cloud in the west would bring foul weather.

And Maud forgot her brier-torn gown,
And her graceful ankles bare and brown;

And listened, while a pleased surprise
Looked from her long-lashed hazel eyes.

At last, like one who for delay
Seeks a vain excuse, he rode away.

Maud Muller looked and sighed: "Ah me!
That I the Judge's bride might be!

"He would dress me up in silks so fine,
And praise and toast me at his wine.

"My father should wear a broadcloth coat;
My brother should sail a painted boat.

"I'd dress my mother so grand and gay,
And the baby should have a new toy each day.

"And I'd feed the hungry and clothe the poor,
And all should bless me who left our door."

The Judge looked back as he climbed the hill,
And saw Maud Muller standing still.

"A form more fair, a face more sweet,
Ne'er hath it been my lot to meet.

"And her modest answer and graceful air
Show her wise and good as she is fair.

"Would she were mine, and I to-day,
Like her, a harvester of hay;

"No doubtful balance of rights and wrongs,
Nor weary lawyers with endless tongues,

"But low of cattle and song of birds,
And health and quiet and loving words."

But he thought of his sisters, proud and cold,
And his mother, vain of her rank and gold.

So, closing his heart, the Judge rode on,
And Maud was left in the field alone.

But the lawyers smiled that afternoon,
When he hummed in court an old love-tune;

And the young girl mused beside the well
Till the rain on the unraked clover fell.

He wedded a wife of richest dower,
Who lived for fashion, as he for power.

Yet oft, in his marble hearth's bright glow,
He watched a picture come and go;

And sweet Maud Muller's hazel eyes
Looked out in their innocent surprise.

Oft, when the wine in his glass was red,
He longed for the wayside well instead;

And closed his eyes on his garnished rooms
To dream of meadows and clover-blooms.

And the proud man sighed, with a secret pain,
"Ah, that I were free again!

"Free as when I rode that day,
Where the barefoot maiden raked her hay."

She wedded a man unlearned and poor,
And many children played round her door.

But care and sorrow, and childbirth pain,
Left their traces on heart and brain.

And oft, when the summer sun shone hot
On the new-mown hay in the meadow lot,

And she heard the little spring brook fall
Over the roadside, through the wall,

In the shade of the apple-tree again
She saw a rider draw his rein;

And, gazing down with timid grace,
She felt his pleased eyes read her face.

Sometimes her narrow kitchen walls
Stretched away into stately halls;

The weary wheel to a spinet turned,
The tallow candle an astral burned,

And for him who sat by the chimney lug,
Dozing and grumbling o'er pipe and mug,

A manly form at her side she saw,
And joy was duty and love was law.

Then she took up her burden of life again,
Saying only, "It might have been."

Alas for maiden, alas for Judge,
For rich repiner and household drudge!

God pity them both! and pity us all,
Who vainly the dreams of youth recall.

For of all sad words of tongue or pen,
The saddest are these: "It might have been!"

Ah, well! for us all some sweet hope lies
Deeply buried from human eyes;

And, in the hereafter, angels may
Roll the stone from its grave away!

JOHN GREENLEAF WHITTIER

WALK, DAMN YOU, WALK!

Up the dusty way from Frisco town,
  To where the mines their treasures hide,
The road is long and many miles
  The golden store and town divide.

Along this road, one summer day
  There toiled a tired man;

Begrimed with dust, the weary way
  He cussed as some folks can.

Our traveler hailed a passing team
  That slowly dragged its load along;
His hail roused up the teamster old
  And checked his jolly song.

  "Say, stranger!"
                "Wa'l, whoa!"
  "Kin I walk
    Behind yer load
    A spell on this road?"

  "Wa'l, no, ye can't walk;
    But git up on this seat
  An' we'll jest talk.
    Git up hyar!"

  "That ain't what I want;
    I ain't that kind;
    Fer it's on behind,
  Right in yer dust,
    That's like a smudge,
    I want to trudge,
  Fer I desarve it!"

"Wa'l, pard, I ain't no hog;
  I don't own this road afore nor 'hind,
So jest git right in the dirt and walk,
  If that's the way yer 'clined!"

"Yeh, hup! gelang!" the driver said;
  The creeping wagon moved amain;
While close behind the stranger toiled,
  And clouds of dust rose up again.

The teamster heard the stranger talk,
  As if two trudged behind his van;
Yet, looking round, could only spy
  A solitary man.

Yet heard the teamster words like these,
  Come out the dust as from a cloud;
For the weary footman spoke his mind,
  His thoughts he uttered loud.

And this the burden of his talk:
  "Walk now, damn you, walk!
    No use to talk;
    Don't like it, eh?
    Not the way
      Ye went at Frisco?
    Walk, damn you, walk!

"Went up in the mines,
    An' made yer stake;
    'Nough to take
    Ye back to the state
    Where ye wuz born;
    Where now is yer corn?
      Walk, damn you, walk!

"Dust in yer eyes,
    Dust in yer nose,
  Dust down yer throat,
    An' thick on yer clothes;
  Can't hardly talk.
    I know it! But you jest
  Walk, damn you, walk!

"Wot did ye do with yer tin?
    Oh, blowed every ounce of it in!
  Got drunk, got sober, got drunk ag'in.
  Wa'l, walk, damn you, walk!

"Wot did ye do? Wa'l, I sw'ar
    When ye was down thar,
      Tell me wot ye didn't do?
      Yer gold-dust flew;
  Ye thought it fine
  To keep a-openin' wine.
      Now walk, damn you, walk!

"Every one wuz yer friend,
  When ye had the dust to spend
  And the coin fer to lend—
  Didn't think of the end;
    Tried to buck a queer game—
    Nary a red, now, to yer name.
Wa'l, walk, damn you, walk!

"Had a cool forty thousand or so.
  Now wot ye got to show
    Fer all that?
  Not a cussed red cent.
  Ye let her went—
    Nothin' too good
    For yer youthful blood.
Now walk, damn you, walk!

"Chokes ye, this dust?
  Wa'l, that ain't the wust—
    When ye git thar,
    Where the diggin's are,
  No pick, no shovel, no pan!
  Wa'l, ye're a healthy man—
    Jest walk, damn you, walk!

"Wisht ye could stop to drink—
  What? Water? Wa'l, jest think
    How, at Frisco—wa'l, water thar
    With ye, wa'nt anywhar—
  It was wine—Extra Dry!
  Oh, you flew high!
    Now walk, damn you, walk!

"Ye say ye've somethin' larned?
  Wa'l, I be darned!
    Hearn ye say that afore;
    Yet ye tried—jest onct more.

"Wa'l, that's so; but this is the last!
  I'm done! Jig's up! All's past!
    Ye hear me talk?
    Walk, damn you, walk!

"I've sworn off."
        "Guess ye're late."
"No more on my plate.
        If I ag'in my pile—
        Wa'l, I should smile!
            Let me ag'in salt her down,
            I'll go round that Frisco town,
        If I walk—
            Yes, damn me, walk!"

. . . .

The fools don't all go to Frisco town;
Nor do they all from the mines come down.
About all of us have, in our day,
In some sort of shape, some kind of way,
Painted the town with the "old stuff"
Dipped in stocks or made some bluff;
Got caught in wedlock by a shrew;
Mixed wines, old and new;
Seen the sights, been out all night,
Rolled home in the morning light,
With crumpled shirt and went to bed,
Waked up at noon with an awful head;
Then how we walked, Hell! how we walked!
Now don't try to yank every bun;
Don't try to have *all* the fun;
    Don't think you know it all;
    Don't know that stocks will fall;
Don't try to bluff on an ace;
Don't know *the* horse in the race;
Don't get scooped by a pretty face;
    Lest when you awake,
        You may talk,
    And the burden be,
        "Walk, damn you, walk!"

                        WILLIAM DE VERE

ALUMNUS FOOTBALL

Bill Jones had been the shining star upon his college team.
His tackling was ferocious and his bucking was a dream.
When husky Williams took the ball beneath his brawny arm
They had two extra men to ring the ambulance alarm.

Bill hit the line and ran the ends like some mad bull amuck.
The other team would shiver when they saw him start to buck.
And when some rival tackler tried to block his dashing pace,
On waking up, he'd ask, "Who drove that truck across my face?"

Bill had the speed—Bill had the weight—Bill never bucked in vain;
From goal to goal he whizzed along while fragments strewed the
    plain,
And there had been a standing bet, which no one tried to call,
That he could make his distance through a ten-foot granite wall.

When he wound up his college course each student's heart was sore.
They wept to think bull-throated Bill would sock the line no more.
Not so with William—in his dreams he saw the Field of Fame,
Where he would buck to glory in the swirl of Life's big game.

Sweet are the dreams of college life, before our faith is nicked—
The world is but a cherry tree that's waiting to be picked;
The world is but an open road—until we find, one day,
How far away the goal posts are that called us to the play.

So, with the sheepskin tucked beneath his arm in football style,
Bill put on steam and dashed into the thickest of the pile;
With eyes ablaze, he sprinted where the laureled highway led—
When Bill woke up his scalp hung loose and knot adorned his head.

He tried to run the ends of life but with rib-crushing toss
A rent-collector tackled him and threw him for a loss.
And when he switched his course again and dashed into the line
The massive Guard named Failure did a toddle on his spine.

Bill tried to punt out of the rut, but ere he turned the trick
Right Tackle Competition scuttled through and blocked the kick.

And when he tackled at Success in one long, vicious prod
The Fullback Disappointment steered his features in the sod.

Bill was no quitter, so he tried a buck in higher gear,
But Left Guard Envy broke it up and stood him on his ear.
Whereat he aimed a forward pass, but in a vicious bound
Big Center Greed slipped through a hole and slammed him to the
  ground.

But one day, when across the Field of Fame the goal seemed dim,
The wise old coach, Experience, came up and spoke to him.
"Oh boy," he said, "the main point now before you win your bout
Is keep on bucking Failure till you've worn the piker out!

"And, kid, cut out this fancy stuff—go in there, low and hard;
Just keep your eye upon the ball and plug on, yard by yard,
And more than all—when you are thrown or tumbled with a crack,
Don't sit there whining—hustle up and keep on coming back;

"Keep coming back with all you've got, without an alibi,
If Competition trips you up or lands upon your eye,
Until at last above the din you hear this sentence spilled:
'We might as well let this bird through before we all get killed.'

"You'll find the road is long and rough, with soft spots far apart,
Where only those can make the grade who have the Uphill Heart.
And when they stop you with a thud or halt you with a crack,
Let Courage call the signals as you keep on coming back.

"Keep coming back, and though the world may romp across your
  spine,
Let every game's end find you still upon the battling line;
For when the One Great Scorer comes to mark against your name,
He writes—not that you won or lost—but how you played the
  Game."

GRANTLAND RICE

THE COTTER'S SATURDAY NIGHT

INSCRIBED TO ROBERT AIKEN, ESQ.

Let not Ambition mock their useful toil,
    Their homely joys, and destiny obscure;
Nor Grandeur hear with a disdainful smile
    The short and simple annals of the poor.—GRAY

My loved, my honored, much-respected friend!
    No mercenary bard his homage pays;
With honest pride, I scorn each selfish end;
    My dearest meed, a friend's esteem and praise.
To you I sing, in simple Scottish lays,
The lowly train in life's sequestered scene;
    The native feelings strong, the guileless ways;
What Aiken in a cottage would have been;
Ah! though his worth unknown, far happier there, I ween.

November chill blaws loud wi' angry sugh;
    The shortening winter-day is near a close;
The miry beasts retreating frae the pleugh,
    The blackening trains o' craws to their repose:
    The toilworn cotter frae his labor goes,—
This night his weekly moil is at an end,—
    Collects his spades, his mattocks, and his hoes,
Hoping the morn in ease and rest to spend,
And weary, o'er the moor, his course does hameward bend.

At length his lonely cot appears in view,
    Beneath the shelter of an aged tree;
The expectant wee things, toddlin', stacher through
    To meet their dad, wi' flichterin' noise an' glee.
    His wee bit ingle, blinking bonnily,
His clean hearthstane, his thriftie wifie's smile,
    The lisping infant prattling on his knee,
Does a' his weary kiaugh and care beguile,
And makes him quite forget his labor and his toil.

Belyve, the elder bairns come drapping in,
    At service out, amang the farmers roun';
Some ca' the pleugh, some herd, some tentie rin

A cannie errand to a neibor town;
   Their eldest hope, their Jenny, woman grown,
In youthfu' bloom, love sparkling in her e'e,
   Comes hame, perhaps to shew a braw new gown,
Or deposit her sair-won penny-fee,
To help her parents dear, if they in hardship be.

With joy unfeigned, brothers and sisters meet,
   And each for other's weelfare kindly spiers:
The social hours, swift-winged, unnoticed fleet;
   Each tells the uncos that he sees or hears;
   The parents, partial, eye their hopeful years;
Anticipation forward points the view.
   The mother, wi' her needle and her shears,
Gars auld claes look amaist as weel's the new;
The father mixes a' wi' admonition due.

Their master's and their mistress's command,
   The younkers a' are warned to obey;
And mind their labors wi' an eydent hand,
   And ne'er, though out o' sight, to jauk or play:
"And oh! be sure to fear the Lord alway!
And mind your duty, duly, morn and night!
   Lest in temptation's path ye gang astray,
Implore His counsel and assisting might:
They never sought in vain that sought the Lord aright!"

But, hark! a rap comes gently to the door;
   Jenny, wha kens the meaning o' the same,
Tells how a neibor lad cam o'er the moor,
   To do some errands, and convoy her hame.
   The wily mother sees the conscious flame
Sparkle in Jenny's e'e, and flush her cheek;
   With heart-struck anxious care inquires his name,
While Jenny hafflins is afraid to speak;
Weel pleased the mother hears it's nae wild, worthless rake.

Wi' kindly welcome, Jenny brings him ben;
   A strappin' youth; he taks the mother's eye;
Blithe Jenny sees the visit's no ill-ta'en;
   The father cracks of horses, pleughs, and kye.
   The youngster's artless heart o'erflows wi' joy,

But blate and lathefu', scarce can weel behave;
    The mother, wi' a woman's wiles, can spy
What makes the youth sae bashfu' an' sae grave:
Weel pleased to think her bairn's respected like the lave.

O happy love! where love like this is found!
    O heartfelt raptures! bliss beyond compare!
I've paced much this weary, mortal round,
    And sage experience bids me this declare:—
    If Heaven a draught of heavenly pleasure spare,
One cordial in this melancholy vale,
    'Tis when a youthful, loving, modest pair
In other's arms breathe out the tender tale,
Beneath the milk-white thorn that scents the evening gale.

Is there, in human form, that bears a heart,
    A wretch, a villain, lost to love and truth,
That can, with studied, sly, ensnaring art,
    Betray sweet Jenny's unsuspecting youth?
    Curse on his perjured arts! dissembling smooth!
Are honor, virtue, conscience, all exiled?
    Is there no pity, no relenting ruth,
Points to the parents fondling o'er their child?
Then paints the ruined maid, and their distraction wild?

But now the supper crowns their simple board,
    The halesome parritch, chief o' Scotia's food,
The soupe their only hawkie does afford,
    That 'yont the hallan snugly chows her cood:
    The dame brings forth, in complimental mood,
To grace the lad, her weel-hained kebbuck, fell,
    And aft he's pressed, and aft he ca's it guid;
The frugal wifie, garrulous, will tell
How 'twas a towmond auld, sin' lint was i' the bell.

The cheerfu' supper done, wi' serious face,
    They, round the ingle, form a circle wide;
The sire turns o'er, wi' patriarchal grace,
    The big ha' Bible, ance his father's pride;
    His bonnet reverently is laid aside,
His lyart haffets wearing thin and bare;
    Those strains that once did sweet in Zion glide,

He wales a portion with judicious care;
And "Let us worship God!" he says, with solemn air.

They chant their artless notes in simple guise;
   They tune their hearts, by far the noblest aim:
Perhaps "Dundee's" wild-warbling measures rise,
   Or plaintive "Martyrs," worthy of the name,
   Or noble "Elgin" beets the heavenward flame,
The sweetest far of Scotia's holy lays:
   Compared with these, Italian trills are tame;
The tickled ear no heartfelt raptures raise;
Nae unison hae they with our Creator's praise.

The priest-like father reads the sacred page,—
   How Abram was the friend of God on high;
Or Moses bade eternal warfare wage
   With Amalek's ungracious progeny;
   Or how the royal bard did groaning lie
Beneath the stroke of Heaven's avenging ire;
   Or Job's pathetic plaint, and wailing cry;
Or rapt Isaiah's wild, seraphic fire;
Or other holy seers that tune the sacred lyre.

Perhaps the Christian volume is the theme,—
   How guiltless blood for guilty man was shed;
How He, who bore in heaven the second name,
   Had not on earth whereon to lay his head:
   How his first followers and servants sped
The precepts sage they wrote to many a land;
   How he, who lone in Patmos banished,
Saw in the sun a mighty angel stand,
And heard great Babylon's doom pronounced by Heaven's command.

Then kneeling down to Heaven's Eternal King,
   The saint, the father, and the husband prays:
Hope "springs exulting on triumphant wing,"
   That thus they all shall meet in future days:
   There ever bask in uncreated rays,
No more to sigh, or shed the bitter tear,
   Together hymning their Creator's praise,
In such society, yet still more dear;
While circling Time moves round in an eternal sphere.

Compared with this, how poor Religion's pride,
  In all the pomp of method and of art,
When men display to congregations wide,
  Devotion's every grace, except the heart!
The Power, incensed, the pageant will desert,
  The pompous strain, the sacerdotal stole;
But, haply, in some cottage far apart,
May hear, well pleased, the language of the soul;
And in His Book of Life the inmates poor enroll.

Then homeward all take off their several way;
  The youngling cottagers retire to rest:
The parent-pair their secret homage pay,
  And proffer up to Heaven the warm request,
  That He, who stills the raven's clamorous nest,
And decks the lily fair in flowery pride,
  Would, in the way His wisdom sees the best,
For them and for their little ones provide;
But, chiefly, in their hearts with grace divine preside.

From scenes like these old Scotia's grandeur springs,
  That makes her loved at home, revered abroad;
Princes and lords are but the breath of kings,
  "An honest man's the noblest work of God";
  And certes, in fair Virtue's heavenly road,
The cottage leaves the palace far behind:
  What is a lordling's pomp?—a cumbrous load,
Disguising oft the wretch of human kind,
Studied in arts of hell, in wickedness refined.

O Scotia! my dear, my native soil!
  For whom my warmest wish to Heaven is sent,
Long may thy hardy sons of rustic toil
  Be blest with health, and peace, and sweet content!
  And, oh, may Heaven their simple lives prevent
From luxury's contagion, weak and vile!
  Then, howe'er crowns and coronets be rent,
A virtuous populace may rise the while,
And stand a wall of fire around their much-loved isle.

O Thou! who poured the patriotic tide,
  That streamed through Wallace's undaunted heart;
Who dared to nobly stem tyrannic pride,
  Or nobly die, the second glorious part,
  (The patriot's God peculiarly thou art,
His friend, inspirer, guardian, and reward!)
  O, never, never Scotia's realm desert;
But still the patriot, and the patriot bard,
In bright succession raise, her ornament and guard!

ROBERT BURNS

THE LORDS OF CREATION

Ye lords of creation, men you are called,
You think you rule the whole.
You are much mistaken, after all,
For you are under woman's control.
For ever since the world began
It's always been the way—
Now did not Adam, the very first man,
The very first woman obey, obey, obey,
The very first woman obey?

Ye lords who are present, hear my call.
I know you will quickly say:
Our size much larger, our nerves more strong,
Shall the stronger the weaker obey?
Now think not, though these words we hear,
We'll mind one word you say;
For as long as a woman's possessed of a tear,
Your power will vanish away, away, away,
Your power will vanish away.

But should there be so strange a wight
As not to be moved by a tear,
Do not be astonished at the sight,
We still have no cause to fear;
Let us leave themselves to muse

Upon their fancied sway—
For as long as a woman's possessed of a smile,
She will certainly have her own way, way, way,
She will certainly have her own way.

Now, ladies, since I've made it plain
That the thing is really so,
We'll not let them have their way,
But we'll show them the way to go.
For ever since the world began
It's always been the way,
And we'll manage it so that the very last man
Shall the very last woman obey, obey, obey,
Shall the very last woman obey.

UNKNOWN

HORATIUS

(c. 496 B.C.)

Lars Porsena of Clusium
  By the Nine Gods he swore
That the great house of Tarquin
  Should suffer wrong no more.
By the Nine Gods he swore it,
  And named a trysting-day,
And bade his messengers ride forth,
East and west and south and north,
  To summon his array.

East and west and south and north
  The messengers ride fast,
And tower and town and cottage
  Have heard the trumpet's blast.
Shame on the false Etruscan
  Who lingers in his home,
When Porsena of Clusium
  Is on the march for Rome.

The horsemen and the footmen
  Are pouring in amain

From many a stately market-place,
  From many a fruitful plain,
From many a lonely hamlet,
  Which, hid by beech and pine,
Like an eagle's nest, hangs on the crest
  Of purple Apennine;

From lordly Volaterrae
  Where scowls the far-famed hold
Piled by the hands of giants
  For godlike kings of old;
From sea-girt Populonia,
  Whose sentinels descry
Sardinia's snowy mountain-tops
  Fringing the southern sky;

From the proud mart of Pisae,
  Queen of the western waves,
Where ride Massilia's triremes
  Heavy with fair-haired slaves,
From where sweet Clanis wanders
  Through corn and vines and flowers,
From where Cortona lifts to heaven
  Her diadem of towers.

Tall are the oaks whose acorns
  Drop in dark Auser's rill;
Fat are the stags that champ the boughs
  Of the Ciminian hill;
Beyond all streams, Clitumnus
  Is to the herdsman dear;
Best of all pools the fowler loves
  The great Volsinian mere.

But now no stroke of woodman
  Is heard by Auser's rill;
No hunter tracks the stag's green path
  Up the Ciminian hill;
Unwatched along Clitumnus
  Grazes the milk-white steer;
Unharmed the water-fowl may dip
  In the Volsinian mere.

The harvests of Arretium,
  This year, old men shall reap;
This year, young boys in Umbro
  Shall plunge the struggling sheep;
And in the vats of Luna,
  This year, the must shall foam
Round the white feet of laughing girls
  Whose sires have marched to Rome.

There be thirty chosen prophets,
  The wisest of the land,
Who alway by Lars Porsena
  Both morn and evening stand:
Evening and morn the Thirty
  Have turned the verses o'er,
Traced from the right on linen white
  By mighty seers of yore.

And with one voice the Thirty
  Have their glad answer given:
"Go forth, go forth, Lars Porsena,—
  Go forth, beloved of Heaven!
Go, and return in glory
  To Clusium's royal dome,
And hang round Nurscia's altars
  The golden shields of Rome!"

And now hath every city
  Sent up her tale of men;
The foot are fourscore thousand,
  The horse are thousands ten.
Before the gates of Sutrium
  Is met the great array;
A proud man was Lars Porsena
  Upon the trysting-day.

For all the Etruscan armies
  Were ranged beneath his eye,
And many a banished Roman,
  And many a stout ally;
And with a mighty following,

To join the muster, came
The Tusculan Mamilius,
   Prince of the Latian name.

But by the yellow Tiber
   Was tumult and affright:
From all the spacious champaign
   To Rome men took their flight.
A mile around the city,
   The throng stopped up the ways;
A fearful sight it was to see
   Through two long nights and days.

For aged folk on crutches,
   And women great with child,
And mothers, sobbing over babes
   That clung to them and smiled,
And sick men borne in litters
   High on the necks of slaves,
And troops of sunburned husbandmen
   With reaping-hooks and staves,

And droves of mules and asses
   Laden with skins of wine,
And endless flocks of goats and sheep,
   And endless herds of kine,
And endless trains of wagons,
   That creaked beneath the weight
Of corn-sacks and of household goods,
   Choked every roaring gate.

Now, from the rock Tarpeian,
   Could the wan burghers spy
The line of blazing villages
   Red in the midnight sky.
The Fathers of the City,
   They sat all night and day,
For every hour some horseman came
   With tidings of dismay.

To eastward and to westward
   Have spread the Tuscan bands,
Nor house, nor fence, nor dovecote

In Crustumerium stands.
Verbenna down to Ostia
  Hath wasted all the plain;
Astur hath stormed Janiculum,
  And the stout guards are slain.

I wis, in all the Senate
  There was no heart so bold
But sore it ached, and fast it beat,
  When that ill news was told.
Forthwith up rose the Consul,
  Up rose the Fathers all;
In haste they girded up their gowns,
  And hied them to the wall.

They held a council, standing
  Before the River-Gate;
Short time was there, ye well may guess,
  For musing or debate.
Out spake the Consul roundly:
  "The bridge must straight go down;
For, since Janiculum is lost,
  Naught else can save the town."

Just then a scout came flying,
  All wild with haste and fear:
"To arms! to arms! Sir Consul,—
  Lars Porsena is here."
On the low hills to westward
  The Consul fixed his eye,
And saw the swarthy storm of dust
  Rise fast along the sky.

And nearer fast and nearer
  Doth the red whirlwind come;
And louder still, and still more loud,
From underneath that rolling cloud,
Is heard the trumpet's war-note proud,
  The trampling and the hum.
And plainly and more plainly
  Now through the gloom appears,
Far to left and far to right,

In broken gleams of dark-blue light,
The long array of helmets bright,
  The long array of spears.

And plainly and more plainly,
  Above that glimmering line,
Now might ye see the banners
  Of twelve fair cities shine;
But the banner of proud Clusium
  Was highest of them all,—
The terror of the Umbrian,
  The terror of the Gaul.

And plainly and more plainly
  Now might the burghers know,
By port and vest, by horse and crest,
  Each warlike Lucumo:
There Cilnius of Arretium
  On his fleet roan was seen;
And Astur of the fourfold shield,
Girt with the brand none else may wield;
Tolumnius with the belt of gold,
And dark Verbenna from the hold
  By reedy Thrasymene.

Fast by the royal standard,
  O'erlooking all the war,
Lars Porsena of Clusium
  Sat in his ivory car.
By the right wheel rode Mamilius,
  Prince of the Latian name;
And by the left false Sextus,
  That wrought the deed of shame.

But when the face of Sextus
  Was seen among the foes,
A yell that rent the firmament
  From all the town arose.
On the house-tops was no woman
  But spat towards him and hissed,
No child but screamed out curses,
  And shook its little fist.

But the Consul's brow was sad,
　　And the Consul's speech was low,
And darkly looked he at the wall,
　　And darkly at the foe:
"Their van will be upon us
　　Before the bridge goes down;
And if they once may win the bridge,
　　What hope to save the town?"

Then out spake brave Horatius,
　　The Captain of the Gate:
"To every man upon this earth
　　Death cometh soon or late.
And how can man die better
　　Than facing fearful odds
For the ashes of his fathers
　　And the temples of his Gods,

"And for the tender mother
　　Who dandled him to rest,
And for the wife who nurses
　　His baby at her breast,
And for the holy maidens
　　Who feed the eternal flame,—
To save them from false Sextus
　　That wrought the deed of shame?

"Hew down the bridge, Sir Consul,
　　With all the speed ye may;
I, with two more to help me,
　　Will hold the foe in play.
In yon strait path a thousand
　　May well be stopped by three:
Now who will stand on either hand,
　　And keep the bridge with me?"

Then out spake Spurius Lartius,—
　　A Ramnian proud was he:
"Lo, I will stand at thy right hand,
　　And keep the bridge with thee."
And out spake strong Herminius,—

Of Titian blood was he:
"I will abide on thy left side,
   And keep the bridge with thee."

"Horatius," quoth the Consul,
   "As thou sayest so let it be."
And straight against that great array
   Forth went the dauntless Three.
For Romans in Rome's quarrel
   Spared neither land nor gold,
Nor son nor wife, nor limb nor life,
   In the brave days of old.

Then none was for a party;
   Then all were for the state;
Then the great man helped the poor,
   And the poor man loved the great:
Then lands were fairly portioned;
   Then spoils were fairly sold:
The Romans were like brothers
   In the brave days of old.

Now Roman is to Roman
   More hateful than a foe,
And the Tribunes beard the high,
   And the Fathers grind the low.
As we wax hot in faction,
   In battle we wax cold;
Wherefore men fight not as they fought
   In the brave days of old.

Now while the Three were tightening
   Their harness on their backs,
The Consul was the foremost man
   To take in hand an axe;
And Fathers, mixed with Commons,
   Seized hatchet, bar, and crow,
And smote upon the planks above,
   And loosed the props below.

Meanwhile the Tuscan army,
   Right glorious to behold,
Came flashing back the noonday light,

Rank behind rank, like surges bright
  Of a broad sea of gold.
Four hundred trumpets sounded
  A peal of warlike glee,
As that great host with measured tread,
And spears advanced, and ensigns spread,
Rolled slowly towards the bridge's head,
  Where stood the dauntless Three.

The Three stood calm and silent,
  And looked upon the foes,
And a great shout of laughter
  From all the vanguard rose;
And forth three chiefs came spurring
  Before that deep array;
To earth they sprang, their swords they drew,
And lifted high their shields, and flew
  To win the narrow way:

Aunus, from green Tifernum,
  Lord of the Hill of Vines;
And Seius, whose eight hundred slaves
  Sicken in Ilva's mines;
And Picus, long to Clusium
  Vassal in peace and war,
Who led to fight his Umbrian powers
From that gray crag where, girt with towers,
The fortress of Nequinum lowers
  O'er the pale waves of Nar.

Stout Lartius hurled down Aunus
  Into the stream beneath;
Herminius struck at Seius;
  And clove him to the teeth;
At Picus brave Horatius
  Darted one fiery thrust,
And the proud Umbrian's gilded arms
  Clashed in the bloody dust.

Then Ocnus of Falerii
  Rushed on the Roman Three;
And Lausulus of Urgo,

The rover of the sea;
And Aruns of Volsinium,
  Who slew the great wild boar,—
The great wild boar that had his den
Amidst the reeds of Cosa's fen,
And wasted fields, and slaughtered men,
  Along Albinia's shore.

Herminius smote down Aruns;
  Lartius laid Ocnus low;
Right to the heart of Lausulus
  Horatius sent a blow:
"Lie there," he cried, "fell pirate!
  No more, aghast and pale,
From Ostia's walls the crowd shall mark
The track of thy destroying bark;
No more Campania's hinds shall fly
To woods and caverns, when they spy
  Thy thrice-accursed sail!"

But now no sound of laughter
  Was heard among the foes;
A wild and wrathful clamor
  From all the vanguard rose.
Six spears' lengths from the entrance,
  Halted that deep array,
And for a space no man came forth
  To win the narrow way.

But, hark! the cry is Astur:
  And lo! the ranks divide;
And the great Lord of Luna
  Comes with his stately stride.
Upon his ample shoulders
  Clangs loud the fourfold shield,
And in his hand he shakes the brand
  Which none but he can wield.

He smiled on those bold Romans,
  A smile serene and high;
He eyed the flinching Tuscans,
  And scorn was in his eye.

Quoth he, "The she-wolf's litter
　　Stand savagely at bay;
But will ye dare to follow,
　　If Astur clears the way?"

Then, whirling up his broadsword
　　With both hands to the height,
He rushed against Horatius,
　　And smote with all his might.
With shield and blade Horatius
　　Right deftly turned the blow.
The blow, though turned came yet too nigh;
It missed his helm, but gashed his thigh.
The Tuscans raised a joyful cry
　　To see the red blood flow.

He reeled, and on Herminius
　　He leaned one breathing-space,
Then, like a wild-cat mad with wounds,
　　Sprang right at Astur's face.
Through teeth, and skull, and helmet
　　So fierce a thrust he sped,
The good sword stood a hand-breadth out
　　Behind the Tuscan's head.

And the great lord of Luna
　　Fell at that deadly stroke,
As falls on Mount Avernus
　　A thunder-smitten oak.
Far o'er the crashing forest
　　The giant arms lie spread;
And the pale augurs, muttering low,
　　Gaze on the blasted head.

On Astur's throat Horatius
　　Right firmly pressed his heel,
And thrice and four times tugged amain,
　　Ere he wrenched out the steel.
"And see," he cried, "the welcome,
　　Fair guests, that waits you here!
What noble Lucumo comes next
　　To taste our Roman cheer?"

But at his haughty challenge
  A sullen murmur ran,
Mingled of wrath, and shame, and dread,
  Along that glittering van.
There lacked not men of prowess,
  Nor men of lordly race,
For all Etruria's noblest
  Were round the fatal place.

But all Etruria's noblest
  Felt their hearts sink to see
On the earth the bloody corpses,
  In the path the dauntless Three;
And, from the ghastly entrance
  Where those bold Romans stood,
All shrank, like boys who, unaware,
Ranging the woods to start a hare,
Come to the mouth of the dark lair
Where, growling low, a fierce old bear
  Lies amidst bones and blood.

Was none who would be foremost
  To lead such dire attack;
But those behind cried "Forward!"
  And those before cried "Back!"
And backward now and forward
  Wavers the deep array;
And on the tossing sea of steel
To and fro the standards reel,
And the victorious trumpet-peal
  Dies fitfully away.

Yet one man for one moment
  Stood out before the crowd;
Well known was he to all the Three,
  And they gave him greeting loud:
"Now welcome, welcome, Sextus!
  Now welcome to thy home!
Why dost thou stay, and turn away?
  Here lies the road to Rome."

Thrice looked he at the city;
  Thrice looked he at the dead;
And thrice came on in fury,
  And thrice turned back in dread;
And, white with fear and hatred,
  Scowled at the narrow way
Where, wallowing in a pool of blood,
  The bravest Tuscans lay.

But meanwhile axe and lever
  Have manfully been plied;
And now the bridge hangs tottering
  Above the boiling tide.
"Come back, come back, Horatius!"
  Loud cried the Fathers all.—
"Back, Lartius! back, Herminius!
  Back, ere the ruin fall!"

Back darted Spurius Lartius;—
  Herminius darted back;
And, as they passed, beneath their feet
  They felt the timbers crack.
But when they turned their faces,
  And on the farther shore
Saw brave Horatius stand alone,
  They would have crossed once more;

But with a crash like thunder
  Fell every loosened beam,
And, like a dam, the mighty wreck
  Lay right athwart the stream:
And a long shout of triumph
  Rose from the walls of Rome,
As to the highest turret-tops
  Was splashed the yellow foam.

And, like a horse unbroken,
  When first he feels the rein,
The furious river struggled hard,
  And tossed his tawny mane,
And burst the curb, and bounded,

Rejoicing to be free;
And whirling down, in fierce career,
Battlement, and plank, and pier,
  Rushed headlong to the sea.

Alone stood brave Horatius,
  But constant still in mind,—
Thrice thirty thousand foes before,
  And the broad flood behind.
"Down with him!" cried false Sextus,
  With a smile on his pale face;
"Now yield thee," cried Lars Porsena,
  "Now yield thee to our grace."

Round turned he, as not deigning
  Those craven ranks to see;
Naught spake he to Lars Porsena,
  To Sextus naught spake he;
But he saw on Palatinus
  The white porch of his home;
And he spake to the noble river
  That rolls by the towers of Rome:

"O Tiber! Father Tiber!
  To whom the Romans pray,
A Roman's life, a Roman's arms,
  Take thou in charge this day!"
So he spake, and, speaking, sheathed
  The good sword by his side,
And, with his harness on his back,
  Plunged headlong in the tide.

No sound of joy or sorrow
  Was heard from either bank,
But friends and foes in dumb surprise,
With parted lips and straining eyes,
  Stood gazing where he sank;
And when above the surges
  They saw his crest appear,
All Rome sent forth a rapturous cry,
And even the ranks of Tuscany
  Could scarce forbear to cheer.

But fiercely ran the current,
  Swollen high by months of rain;
And fast his blood was flowing,
  And he was sore in pain,
And heavy with his armor,
  And spent with changing blows;
And oft they thought him sinking,
  But still again he rose.

Never, I ween, did swimmer,
  In such an evil case,
Struggle through such a raging flood
  Safe to the landing-place;
But his limbs were borne up bravely
  By the brave heart within,
And our good Father Tiber
  Bore bravely up his chin.

"Curse on him!" quoth false Sextus;—
  "Will not the villain drown?
But for this stay, ere close of day
  We should have sacked the town!"
"Heaven help him!" quoth Lars Porsena,
  "And bring him safe to shore;
For such a gallant feat of arms
  Was never seen before."

And now he feels the bottom;
  Now on dry earth he stands;
Now round him throng the Fathers
  To press his gory hands;
And now, with shouts and clapping,
  And noise of weeping loud,
He enters through the River-Gate,
  Borne by the joyous crowd.

They gave him of the corn-land,
  That was of public right,
As much as two strong oxen
  Could plough from morn till night;
And they made a molten image,

And set it up on high,
And there it stands unto this day
  To witness if I lie.

It stands in the Comitium,
  Plain for all folk to see,—
Horatius in his harness,
  Halting upon one knee;
And underneath is written,
  In letters all of gold,
How valiantly he kept the bridge
  In the brave days of old.

And still his name sounds stirring
  Unto the men of Rome,
As the trumpet-blast that cries to them
  To charge the Volscian home;
And wives still pray to Juno
  For boys with hearts as bold
As his who kept the bridge so well
  In the brave days of old.

And in the nights of winter
  When the cold north-winds blow,
And the long howling of the wolves
  Is heard amidst the snow;
When round the lonely cottage
  Roars loud the tempest's din,
And the good logs of Algidus
  Roar louder yet within;

When the oldest cask is opened,
  And the largest lamp is lit;
When the chestnuts glow in the embers,
  And the kid turns on the spit;
When young and old in circle
  Around the firebrands close;
When the girls are weaving baskets,
  And the lads are shaping bows;

When the goodman mends his armor,
  And trims his helmet's plume;

When the goodwife's shuttle merrily
  Goes flashing through the loom;
With weeping and with laughter
  Still is the story told,
How well Horatius kept the bridge
  In the brave days of old.

            THOMAS BABINGTON MACAULAY

RHYME OF THE RAILS

Singing through the forests,
  Rattling over ridges,
Shooting under arches,
  Rumbling over bridges,
Whizzing through the mountains,
  Buzzing o'er the vale—
Bless me! this is pleasant,
  Riding on the Rail.

Men of different "stations"
  In the eye of Fame,
Here are very quickly
  Coming to the same.
High and lowly people,
  Birds of every feather,
On a common level
  Traveling together.

Gentlemen in shorts,
  Looming very tall;
Gentlemen at large,
  Talking very small;
Gentlemen in tights,
  With a loose-ish mien;
Gentlemen in gray,
  Looking rather green;

Gentlemen quite old,
  Asking for the news;
Gentlemen in black,

In a fit of blues;
Gentlemen in claret,
    Sober as a vicar;
Gentlemen in tweed,
    Dreadfully in liquor!

Stranger on the right
    Looking very sunny,
Obviously reading
    Something rather funny.
Now the smiles are thicker,
    Wonder what they mean!
Faith he's got the *Knicker-*
    Bocker Magazine!

Stranger on the left,
    Closing up his peepers;
Now he snores again,
    Like the Seven Sleepers;
At the feet a volume
    Gives the explanation,
How the man grew stupid
    From "Association."

Ancient maiden lady
    Anxiously remarks,
That there must be peril
    'Mong so many sparks;
Roguish-looking fellow,
    Turning to the stranger,
Says it's his opinion
    She is out of danger!

Woman with her baby,
    Sitting *vis-à vis*,
Baby keeps a-squalling,
    Woman looks at me;
Asks about the distance,
    Says it's tiresome talking,
Noises of the cars
    Are so very shocking.

Market-woman, careful
    Of the precious casket,
Knowing eggs are eggs,
    Tightly holds her basket;
Feeling that a smash,
    If it came, would surely
Send her eggs to pot
    Rather prematurely.

Singing through the forests,
    Ratting over ridges,
Shooting under arches,
    Rumbling over bridges,
Whizzing through the mountains,
    Buzzing o'er the vale;
Bless me! this is pleasant,
    Riding on the Rail!

JOHN GODFREY SAXE

MY LAST DUCHESS

FERRARA

That's my last Duchess painted on the wall,
Looking as if she were alive. I call
That piece a wonder, now: Fra Pandolf's hands
Worked busily a day, and there she stands.
Will't please you sit and look at her? I said
"Fra Pandolf" by design, for never read
Strangers like you that pictured countenance,
The depth and passion of its earnest glance,
But to myself they turned (since none puts by
The curtain I have drawn for you, but I)
And seemed as they would ask me, if they durst,
How such a glance came there; so, not the first
Are you to turn and ask thus. Sir, 'twas not
Her husband's presence only, called that spot
Of joy into the Duchess' cheek: perhaps

Fra Pandolf chanced to say, "Her mantle laps
Over my lady's wrist too much," or "Paint
Must never hope to reproduce the faint
Half-flush that dies along her throat": such stuff
Was courtesy, she thought, and cause enough
For calling up that spot of joy. She had
A heart—how shall I say?—too soon made glad,
Too easily impressed: she liked whate'er
She looked on, and her looks went everywhere.
Sir, 'twas all one! My favor at her breast,
The dropping of the daylight in the West,
The bough of cherries some officious fool
Broke in the orchard for her, the white mule
She rode with round the terrace—all and each
Would draw from her alike the approving speech,
Or blush, at least. She thanked men,—good! but thanked
Somehow—I know not how—as if she ranked
My gift of a nine-hundred-years-old name
With anybody's gift. Who'd stoop to blame
This sort of trifling? Even had you skill
In speech—(which I have not)—to make your will
Quite clear to such an one, and say, "Just this
Or that in you disgusts me; here you miss,
Or there exceed the mark"—and if she let
Herself be lessoned so, nor plainly set
Her wits to yours, forsooth, and made excuse,
—E'en then would be some stooping; and I choose
Never to stoop. Oh sir, she smiled, no doubt,
Whene'er I passed her; but who passed without
Much the same smile? This grew; I gave commands;
Then all smiles stopped together. There she stands
As if alive. Will't please you rise? We'll meet
The company below, then. I repeat,
The Count your master's known munificence
Is ample warrant that no just pretense
Of mine for dowry will be disallowed;
Though his fair daughter's self, as I avowed
At starting, is my object. Nay, we'll go
Together down, sir. Notice Neptune, though,
Taming a sea-horse, thought a rarity,
Which Claus of Innsbruck cast in bronze for me!

ROBERT BROWNING

DANNY DEEVER

"What are the bugles blowin' for?" said Files-on-Parade.
"To turn you out, to turn you out," the Color-Sergeant said.
"What makes you look so white, so white?" said Files-on-Parade.
"I'm dreadin' what I've got to watch," the Color-Sergeant said.
 For they're hangin' Danny Deever, you can 'ear the Dead March
   play,
 The regiment's in 'ollow square—they're hangin' him to-day;
 They've taken of his buttons off an' cut his stripes away,
 An' they're hangin' Danny Deever in the mornin'.

"What makes the rear-rank breathe so 'ard?" said Files-on-Parade.
"It's bitter cold, it's bitter cold," the Color-Sergeant said.
"What makes that front-rank man fall down?" says Files-on-Parade.
"A touch o' sun, a touch o' sun," the Color-Sergeant said.
 They're hangin' Danny Deever, they are marchin' of 'im round,
 They 'ave 'alted Danny Deever by 'is coffin on the ground;
 An' 'e'll swing in 'arf a minute for a sneakin' shootin' hound—
 O they're hangin' Danny Deever in the mornin'!

" 'Is cot was right-'and cot to mine," said Files-on-Parade.
" 'E's sleepin' out an' far to-night," the Color-Sergeant said.
"I've drunk 'is beer a score o' times," said Files-on-Parade.
" 'E's drinkin' bitter beer alone," the Color-Sergeant said.
 They are hangin' Danny Deever, you must mark 'im to 'is place,
 For 'e shot a comrade sleepin'—you must look 'im in the face;
 Nine 'undred of 'is county an' the regiment's disgrace,
 While they're hangin' Danny Deever in the mornin'.

"What's that so black agin the sun?" said Files-on-Parade.
"It's Danny fightin' 'ard fur life," the Color-Sergeant said.
"What's that that whimpers over'ead?" said Files-on-Parade.
"It's Danny's soul that's passin' now," the Color-Sergeant said.
 For they're done with Danny Deever, you can 'ear the quickstep
   play,
 The regiment's in column, an' they're marchin' us away;
 Ho! the young recruits are shakin', an' they'll want their beer to-day,
 After hangin' Danny Deever in the mornin'.

RUDYARD KIPLING

THE DEACON'S MASTERPIECE, OR THE WONDERFUL "ONE-HOSS SHAY"

A LOGICAL STORY

Have you heard of the wonderful one-hoss shay,
That was built in such a logical way
It ran a hundred years to a day,
And then, of a sudden, it—ah, but stay,
I'll tell you what happened without delay,
Scaring the parson into fits,
Frightening people out of their wits,—
Have you ever heard of that, I say?

Seventeen hundred and fifty-five.
Georgius Secundus was then alive,—
Snuffy old drone from the German hive.
That was the year when Lisbon-town
Saw the earth open and gulp her down,
And Braddock's army was done so brown,
Left without a scalp to its crown.
It was on the terrible Earthquake-day
That the Deacon finished the one-hoss shay.

Now in building of chaises, I tell you what,
There is always *somewhere* a weakest spot,—
In hub, tire, felloe, in spring or thill,
In panel, or crossbar, or floor, or sill,
In screw, bolt, thoroughbrace,—lurking still,
Find it somewhere you must and will,—
Above or below, or within or without,—
And that's the reason, beyond a doubt,
That a chaise *breaks down*, but doesn't *wear out*.

But the Deacon swore (as Deacons do,
With an "I dew vum," or an "I tell *yeou*,")
He would build one shay to beat the taown
'N' the keounty 'n' all the kentry raoun';
It should be so built that it *couldn'* break daown:
"Fur," said the Deacon, "'t's mighty plain

Thut the weakes' place mus' stan' the strain;
'N' the way t' fix it, uz I maintain,
    Is only jest
T' make that place uz strong uz the rest."

So the Deacon inquired of the village folk
Where he could find the strongest oak,
That couldn't be split nor bent nor broke,—
That was for spokes and floor and sills;
He sent for lancewood to make the thills;
The crossbars were ash, from the straightest trees,
The panels of white-wood, that cuts like cheese,
But lasts like iron for things like these;
The hubs of logs from the "Settler's ellum,"—
Last of its timber,—they couldn't sell 'em,
Never an axe had seen their chips,
And the wedges flew from between their lips,
Their blunt ends frizzled like celery-tips;
Step and prop-iron, bolt and screw,
Spring, tire, axle, and linchpin too,
Steel of the finest, bright and blue;
Thoroughbrace bison-skin, thick and wide;
Boot, top, dasher, from tough old hide
Found in the pit when the tanner died.
That was the way he "put her through."
"There!" said the Deacon, "naow she'll dew!"

Do! I tell you, I rather guess
She was a wonder, and nothing less!
Colts grew horses, beards turned gray,
Deacon and deaconess dropped away,
Children and grandchildren—where were they?
But there stood the stout old one-hoss shay
As fresh as on Lisbon-earthquake-day!

EIGHTEEN HUNDRED;—it came and found
The Deacon's masterpiece strong and sound.
Eighteen hundred increased by ten;
"Hahnsum kerridge" they called it then.
Eighteen hundred and twenty came;—
Running as usual; much the same.
Thirty and Forty at last arrive,
And then come Fifty, and FIFTY-FIVE.

Little of all we value here
Wakes on the morn of its hundredth year
Without both feeling and looking queer.
In fact, there's nothing that keeps its youth,
So far as I know, but a tree and truth.
(This is a moral that runs at large;
Take it.—You're welcome.—No extra charge.)

FIRST OF NOVEMBER,—the Earthquake-day,—
There are traces of age in the one-hoss shay.
A general flavor of mild decay,
But nothing local, as one may say.
There couldn't be,—for the Deacon's art
Had made it so like in every part
That there wasn't a chance for one to start.
For the wheels were just as strong as the thills,
And the floor was just as strong as the sills,
And the panels just as strong as the floor,
And the whipple-tree neither less nor more,
And the back-crossbar as strong as the fore,
And spring and axle and hub *encore*.
And yet, *as a whole*, it is past a doubt
In another hour it will be *worn out!*

First of November, Fifty-five!
This morning the parson takes a drive.
Now, small boys, get out of the way!
Here comes the wonderful one-hoss shay,
Drawn by a rat-railed, ewe-necked bay.
"Huddup!" said the parson.—Off went they.

The parson was working his Sunday's text,—
Had got to *fifthly*, and stopped perplexed
At what the—Moses—was coming next.
All at once the horse stood still,
Close by the meet'n'-house on the hill.
First a shiver, and then a thrill,
Then something decidedly like a spill,—
And the parson was sitting upon a rock,
At half past nine by the meet'n'-house clock,—
Just the hour of the Earthquake shock!
What do you think the parson found,

When he got up and stared around?
The poor old chaise in a heap or mound,
As if it had been to the mill and ground!
You see, of course, if you're not a dunce,
How it went to pieces all at once,—
All at once, and nothing first,—
Just as bubbles do when they burst.

End of the wonderful one-hoss shay.
Logic is logic. That's all I say.

OLIVER WENDELL HOLMES

TWO SURPRISES

A workman plied his clumsy spade
  As the sun was going down;
The German King, with a cavalcade,
  On his way to Berlin town,

Reined up his steed at the old man's side.
  "My toiling friend," said he,
"Why not cease work at eventide
  When laborer should be free?"

"I do not slave," the old man said,
  "And I am always free!
Though I work from the time I leave my bed
  Till I can hardly see."

"How much," said the King, "is the grain in a day?"
  "Eight groschens," the man replied.
"And thou canst live on this meager pay?"
  "Like a king," he said with pride.

"Two groschens for me and my wife, good friend,
  And two for a debt I owe;
Two groschens to lend and two to spend,
  For those who can't labor, you know."

"Thy debt?" said the King; said the toiler, "Yea,
  To my mother with age oppressed,
Who cared for me, toiled for me, many a day
  And now hath need of rest."

"To whom dost lend thy daily store?"
  "To my boys—for their shooling; you see,
When I am too feeble to toil any more,
  They will care for their mother and me."

"And thy last two groschens?" the monarch said.
  "My sisters are old and lame;
I give them two groschens for raiment and bread,
  All in the Father's name."

Tears welled up in the good King's eyes.
  "Thou knowest me not," said he;
"As thou hast given me one surprise,
  Here is another for thee."

"I am the King; give me thy hand"—
  And he heaped it high with gold.
"When more thou needest, I command
  That I at once be told.

"For I would bless with rich reward
  The man who can proudly say
That eight souls he doth keep and guard
  On eight poor groschens a day."

R. W. MCALPINE

II. Love

HOW DO I LOVE THEE?

(from *Sonnets from the Portuguese*)

How do I love thee? Let me count the ways.
I love thee to the depth and breadth and height
My soul can reach, when feeling out of sight
For the ends of Being and ideal Grace.
I love thee to the level of every day's
Most quiet need, by sun and candlelight.
I love thee freely, as men strive for Right;
I love thee purely, as they turn from Praise.
I love thee with the passion put to use
In my old griefs, and with my childhood's faith.
I love thee with a love I seemed to lose
With my lost saints—I love thee with the breath,
Smiles, tears, of all my life!—and, if God choose,
I shall but love thee better after death.

ELIZABETH BARRETT BROWNING

LOVE NOT ME FOR COMELY GRACE

Love not me for comely grace,
For my pleasing eye or face;
Nor for any outward part,
No, nor for a constant heart:
 For these may fail or turn to ill,
  So thou and I shall sever.
Keep, therefore, a true woman's eye,
And love me still, but know not why;
 So hast thou the same reason still
  To doat upon me ever.

UNKNOWN

WHEN YOU ARE OLD

After Pierre de Ronsard

When you are old and gray and full of sleep,
And nodding by the fire, take down this book,
And slowly read and dream of the soft look
Your eyes had once, and of their shadows deep;

How many loved your moments of glad grace,
And loved your beauty with love false or true;
But one man loved the pilgrim soul in you,
And loved the sorrows of your changing face.

And bending down beside the glowing bars
Murmur, a little sadly, how love fled
And paced upon the mountains overhead
And hid his face amid a crowd of stars.

WILLIAM BUTLER YEATS

A RHYME OF THE DREAM-MAKER MAN

Down near the end of a wandering lane,
   That runs 'round the cares of a day,
Where Conscience and Memory meet and explain
   Their quaint little quarrels away.
A misty air-castle sits back in the dusk
   Where brownies and hobgoblins dwell
      And this is the home
      Of a busy old gnome
   Who is making up dream-things to sell,
      My dear,
   The daintiest dreams to sell.

He makes golden dreams of wicked men's sighs.
   He weaves on the thread of a hope
The airiest fancies of pretty brown eyes,
   And patterns his work with a trope.

The breath of a rose and the blush of a wish
  Boiled down to the ghost of a bliss,
    He wraps in a smile
    Every once in a while,
  And calls it the dream of a kiss,
    Dear heart,
  The dream of an unborn kiss.

Last night when I walked thro' the portals of sleep
  And came to the weird little den,
I looked in the place where the elf-man should keep
  A dream that I buy now and then.
'Tis only the sweet happy dream of a day—
  Yet one that I wish may come true—
    But I learned from the elf
    That you'd been there yourself
  And he'd given my dear dream to you,
    Sweetheart,
  He'd given our dream to you.

WILLIAM ALLEN WHITE

MY SHIPS

If all the ships I have at sea
Should come a-sailing home to me,
From sunny lands, and lands of cold,
Ah, well! the harbor could not hold
So many sails as there would be
If all my ships came in from sea.

If half my ships came home from sea,
And brought their precious freight to me,
Ah, well! I should have wealth as great
As any king who sits in state,
So rich the treasures that would be
In half my ships now out at sea.

If just one ship I have at sea
Should come a-sailing home to me,
Ah, well! the storm clouds then might frown,

For if the others all went down
Still rich and proud and glad I'd be,
If that one ship came back to me.

If that one ship were down at sea,
And all the others came to me,
Weighed down with gems and wealth untold,
With glory, honor, riches, gold,
The poorest soul on earth I'd be
If that one ship came not to me.

O skies be calm! O winds blow free—
Blow all my ships safe home to me.
But if thou sendest some awrack
To never more come sailing back,
Send any—all that skim the sea—
But bring my love-ship home to me.

ELLA WHEELER WILCOX

THE NEWLYWEDS

"What is the thing your eyes hold loveliest
In these, our fields and shores? I'll bring it home."
With tenderness, awaiting her request,
He stood. The dooryard dogwood was a foam
Of wind-tipped flowers, catching at her breath,
But these she did not mention, trying hard
To meet his eagerness. "Come flood, or death
By thunderbolt," he laughed, "I'll heap the yard
With everything you ask for. Name it now."
She made no answer, yet a little smile
Marked for him her compliance. Then, the bough
Tilted its stiffened beauty like a pile
Of snowy cloud above them. "Ah, I know,"
He cried, "Your heart is set on something far
Beyond our present means. Is that not so?"

"I want you and the dogwood as you are,
April forever. Can you heap that here?"
And while she watched, the boy went out of him.
"I think I understand your wifely fear,"

And, reaching up, he shook a weighted limb.
So, like the blossoms, quiet settled there.
"I will not run away to bring you gifts."
He spoke less lightly. "Boys can never bear
The undramatic thing. Their rich blood lifts
Their spirits higher than their hands, but men
May learn where such as you will teach,
How life is spent at try and try again
To keep white-blowing loveliness in reach."

CLOYD MANN CRISWELL

LONGING

Come to me in my dreams, and then
By day I shall be well again!
For then the night will more than pay
The hopeless longing of the day.

Come, as thou cam'st a thousand times,
A messenger from radiant climes,
And smile on thy new world, and be
As kind to others as to me!

Or, as thou never cam'st in sooth,
Come now, and let me dream it truth;
And part my hair, and kiss my brow,
And say: *My love! why sufferest thou?*

Come to me in my dreams, and then
By day I shall be well again!
For then the night will more than pay
The hopeless longing of the day.

MATTHEW ARNOLD

SONG

When I am dead, my dearest,
  Sing no sad songs for me;
Plant thou no roses at my head,
  Nor shady cypress-tree:

Be the green grass above me
  With showers and dewdrops wet;
And if thou wilt, remember,
  And if thou wilt, forget.

I shall not see the shadows,
  I shall not feel the rain;
I shall not hear the nightingale
  Sing on, as if in pain:
And dreaming through the twilight
  That doth not rise nor set,
Haply I may remember
  And haply may forget.

CHRISTINA GEORGINA ROSSETTI

REMEMBER

Remember me when I am gone away,
Gone far away into the silent land;
When you can no more hold me by the hand,
Nor I half turn to go, yet turning stay.
Remember me when no more, day by day,
You tell me of our future that you planned:
Only remember me; you understand
It will be late to counsel then or pray.
Yet if you should forget me for a while
And afterwards remember, do not grieve:
For if the darkness and corruption leave
A vestige of the thoughts that once I had,
Better by far you should forget and smile
Than that you should remember and be sad.

CHRISTINA GEORGINA ROSSETTI

SUDDEN LIGHT

I have been here before,
  But when or how I cannot tell.
I know the grass beyond the door,
  The sweet keen smell,
The sighing sound, the lights around the shore.

You have been mine before—
  How long ago I may not know;
But just when at that swallow's soar
  Your neck turned so,
Some veil did fall—I knew it all of yore.

  Has this been thus before?
  And shall not thus time's eddying flight
Still with our lives our love restore
  In death's despite,
And day and night yield one delight once more?
                              DANTE GABRIEL ROSSETTI

SHALL I COMPARE THEE TO A SUMMER'S DAY?

(SONNET XVIII)

Shall I compare thee to a Summer's day?
Thou art more lovely and more temperate:
Rough winds do shake the darling buds of May,
And Summer's lease hath all too short a date:
Sometime too hot the eye of heaven shines,
And often is his gold complexion dimmed;
And every fair from fair sometime declines,
By chance or nature's changing course untrimmed:
But thy eternal Summer shall not fade
Nor lose possession of that fair thou owest;
Nor shall Death brag thou wanderest in his shade,
When in eternal lines to time thou growest:
So long as men can breathe, or eyes can see,
So long lives this, and this gives life to thee.
                              WILLIAM SHAKESPEARE

SWEET LOVE, RENEW THY FORCE

(SONNET LVI)

Sweet love, renew thy force; be it not said
Thy edge should blunter be than appetite,
Which but today by feeding is allay'd,

Tomorrow sharpen'd in his former might.
So, love, be thou; although today thou fill
Thy hungry eyes even till they wink with fullness,
Tomorrow see again, and do not kill
The spirit of love with a perpetual dullness.
Let this sad int'rim like the ocean be
Which parts the shore where two contracted new
Come daily to the banks, that, when they see
Return of love, more blest may be the view;
Or call it winter, which, being full of care,
Makes summer's welcome thrice more wish'd, more rare.

WILLIAM SHAKESPEARE

ONLY THY DUST . . .

Only thy dust is here, thy dust . . .
    But when chill May uncloses
Her petals and is June, I feel
    A heartbeat shake the roses.

Earth and the sun were sweet to us,
    Green grass and brooks and laughter . . .
And I cannot think of thee a ghost
    Within some strange hereafter.

Dawn and the hills were glad of us,
    Tossed corn and windy meadows . . .
And I should not know thee as a shade,
    Pallid among pale shadows.

Stars and streams were friends to us,
    Clear skies and wintry weather . . .
And it was not wraith and wraith with us,
    But flesh and blood together.

Only the dust of thee is here . . .
    But when mine own day closes
I will lie down beside thee, love,
    And mingle with thy roses.

DON MARQUIS

TO ONE IN PARADISE

Thou wast all that to me, love,
　For which my soul did pine:
A green isle in the sea, love,
　A fountain and a shrine
All wreathed with fairy fruits and flowers,
　And all the flowers were mine.

Ah, dream too bright to last!
　Ah, starry Hope, that didst arise
But to be overcast!
　A voice from out of the Future cries,
"On! on!"—but o'er the Past
　(Dim gulf!) my spirit hovering lies
Mute, motionless, aghast.

For, alas! alas! with me
　The light of Life is o'er!
　No more—no more—no more—
(Such language holds the solemn sea
　To the sands upon the shore)
Shall bloom the thunder-blasted tree,
　Or the stricken eagle soar.

And all my days are trances,
　And all my nightly dreams
Are where thy dark eye glances,
　And where thy footstep gleams—
In what ethereal dances,
　By what eternal streams.

　　　　　　　　　EDGAR ALLEN POE

TO HELEN

Helen, thy beauty is to me
　Like those Nicaean barks of yore,
That gently, o'er a perfumed sea,
　The weary, wayworn wanderer bore
　To his own native shore.

On desperate seas long wont to roam,
  Thy hyacinth hair, thy classic face,
Thy Naiad airs, have brought me home
  To the glory that was Greece
  And the grandeur that was Rome.

Lo! in yon brilliant window-niche
  How statue-like I see thee stand,
The agate lamp within thy hand!
  Ah, Psyche, from the regions which
  Are Holy Land!

EDGAR ALLAN POE

GIVE ALL TO LOVE

Give all to love;
Obey thy heart;
Friends, kindred, days,
Estate, good fame,
Plans, credit, and the Muse,—
Nothing refuse.

'Tis a brave master;
Let it have scope:
Follow it utterly,
Hope beyond hope:
High and more high
It dives into noon,
With wing unspent,
Untold intent;
But it is a god,
Knows its own path
And the outlets of the sky.

It was never for the mean;
It requireth courage stout.
Souls above doubt,
Valor unbending,
It will reward,—
They shall return
More than they were,
And ever ascending.

Leave all for love;
Yet, hear me, yet,
One word more thy heart behoved,
One pulse more of firm endeavor,—
Keep thee to-day,
To-morrow, forever,
Free as an Arab
Of thy beloved.

Cling with life to the maid;
But when the surprise,
First vague shadow of surmise,
Flits across her bosom young,
Of a joy apart from thee,
Free be she, fancy-free;
Nor thou detain her vesture's hem,
Nor the palest rose she flung
From her summer diadem.

Though thou loved her as thyself,
As a self of purer clay,
Though her parting dims the day,
Stealing grace from all alive;
Heartily know,
When half-gods go,
The gods arrive.

RALPH WALDO EMERSON

SEVEN TIMES THREE—LOVE

(from *Songs of Seven*)

I leaned out of window, I smelt the white clover,
  Dark, dark was the garden, I saw not the gate;
"Now, if there be footsteps, he comes, my one lover,—
  Hush, nightingale, hush! O sweet nightingale, wait
    Till I listen and hear
    If a step draweth near,
    For my love he is late!

"The skies in the darkness stoop nearer and nearer,
    A cluster of stars hangs like fruit in the tree,
The fall of the water comes sweeter, comes clearer:
    To what art thou listening, and what dost thou see?
        Let the star-clusters grow,
        Let the sweet waters flow,
        And cross quickly to me.

"You night-moths that hover, where honey brims over
    From sycamore blossoms, or settle or sleep;
You glowworms, shine out, and the pathway discover
    To him that comes darkling along the rough steep.
        Ah, my sailor, make haste,
        For the time runs to waste,
        And my love lieth deep,—

"Too deep for swift telling; and yet, my one lover,
    I've conned thee an answer, it waits thee to-night."
By the sycamore passed he, and through the white clover,
    Then all the sweet speech I had fashioned took flight;
        But I'll love him more, more
        Than e'er wife loved before,
        Be the days dark or bright.

                                        JEAN INGELOW

MEMORY

I can remember our sorrow, I can remember our laughter;
I know that surely we kissed and cried and ate together;
I remember our places and games, and plans we had—
The little house and how all came to naught—
Remember well:
But I cannot remember our love,
I cannot remember our love.

                                        HELEN HOYT

UNDERSTANDING

If I should ever need to reach your heart,
Or feel the firmness of your clasping hand,
I pray that you will always do your part
To guide my groping way, and understand
That sometimes, even in a love like ours,
Dim shadows of unrest may dare to grow,
And in the darkness of these sudden hours
Your gentle touch or words might make them go.

If I should search for reassurance, dear,
Within the quiet depths of your own eyes,
Oh, let their gaze remain as wise and clear,
Without rebuke, or sharpness of surprise;
For if you shut me out to grope in vain,
I may not wish to seek your door again.

PAULINE E. SOROKA

NOT BY BREAD ALONE

If thou of fortune be bereft,
And thou dost find but two loaves left
To thee—sell one, and with the dole
Buy hyacinths to feed thy soul.

But not alone does beauty bide
Where bloom and tint and fragrance hide;
The minstrel's melody may feed
Perhaps a more insistent need.

But even beauty, howe'er blent
To ear and eye, fails to content;
Only the heart, with love afire,
Can satisfy the soul's desire.

JAMES TERRY WHITE

EPITAPH IN SIRMIO

Witness how it comes to pass
That the fevered heart grows cool,
Dark and sweet beneath the grass,
How the grass is beautiful,
How the wind, in going over,
Spreads a cool green on the air . . .
This was once a tortured lover,
Sick to death of hot despair.

DAVID MORTON

CHOICE

I'd rather have the thought of you
To hold against my heart,
My spirit to be taught of you
With west winds blowing,
Than all the warm caresses
Of another love's bestowing,
Or all the glories of the world
In which you had no part.

I'd rather have the theme of you
To thread my nights and days,
I'd rather have the dream of you
With faint stars glowing,
I'd rather have the want of you,
The rich, elusive taunt of you
Forever and forever and forever unconfessed
Than claim the alien comfort
Of any other's breast.

O lover! O my lover,
That this should come to me!
I'd rather have the hope of you,
Ah, Love, I'd rather grope for you
Within the great abyss

Than claim another's kiss—
Alone I'd rather go my way
Throughout eternity.

ANGELA MORGAN

OF CERTAIN IRISH FAIRIES

The Leprechaun—the omadhaun!—that lives in County Clare,
Is one foot wide and three feet high without an inch to spare.
He winks the sea-blue eye of him, like other saucy rogues,
And underneath the blackthorn bush he sits to clout his brogues.
Then, if you catch the Leprechaun and never loose your hold,
He's bound to show you where he's hid a pot of yellow gold,
And give you, too, a fairy purse with tassels down the end
That's never bare but always full no matter what you spend.
'Tis I would catch the Leprechaun; and then what would I do?
I'd take the yellow gold, machree, and give it all to you!

The Cluricawne of Monaghan is mighty seldom seen;
He wears a crimson swallow-tail, a vest of apple-green
And shiny shoes with buckles, too, and silver ones at that,
And on his curly head, askew he claps a steeple-hat.
'Tis I will catch the Cluricawne; and why? Because he knows
The only spot in Eire where the four-leafed shamrock grows,
The shamrock that the fairies tend, that does not spring from seed;
'Twill bring you health and wealth and love,—though love you'll never
   need;
'Twill bring you ribbons, laces, pearls and jewels great and small;
So I will catch the Cluricawne and you shall have them all.

ARTHUR GUITERMAN

NO TIME TO HATE

I had no time to hate, because
The grave would hinder me,
And life was not so ample I
Could finish enmity.

Nor had I time to love, but since
Some industry must be,
The little toil of love, I thought,
Was large enough for me.

EMILY DICKINSON

WE'LL GO NO MORE A ROVING

So, we'll go no more a roving
  So late into the night,
Though the heart be still as loving,
  And the moon be still as bright.

For the sword outwears its sheath,
  And the soul wears out the breast,
And the heart must pause to breathe,
  And Love itself have rest.

Though the night was made for loving,
  And the day returns too soon,
Yet we'll go no more a roving
  By the light of the moon.

GEORGE GORDON BYRON

WHEN WE TWO PARTED

When we two parted
In silence and tears,
Half broken-hearted,
To sever for years,
Pale grew thy cheek and cold,
Colder thy kiss;
Truly that hour foretold
Sorrow to this!

The dew of the morning
Sunk chill on my brow;
It felt like the warning
Of what I feel now.
Thy vows are all broken,
And light is thy fame:

I hear thy name spoken
And share in its shame.

They name thee before me,
A knell to mine ear;
A shudder comes o'er me—
Why wert thou so dear?
They know not I knew thee
Who knew thee too well:
Long, long shall I rue thee
Too deeply to tell.

In secret we met:
In silence I grieve
That thy heart could forget,
Thy spirit deceive.
If I should meet thee
After long years,
How should I greet thee?—
With silence and tears.

GEORGE GORDON BYRON

THE FLIGHT OF LOVE

When the lamp is shattered
The light in the dust lies dead—
When the cloud is scattered,
The rainbow's glory is shed.
When the lute is broken,
Sweet tones are remembered not;
When the lips have spoken,
Loved accents are soon forgot.

As music and splendor
Survive not the lamp and the lute,
The heart's echoes render
No song when the spirit is mute—
No song but sad dirges,
Like the wind through a ruined cell,
Or the mournful surges
That ring the dead seaman's knell.

When hearts have once mingled,
Love first leaves the well-built nest;
The weak one is singled
To endure what it once possessed.
O Love! who bewailest
The frailty of all things here,
Why choose you the frailest
For your cradle, your home, and your bier?

Its passions will rock thee
As the storms rock the ravens on high;
Bright reason will mock thee,
Like the sun from a wintry sky.
From thy nest every rafter
Will rot, and thine eagle home
Leave thee naked to laughter,
When leaves fall and cold winds come.

                              PERCY BYSSHE SHELLEY

TO ——

One word is too often profaned
    For me to profane it,
One feeling too falsely disdained
    For thee to disdain it.
One hope is too like despair
    For prudence to smother,
And Pity from thee more dear
    Than that from another.
I can give not what men call love;
    But wilt thou accept not
The worship the heart lifts above
    And the Heavens reject not:
The desire of the moth for the star,
    Of the night for the morrow,
The devotion to something afar
    From the sphere of our sorrow?

                              PERCY BYSSHE SHELLEY

A RED, RED ROSE

O, my luve's like a red, red rose
  That's newly sprung in June;
O, my luve's like the melodie
  That's sweetly played in tune.

As fair thou art, my bonnie lass,
  So deep in luve am I;
And I will luve thee still, my dear,
  Till a' the seas gang dry.

Till a' the seas gang dry, my dear,
  And the rocks melt wi' the sun;
I will luve thee still, my dear,
  While the sands o' life shall run.

And fare-thee-weel, my only luve!
  And fare-thee-weel a while!
And I will come again, my luve,
  Though it were ten thousand mile.

ROBERT BURNS

AS IN A ROSE-JAR

As in a rose-jar filled with petals sweet
  Blown long ago in some old garden place,
  Mayhap, where you and I a little space
Drank deep of love and knew that love was fleet;
Of leaves once gathered from a lost retreat
  By one who never will again retrace
  Her silent footsteps—one whose gentle face
Was fairer than the roses at her feet;

So, deep within the vase of memory
  I keep my dust of roses fresh and dear
    As in the days before I knew the smart

Of time and death. Nor aught can take from me
The haunting fragrance that still lingers here
As in a rose-jar, so within my heart.

THOMAS S. JONES, JR.

IF I WERE KING

After Villon

If I were king—ah love, if I were king!
What tributary nations would I bring
To stoop before your sceptre and to swear
Allegiance to your lips and eyes and hair.
Beneath your feet what treasures I would fling:—
The stars should be your pearls upon a string,
The world a ruby for your finger ring,
And you should have the sun and moon to wear
If I were king.

Let these wild dreams and wilder words take wing,
Deep in the woods I hear a shepherd sing
A simple ballad to a sylvan air,
Of love that ever finds your face more fair.
I could not give you any godlier thing
If I were king.

JUSTIN HUNTLY MCCARTHY

NOW WHAT IS LOVE

Now what is Love, I pray thee, tell?
  It is that fountain and that well
  Where pleasure and repentance dwell;
  It is, perhaps, the saucing bell
  That tolls all into heaven or hell;
  And this is Love, as I hear tell.

Yet what is Love, I prithee, say?
  It is a work on holiday,
  It is December matched with May,
  When lusty bloods in fresh array

Hear ten months after of the play;
And this is Love, as I hear say.

Yet what is Love, good shepherd, sain?
  It is a sunshine mixed with rain,
  It is a toothache or like pain,
  It is a game where none hath gain;
  The lass saith no, yet would full fain;
  And this is Love, as I hear sain.

Yet, shepherd, what is Love, I pray?
  It is a yes, it is a nay,
  A pretty kind of sporting fray,
  It is a thing will soon away.
  Then, nymphs, take vantage while ye may;
  And this is Love, as I hear say.

Yet what is Love, good shepherd, show?
  A thing that creeps, it cannot go,
  A prize that passeth to and fro,
  A thing for one, a thing for moe,
  And he that proves shall find it so;
  And shepherd, this is Love, I trow.

                    WALTER RALEIGH

THE PASSIONATE SHEPHERD TO HIS LOVE

Come live with me and be my Love,
And we will all the pleasures prove
That hills and valleys, dales and fields,
Or woods or steepy mountain yields.

And we will sit upon the rocks,
And see the shepherds feed their flocks
By shallow rivers, to whose falls
Melodious birds sing madrigals.

And I will make thee beds of roses
And a thousand fragrant posies;
A cap of flowers, and a kirtle
Embroidered all with leaves of myrtle.

A gown made of the finest wool
Which from our pretty lambs we pull;
Fair-lined slippers for the cold,
With buckles of the purest gold.

A belt of straw and ivy-buds
With coral clasps and amber studs:
And if these pleasures may thee move,
Come live with me and be my Love.

The shepherd swains shall dance and sing
For thy delight each May morning:
If these delights thy mind may move,
Then live with me and be my Love.

CHRISTOPHER MARLOWE

TO CELIA

(from *The Forest*)

Drink to me only with thine eyes,
  And I will pledge with mine;
Or leave a kiss but in the cup
  And I'll not look for wine.
The thirst that from the soul doth rise
  Doth ask a drink divine;
But might I of Jove's nectar sup,
  I would not change for thine.

I sent thee late a rosy wreath,
  Not so much honoring thee
As giving it a hope that there
  It could not withered be;
But thou thereon didst only breathe,
  And sent'st it back to me;
Since when it grows, and smells, I swear,
  Not of itself but thee!

BEN JONSON

LOVE

Love bade me welcome; yet my soul drew back,
    Guilty of dust and sin.
But quick-eyed Love, observing me grow slack
    From my first entrance in,
Drew nearer to me, sweetly questioning
    If I lack anything.

"A guest," I answered, "worthy to be here:"
    Love said, "You shall be he."
"I, the unkind, ungrateful? Ah, my dear,
    I cannot look on Thee."
Love took my hand and, smiling, did reply,
    "Who made the eyes but I?"

"Truth, Lord; but I have marred them: let my shame
    Go where it doth deserve."
"And know you not," says Love, "Who bore the blame?"
    "My dear, then I will serve."
"You must sit down," says Love, "and taste my meat."
    So I did sit and eat.

                                GEORGE HERBERT

TO HIS COY MISTRESS

Had we but world enough, and time,
This coyness, Lady, were no crime.
We would sit down and think which way
To walk and pass our long love's day.
Thou by the Indian Ganges' side
Shouldst rubies find: I by the tide
Of Humber would complain. I would
Love you ten years before the Flood,
And you should, if you please, refuse
Till the conversion of the Jews.
My vegetable love should grow
Vaster than empires, and more slow;

An hundred years should go to praise
Thine eyes and on thy forehead gaze;
Two hundred to adore each breast,
But thirty thousand to the rest;
An age at least to every part,
And the last age should show your heart.
For, Lady, you deserve this state,
Nor would I love at lower rate.
　But at my back I always hear
Time's winged chariot hurrying near;
And yonder all before us lie
Deserts of vast eternity.
Thy beauty shall no more be found,
Nor, in thy marble vault, shall sound
My echoing song: then worms shall try
That long preserved virginity,
And your quaint honor turn to dust,
And into ashes all my lust:
The grave's a fine and private place,
But none, I think, do there embrace.
　Now therefore, while the youthful hue
Sits on thy skin like morning dew,
And while thy willing soul transpires
At every pore with instant fires,
Now let us sport us while we may,
And now, like amorous birds of prey,
Rather at once our time devour
Than languish in his slow-chapt power.
Let us roll all our strength and all
Our sweetness up into one ball,
And tear our pleasures with rough strife
Through the iron gates of life:
Thus, though we cannot make our sun
Stand still, yet we will make him run.

ANDREW MARVELL

LESBIA

Grow weary if you will, let me be sad.
Use no more speech now;
Let the silence spread gold hair above us,

Fold on delicate fold.
Use no more speech;
You had the ivory of my life to carve . . .

And Picus of Mirandola is dead;
And all the gods they dreamed and fabled of,
Hermes and Thoth and Christ are rotten now,
Rotten and dank . . .
And through it all I see your pale Greek face;
Tenderness
Makes me as eager as a little child to love you;
You morsel left half-cold on Caesar's plate.

RICHARD ALDINGTON

THE WOMAN WHO UNDERSTANDS

*Somewhere she waits to make you win, your soul in her firm, white
hands—*
*Somewhere the gods have made for you, the Woman Who Under-
stands!*

As the tide went out she found him
  Lashed to a spar of Despair,
The wreck of his Ship around him—
  The wreck of his Dreams in the air;
Found him and loved him and gathered
  The soul of him close to her heart—
The soul that had sailed an uncharted sea,
The soul that had sought to win and be free—
  The soul of which *she* was part!
    And there in the dusk she cried to the man,
   "Win your battle—you can, you can!"

Broken by Fate, unrelenting,
  Scarred by the lashings of Chance;
Bitter his heart—unrepenting—
  Hardened by Circumstance;
Shadowed by Failure ever,
  Cursing, he would have died,
But the touch of her hand, her strong warm hand,

And her love of his soul, took full command,
  Just at the turn of the tide!
    Standing beside him, filled with trust,
    "Win!" she whispered, "you must, you must!"

Helping and loving and guiding,
  Urging when that were best,
Holding her fears in hiding
  Deep in her quiet breast;
This is the woman who kept him
  True to his standards lost,
When tossed in the storm and stress of strife,
He thought himself through with the game of life
  And ready to pay the cost.
    Watching and guarding, whispering still,
    "Win you can—and you will, you will!"

This is the story of ages
  This is the Woman's way;
Wiser than seers or sages,
  Lifting us day by day;
Facing all things with a courage
  Nothing can daunt or dim,
    Treading Life's path, wherever it leads—
Lined with flowers or choked with weeds,
  But ever with him—with him!
    Guidon—comrade—golden spur—
    The men who win are helped by *her!*

Somewhere she waits, strong in belief, your
  Soul in her firm, white hands:
Thank well the gods, when she comes to you,
  The Woman Who Understands!

EVERARD JACK APPLETON

WHEN I WAS ONE-AND-TWENTY

When I was one-and-twenty
  I heard a wise man say,
"Give crowns and pounds and guineas
  But not your heart away;

Give pearls away and rubies
But keep your fancy free."
But I was one-and-twenty,
No use to talk to me.

When I was one-and-twenty
I heard him say again,
"The heart out of the bosom
Was never given in vain;
'Tis paid with sighs a plenty
And sold for endless rue."
And I am two-and-twenty,
And oh, 'tis true, 'tis true.

A. E. HOUSMAN

A LEAVE-TAKING

Let us go hence, my songs; she will not hear.
Let us go hence together without fear;
Keep silence now, for singing-time is over,
And over all old things and all things dear.
She loves not you nor me as all we love her.
Yes, though we sang as angels in her ear,
   She would not hear.

Let us rise up and part; she will not know.
Let us go seaward as the great winds go,
Full of blown sand and foam; what help is there?
There is no help, for all these things are so,
And all the world is bitter as a tear.
And how these things are, though ye strove to show,
   She would not know.

Let us go home and hence; she will not weep.
We gave love many dreams and days to keep,
Flowers without scent, and fruits that would not grow,
Saying, "If thou wilt, thrust in thy sickle and reap."
All is reaped now; no grass is left to mow;
And we that sowed, though all we fell on sleep,
   She would not weep.

Let us go hence and rest; she will not love.
She shall not hear us if we sing hereof,
Nor see love's ways, how sore they are and steep.
Come hence, let be, lie still; it is enough.
Love is a barren sea, bitter and deep;
And though she saw all heaven in flower above,
    She would not love.

Let us give up, go down; she will not care.
Though all the stars made gold of all the air,
And the sea moving saw before it move
One moonflower making all the foamflowers fair;
Though all those waves went over us, and drove
Deep down the stifling lips and drowning hair,
    She would not care.

Let us go hence, go hence; she will not see.
Sing all once more together; surely she,
She too, remembering days and words that were,
Will turn a little toward us, sighing; but we,
We are hence, we are gone, as though we had not been there.
Nay, and though all men seeing had pity on me,
    She would not see.

ALGERNON CHARLES SWINBURNE

EARTH TREMBLES WAITING

I wait for his foot fall,
    Eager, afraid,
Each evening hour
    When the lights fade . . .

I wait for his voice
    To speak low to me—
As a mariner lost
    Dreams of harbor, at sea . . .

I wait for his lips
    When the dusk falls.
Life holds my longing
    Behind dark walls.

I wait for his face—
    As after rain
Earth trembles waiting
    For the sun again . . .
        BLANCHE SHOEMAKER WAGSTAFF

OF LOVE

(from *The Prophet*)

Then said Almitra, Speak to us of Love.
    And he raised his head and looked upon
the people, and there fell a stillness upon
them. And with a great voice he said:
    When love beckons to you, follow him,
    Though his ways are hard and steep.
    And when his wings enfold you yield to him,
    Though the sword hidden among his pinions
may wound you.
    And when he speaks to you believe in him,
    Though his voice may shatter your dreams
as the north wind lays waste the garden.

    For even as love crowns you so shall he
crucify you. Even as he is for your growth
so is he for your pruning.
    Even as he ascends to your height and
caresses your tenderest branches that quiver
in the sun,
    So shall he descend to your roots and
shake them in their clinging to the earth.

    Like sheaves of corn he gathers you unto
himself.
    He threshes you to make you naked.
    He sifts you to free you from your husks.
    He grinds you to whiteness.
    He kneads you until you are pliant;
    And then he assigns you to his sacred fire, that
you may become sacred bread for God's sacred feast.

All these things shall love do unto you that
you may know the secrets of your heart, and in that
knowledge become a fragment of Life's heart.

But if in your fear you would seek only love's
peace and love's pleasure,
Then it is better for you that you cover your
nakedness and pass out of love's threshing-floor,
Into the seasonless world where you shall laugh,
but not all of your laughter, and weep, but not
all of your tears.

Love gives naught but itself and takes naught
but from itself.
Love possesses not nor would it be possessed;
For love is sufficient unto love.

When you love you should not say, "God is in
my heart" but rather, "I am in the heart of God."
And think not you can direct the course of love,
for love, if it finds you worthy, directs your course.

Love has no other desire but to fulfil itself.
But if you love and must needs have desires, let
these be your desires:
To melt and be like a running brook that sings
its melody to the night.
To know the pain of too much tenderness.
To be wounded by your own understanding of love;
And to bleed willingly and joyfully.
To wake at dawn with a winged heart and give
thanks for another day of loving;
To rest at the noon hour and meditate love's
ecstasy;
To return home at eventide with gratitude;
And then to sleep with a prayer for the beloved
in your heart and a song of praise upon your lips.

KAHLIL GIBRAN

III. Friendship

A FRIEND OR TWO

There's all of pleasure and all of peace
    In a friend or two;
And all your troubles may find release
    Within a friend or two;
It's in the grip of the sleeping hand
On native soil or in alien land,
But the world is made—do you understand—
    Of a friend or two.

A song to sing, and a crust to share
    With a friend or two;
A smile to give and a grief to bear
    With a friend or two;
A road to walk and a goal to win,
An inglenook to find comfort in,
The gladdest hours that we know begin
    With a friend or two.

A little laughter; perhaps some tears
    With a friend or two;
The days, the weeks, and the months and years
    With a friend or two;
A vale to cross and a hill to climb,
A mock at age and a jeer at time—
The prose of life takes the lilt of rhyme
    With a friend or two.

The brother-soul and the brother-heart
    Of a friend or two
Make us drift on from the crowd apart,
    With a friend or two;
For come days happy or come days sad
We count no hours but the ones made glad
By the hale good times we have ever had
    With a friend or two.

Then brim the goblet and quaff the toast
    To a friend or two,
For glad the man who can always boast
    Of a friend or two;
But fairest sight is a friendly face,
The blithest tread is a friendly pace,
And heaven will be a better place
    For a friend or two.

                  WILBUR D. NESBIT

THE FRIEND WHO JUST STANDS BY

When trouble comes your soul to try,
You love the friend who just "stands by."
Perhaps there's nothing he can do—
The thing is strictly up to you;
For there are troubles all your own,
And paths the soul must tread alone;
Times when love cannot smooth the road
Nor friendship lift the heavy load,
But just to know you have a friend
Who will "stand by" until the end,
Whose sympathy through all endures,
Whose warm handclasp is always yours—
It helps, someway, to pull you through,
Although there's nothing he can do.
And so with fervent heart you cry,
"God bless the friend who just 'stands by'!"

                  B. Y. WILLIAMS

THEY SAY THAT IN THE UNCHANGING PLACE

(from *Dedicatory Ode*)

They say that in the unchanging place,
    Where all we loved is always dear,
We meet our morning face to face
    And find at last our twentieth year . . .

They say (and I am glad they say)
  It is so; and it may be so:
It may be just the other way,
  I cannot tell. But this I know:

From quiet homes and first beginning,
  Out to the undiscovered ends,
There's nothing worth the wear of winning,
  But laughter and the love of friends.

                                    HILAIRE BELLOC

TO A FRIEND

I ask but one thing of you, only one,
  That always you will be my dream of you;
  That never shall I wake to find untrue
All this I have believed and rested on,
Forever vanished, like a vision gone
  Out into the night. Alas how few
  There are who strike in us a chord we knew
Existed, but so seldom heard its tone
  We tremble at the half-forgotten sound.
The world is full of rude awakenings
  And heaven-born castles shattered to the ground,
Yet still our human longing vainly clings
  To a belief in beauty through all wrongs.
  O stay your hand, and leave my heart its songs!

                                    AMY LOWELL

THE ENGLISH ARE FROSTY

(from *The White Cliffs*)

The English are frosty
  When you're no kith or kin
Of their's, but how they alter,
  When once they take you in!
The kindest, the truest,
  The best friends ever known,

It's hard to remember
    How they froze you to a bone.
They showed me all London,
    Johnnie and his friends;
They took me to the country
    For long weekends;
I never was so happy,
    I never had such fun,
I stayed many weeks in England
    Instead of just one.

                      ALICE DUER MILLER

AROUND THE CORNER

Around the corner I have a friend,
In this great city that has no end;
Yet days go by, and weeks rush on,
And before I know it, a year is gone,
And I never see my old friend's face,
For Life is a swift and terrible race.
He knows I like him just as well
As in the days when I rang his bell
And he rang mine.
We were younger then,
And now we are busy, tired men:
Tired with playing a foolish game,
Tired with trying to make a name.
"To-morrow," I say, "I will call on Jim,
Just to show that I'm thinking of him."
But to-morrow comes—and to-morrow goes,
And the distance between us grows and grows.

Around the corner!—yet miles away . . .
"Here's a telegram, sir,"
     "Jim died to-day."

And that's what we get, and deserve in the end:
Around the corner, a vanished friend.

                CHARLES HANSON TOWNE

AULD LANG SYNE

Should auld acquaintance be forgot,
  And never brought to min'?
Should auld acquaintance be forgot,
  And days o' lang syne?

    For auld lang syne, my dear,
      For auld lang syne,
    We'll tak a cup o' kindness yet
      For auld lang syne.

We twa hae rin about the braes,
  And pu'd the gowans fine;
But we've wandered monie a weary fit
  Sin' auld lang syne.

We twa hae paidl't i' the burn,
  Frae mornin' sun till dine;
But seas between us braid hae roared
  Sin' auld lang syne.

And here's a hand, my trusty fiere,
  And gie's a hand o' thine;
And we'll tak a right guid willie-waught
  For auld lang syne.

And surely ye'll be your pint-stowp,
  And surely I'll be mine,
And we'll take a cup o' kindness yet
  For auld lang syne!

                    ROBERT BURNS

TO A FRIEND

When we were idlers with the loitering rills,
  The need of human love we little noted:
  Our love was nature; and the peace that floated
On the white mist, and dwelt upon the hills,

To sweet accord subdued our wayward wills:
   One soul was ours, one mind, one heart devoted,
   That, wisely doting, asked not why it doted,
And ours the unknown joy, which knowing kills.
But now I find how dear thou wert to me;
   That man is more than half of nature's treasure,
Of that fair beauty which no eye can see,
   Of that sweet music which no ear can measure;
   And now the streams may sing for others' pleasure,
The hills sleep on in their eternity.

HARTLEY COLERIDGE

WHEN TO THE SESSIONS OF SWEET SILENT THOUGHT

(SONNET XXX)

When to the sessions of sweet silent thought
I summon up remembrance of things past,
I sigh the lack of many a thing I sought
And with old woes new wail my dear time's waste.
Then can I drown an eye (unus'd to flow)
For precious friends hid in death's dateless night,
And weep afresh love's long since cancell'd woe,
And moan th' expense of many a vanish'd sight.
Then can I grieve at grievances foregone,
And heavily from woe to woe tell o'er
The sad account of fore-bemoaned moan.
Which I new pay as if not paid before.
But if the while I think on thee, dear friend,
All losses are restor'd and sorrows end.

WILLIAM SHAKESPEARE

SALAAM ALAIKUM

(Peace Be with You)

I pray the prayer the Easterners do,
May the peace of Allah abide with you.
Wherever you stay, wherever you go,

May the beautiful palms of Allah grow.
Through days of labor and nights of rest,
The love of good Allah make thee blest.
So I touch my heart as the Easterners do,
May the peace of Allah abide with you.

UNKNOWN

IV. Home and Family

ROOFS

(FOR AMELIA JOSEPHINE BURR)

The road is wide and the stars are out and the breath of the night is
    sweet,
And this is the time when wanderlust should seize upon my feet.
But I'm glad to turn from the open road and the starlight on my
    face,
And leave the splendor of out-of-doors for a human dwelling place.

I never have seen a vagabond who really liked to roam
All up and down the streets of the world and not to have a home:
The tramp who slept in your barn last night and left at break of
    day
Will wander only until he finds another place to stay.

A gypsy-man will sleep in his cart with canvas overhead;
Or else he'll go into his tent when it is time for bed.
He'll sit on the grass and take his ease so long as the sun is high,
But when it is dark he wants a roof to keep away the sky.

If you call a gypsy a vagabond, I think you do him wrong,
For he never goes a-travelling but he takes his home along.
And the only reason a road is good, as every wanderer knows,
Is just because of the homes, the homes, the homes to which it goes.

They say that life is a highway and its milestones are the years,
And now and then there's a toll-gate where you buy your way with
    tears.
It's a rough road and a steep road and it stretches broad and far,
But it leads at last to a golden Town where golden Houses are.

JOYCE KILMER

PRAYER FOR THIS HOUSE

May nothing evil cross this door,
And may ill fortune never pry
About these windows; may the roar
    And rain go by.

Strengthened by faith, these rafters will
Withstand the batt'ring of the storm;
This hearth, though all the world grow chill,
    Will keep us warm.

Peace shall walk softly through these rooms,
Touching our lips with holy wine,
Till ev'ry casual corner blooms
    Into a shrine.

Laughter shall drown the raucous shout;
And, though these shelt'ring walls are thin,
May they be strong to keep hate out
    And hold love in.

               LOUIS UNTERMEYER

FRUIT OF THE FLOWER

My father is a quiet man
  With sober, steady ways;
For simile, a folded fan;
  His nights are like his days.

My mother's life is puritan,
  No hint of cavalier,
A pool so calm you're sure it can
  Have little depth to fear.

And yet my father's eyes can boast
  How full his life has been;
There haunts them yet the languid ghost
  Of some still sacred sin.

And though my mother chants of God,
  And of the mystic river,
I've seen a bit of checkered sod
  Set all her flesh aquiver.

Why should he deem it pure mischance
  A son of his is fain
To do a naked tribal dance
  Each time he hears the rain?

Why should she think it devil's art
  That all my songs should be
Of love and lovers, broken heart,
  And wild sweet agony?

Who plants a seed begets a bud,
  Extract of that same root;
Why marvel at the hectic blood
  That flushes this wild fruit?

                          COUNTEE CULLEN

A PRAYER FOR MY DAUGHTER

Once more the storm is howling, and half hid
Under this cradle-hood and coverlid
My child sleeps on. There is no obstacle
But Gregory's wood and one bare hill
Whereby the haystack and roof levelling wind,
Bred on the Atlantic, can be stayed;
And for an hour I have walked and prayed
Because of the great gloom that is in my mind.

I have walked and prayed for this young child an hour
And heard the sea-wind scream upon the tower,
And under the arches of the bridge, and scream
In the elms above the flooded stream;
Imagining in excited reverie
That in the future years had come,
Dancing to a frenzied drum,
Out of the murderous innocence of the sea.

May she be granted beauty and yet not
Beauty to make a stranger's eye distraught,
Or hers before a looking-glass, for such,
Being made beautiful overmuch,
Consider beauty a sufficient end,
Lose natural kindness and maybe
The heart-revealing intimacy
That chooses right, and never finds a friend.

Helen being chosen found life flat and dull
And later had much trouble from a fool,
While that great Queen, that rose out of the spray,
Being fatherless could have her way,
Yet chose a bandy-legged smith for man.
It's certain that fine women eat
A crazy salad with their meat,
Whereby the Horn of Plenty is undone.

In courtesy I'd have her chiefly learned,
Hearts are not had as a gift, but hearts are earned
By those that are not entirely beautiful;
Yet many, that have played the fool
For beauty's very self, has charm made wise,
And many a poor man that has roved,
Loved and thought himself beloved,
From a glad kindness cannot take his eyes.

May she become a flourishing hidden tree
That all her thoughts may like the linnet be
And have no business but dispensing round
Their magnanimities of sound,
Nor but in merriment begin a chase,
Nor but in merriment a quarrel.
Oh, may she live like some green laurel
Rooted in one dear perpetual place.

My mind, because the minds that I have loved,
The sort of beauty that I have approved,
Prosper but little, has dried up of late,
Yet knows that to be choked with hate
May well be of all evil chances chief.

If there's no hatred in a mind
Assault and battery of the wind
Can never tear the linnet from the leaf.

An intellectual hatred is the worst,
So let her think opinions are accursed.
Have I not seen the loveliest woman born
Out of the mouth of Plenty's horn,
Because of her opinionated mind
Barter that horn and every good
By quiet natures understood
For an old bellows full of angry wind?

Considering that, all hatred driven hence,
The soul recovers radical innocence
And learns at last that it is self-delighting,
Self-appeasing, self-affrighting,
And that its own sweet will is heaven's will;
She can, though every face should scowl
And every windy quarter howl
Or every bellows burst, be happy still.

And may her bridegroom bring her to a house
Where all's accustomed, ceremonious;
For arrogance and hatred are the wares
Peddled in the thoroughfares.
How but in custom and in ceremony
Are innocence and beauty born?
Ceremony's a name for the rich horn,
And custom for the spreading laurel tree.

WILLIAM BUTLER YEATS

A PARENTAL ODE TO MY SON

AGED THREE YEARS AND FIVE MONTHS

Thou happy, happy elf!
(But stop,—first let me kiss away that tear!)
Thou tiny image of myself!
(My love, he's poking peas into his ear!)
Thou merry, laughing sprite,

With spirits feather-light,
Untouched by sorrow, and unsoiled by sin,—
(My dear, the child is swallowing a pin!)

Thou little tricksy Puck!
With antic toys so funnily bestuck,
Light as the singing bird that wings the air,—
(The door! the door! he'll tumble down the stair!)
Thou darling of thy sire!
(Why, Jane, he'll set his pinafore afire!)
    Thou imp of mirth and joy!
In Love's dear chain so strong and bright a link,
    Thou idol of thy parents,—(Drat the boy!
There goes my ink!)

    Thou cherub,—but of earth;
Fit playfellow for Fays, by moonlight pale,
    In harmless sport and mirth,
(That dog will bite him, if he pulls its tail!)
    Thou human humming-bee, extracting honey
From every blossom in the world that blows,
    Singing in youth's Elysium ever sunny.—
(Another tumble! That's his precious nose!)

Thy father's pride and hope!
(He'll break the mirror with that skipping-rope!)
With pure heart newly stamped from nature's mint,
(Where *did* he learn that squint?)
Thou young domestic dove!
(He'll have that jug off with another shovel!)
Dear nursling of the hymeneal nest!
(Are these torn clothes his best?)
Little epitome of man!
(He'll climb upon the table, that's his plan!)
Touched with the beauteous tints of dawning life,—
    (He's got a knife!)

Thou enviable being!
No storms, no clouds, in thy blue sky foreseeing,
    Play on, play on,
    My elfin John!
Toss the light ball, bestride the stick,—

(I knew so many cakes would make him sick!)
  With fancies, buoyant as the thistle-down,
Prompting the face grotesque, and antic brisk,
With many a lamb-like frisk!
  (He's got the scissors, snipping at your gown!)

Thou pretty opening rose!
(Go to your mother, child, and wipe your nose!)
Balmy and breathing music like the South,—
(He really brings my heart into my mouth!)
Fresh as the morn, and brilliant as its star,—
(I wish that window had an iron bar!)
Bold as the hawk, yet gentle as the dove;—
(I'll tell you what, my love,
I cannot write unless he's sent above.)

THOMAS HOOD

BECOMING A DAD

Old women say that men don't know
The pain through which all mothers go,
And maybe that is true, and yet
I vow I never shall forget
The night he came. I suffered, too,
Those bleak and dreary long hours through;
I paced the floor and mopped my brow
And waited for his glad wee-ow!
I went upstairs and then came down,
Because I saw the doctor frown
And knew beyond the slightest doubt
He wished to goodness I'd clear out.

I walked into the yard for air
And back again to hear her there,
And met the nurse, as calm as though
My world was not in deepest woe,
And when I questioned, seeking speech
Of consolation that would reach
Into my soul and strengthen me
For dreary hours that were to be:
"Progressing nicely!" that was all

She said and tip-toed down the hall;
"Progressing nicely!" nothing more,
And left me there to pace the floor.

And once the nurse came out in haste
For something that had been misplaced,
And I that had been growing bold
Then felt my blood grow icy cold;
And fear's stern chill swept over me.
I stood and watched and tried to see
Just what it was she came to get.
I haven't learned that secret yet.
I half-believe that nurse in white
Was adding fuel to my fright
And taking an unholy glee,
From time to time, in torturing me.

Then silence! To her room I crept
And was informed the doctor slept!
The doctor slept! Oh, vicious thought,
While she at death's door bravely fought
And suffered untold anguish deep,
The doctor lulled himself to sleep.
I looked and saw him stretched out flat
And could have killed the man for that.
Then morning broke, and oh, the joy:
With dawn there came to us our boy.
And in a glorious little while
I went in there and saw her smile!

I must have looked a human wreck,
My collar wilted at my neck,
My hair awry, my features drawn
With all the suffering I had borne.
She looked at me and softly said,
"If I were you, I'd go to bed."
Her's was the bitterer part, I know;
She traveled through the vale of woe.
But now when women folks recall
The pain and anguish of it all
I answer them in manner sad:
"It's no cinch to become a dad."

EDGAR A. GUEST

WASHING THE DISHES

When we on simple rations sup
How easy is the washing up!
But heavy feeding complicates
The task by soiling many plates.

And though I grant that I have prayed
That we might find a serving-maid,
I'd scullion all my days, I think,
To see Her smile across the sink!

I wash, she wipes. In water hot
I souse each dish and pan and pot;
While Taffy mutters, purrs, and begs,
And rubs himself against my legs.

The man who never in his life
Has washed the dishes with his wife
Or polished up the silver plate—
He still is largely celibate.

One warning: there is certain ware
That must be handled with all care:
The Lord Himself will give you up
If you should drop a willow cup!

CHRISTOPHER MORLEY

MY OLD KENTUCKY HOME

The sun shines bright in the old Kentucky home;
  'Tis summer, the darkeys are gay;
The corn-top's ripe, and the meadow's in the bloom,
  While the birds make music all the day.
The young folks roll on the little cabin floor,
  All merry, all happy and bright;
By-'n'-by hard times comes a-knocking at the door:—
  Then my old Kentucky home, good-night!

Weep no more, my lady,
O, weep no more to-day!
We will sing one song for the old Kentucky home,
For the old Kentucky home, far away.

They hunt no more for the possum and the coon,
On the meadow, the hill, and the shore;
They sing no more by the glimmer of the moon,
On the bench by the old cabin door.
The day goes by like a shadow o'er the heart,
With sorrow, where all was delight;
The time has come when the darkeys have to part:—
Then my old Kentucky home, good-night!

The head must bow, and the back will have to bend,
Wherever the darkey may go;
A few more days and the troubles all will end,
In the field where the sugar-canes grow.
A few more days for to tote the weary load,—
No matter, 'twill never be light;
A few more days till we totter on the road:—
Then my old Kentucky home, good-night!

Weep no more, my lady,
O, weep no more to-day!
We will sing one song for the old Kentucky home,
For the old Kentucky home, far away.

STEPHEN FOSTER

THE CHILDREN'S HOUR

Between the dark and the daylight,
When the night is beginning to lower,
Comes a pause in the day's occupations,
That is known as the Children's Hour.

I hear in the chamber above me
The patter of little feet,
The sound of a door that is opened,
And voices soft and sweet.

From my study I see in the lamplight,
  Descending the broad hall stair,
Grave Alice, and laughing Allegra,
  And Edith with golden hair.

A whisper, and then a silence:
  Yet I know by their merry eyes
They are plotting and planning together
  To take me by surprise.

A sudden rush from the stairway,
  A sudden raid from the hall!
By three doors left unguarded
  They enter my castle wall!

They climb up into my turret
  O'er the arms and back of my chair;
If I try to escape, they surround me;
  They seem to be everywhere.

They almost devour me with kisses,
  Their arms about me entwine,
Till I think of the Bishop of Bingen
  In his Mouse-Tower on the Rhine!

Do you think, O blue-eyed banditti,
  Because you have scaled the wall,
Such an old mustache as I am
  Is not a match for you all!

I have you fast in my fortress,
  And will not let you depart,
But put you down into the dungeon
  In the round-tower of my heart.

And there will I keep you forever,
  Yes, forever and a day,
Till the walls shall crumble to ruin,
  And moulder in dust away.
                HENRY WADSWORTH LONGFELLOW

MY EARLY HOME

Here sparrows build upon the trees,
  And stock-dove hides her nest;
The leaves are winnowed by the breeze
  Into a calmer rest:
The blackcap's song was very sweet,
  That used the rose to kiss;
It made the paradise complete:
  My early home was this.

The redbreast from the sweetbrier bush
  Dropt down to pick the worm;
On the horse-chestnut sang the thrush,
  O'er the house where I was born;
The moonlight, like a shower of pearls,
  Fell o'er this "bower of bliss,"
And on the bench sat boys and girls:
  My early home was this.

The old house stooped just like a cave,
  Thatched o'er with mosses green;
Winter around the walls would rave,
  But all was calm within;
The trees are here all green agen,
  Here bees the flowers still kiss,
But flowers and trees seemed sweeter then:
  My early home was this.

JOHN CLARE

HEART'S CONTENT

"A sail! a sail! Oh, whence away,
  And whither, o'er the foam?
Good brother mariners, we pray,
  God speed you safely home!"
"Now wish us not so foul a wind,

Until the fair be spent;
For hearth and home we leave behind:
We sail for Heart's Content."

"For Heart's Content! And sail ye so,
    With canvas flowing free?
But, pray you, tell us, if ye know,
    Where may that harbor be?
For we that greet you, worn of time,
    Wave-racked, and tempest-rent,
By sun and star, in every clime,
    Have searched for Heart's Content.

"In every clime the world around,
    The waste of waters o'er;
An El Dorado have we found,
    That ne'er was found before.
The isles of spice, the lands of dawn,
    Where East and West are blent—
All these our eyes have looked upon,
    But where is Heart's Content?

"Oh, turn again, while yet ye may,
    And ere the hearths are cold,
And all the embers ashen-gray,
    By which ye sat of old,
And dumb in death the loving lips
    That mourned as forth ye went
To join the fleet of missing ships,
    In quest of Heart's Content;

"And seek again the harbor-lights,
    Which faithful fingers trim,
Ere yet alike the days and nights
    Unto your eyes are dim!
For woe, alas! to those that roam
    Till time and tide are spent,
And win no more the port of home—
    The only Heart's Content!"

                                        UNKNOWN

HOME

O, Falmouth is a fine town with ships in the bay,
And I wish from my heart it's there I was to-day;
I wish from my heart I was far away from here,
Sitting in my parlor and talking to my dear.
For it's home, dearie, home—it's home I want to be.
Our topsails are hoisted, and we'll away to sea.
O, the oak and the ash and the bonnie birken tree
They're all growing green in the old countrie.

In Baltimore a-walking a lady I did meet
With her babe on her arm as she came down the street;
And I thought how I sailed, and the cradle standing ready
For the pretty little babe that had never seen its daddie.
    And it's home, dearie, home,—

O, if it be a lass, she shall wear a golden ring;
And if it be a lad, he shall fight for his king;
With his dirk and his hat and his little jacket blue
He shall walk the quarter-deck as his daddie used to do.
    And it's home, dearie, home,—

O, there's a wind a-blowing, a-blowing from the west,
And that of all the winds is the one I like the best,
For it blows at our backs, and it shakes our pennon free,
And it soon will blow us home to the old countrie.
For it's home, dearie, home—it's home I want to be.
Our topsails are hoisted, and we'll away to sea.
O, the oak and the ash and the bonnie birken tree
They're all growing green in the old countrie.

WILLIAM ERNEST HENLEY

TO MY DEAR AND LOVING HUSBAND

If ever two were one, then surely we.
If ever man were loved by wife, then thee;
If ever wife was happy in a man,

Compare with me ye women if you can.
I prize thy love more than whole mines of gold,
Or all the riches that the East doth hold.
My love is such that rivers cannot quench,
Nor ought but love from thee give recompense.
Thy love is such I can no way repay;
The heavens reward thee manifold, I pray.
Then while we live, in love let's so persever,
That when we live no more we may live ever.

ANNE BRADSTREET

THE HAND THAT ROCKS THE CRADLE IS THE HAND THAT RULES THE WORLD

Blessing on the hand of women!
  Angels guard its strength and grace,
In the palace, cottage, hovel,
  Oh, no matter where the place;
Would that never storms assailed it,
  Rainbows ever gently curled;
For the hand that rocks the cradle
  Is the hand that rules the world.

Infancy's the tender fountain,
  Power may with beauty flow,
Mother's first to guide the streamlets,
  From them souls unresting grow—
Grow on for the good or evil,
  Sunshine streamed or evil hurled;
For the hand that rocks the cradle
  Is the hand that rules the world.

Woman, how divine your mission
  Here upon our natal sod!
Keep, oh, keep the young heart open
  Always to the breath of God!
All true trophies of the ages
  Are from mother-love impearled;
For the hand that rocks the cradle
  Is the hand that rules the world.

Blessings on the hand of women!
　Fathers, sons, and daughters cry,
And the sacred song is mingled
　With the worship in the sky—
Mingles where no tempest darkens,
　Rainbows evermore are hurled;
For the hand that rocks the cradle
　Is the hand that rules the world.

WILLIAM ROSS WALLACE

V. Patriotism and War

THE NEW COLOSSUS

Not like the brazen giant of Greek fame,
With conquering limbs astride from land to land;
Here at our sea-washed, sunset gates shall stand
A mighty woman with a torch, whose flame
Is the imprisoned lightning, and her name
Mother of Exiles. From her beacon-hand
Glows world-wide welcome; her mild eyes command
The air-bridged harbor that twin cities frame.
"Keep, ancient lands, your storied pomp!" cries she
With silent lips. "Give me your tired, your poor,
Your huddled masses yearning to breathe free,
The wretched refuse of your teeming shore.
Send these, the homeless, tempest-tost to me,
I lift my lamp beside the golden door!"

EMMA LAZARUS

A VICTORY DANCE

The cymbals crash,
  And the dancers walk,
With long silk stockings
  And arms of chalk,
Butterfly skirts,
  And white breasts bare,
And shadows of dead men
  Watching 'em there.

Shadows of dead men
  Stand by the wall,
Watching the fun
  Of the Victory Ball
They do not reproach,
  Because they know,
If they're forgotten,
  It's better so.

Under the dancing
  Feet are the graves.
Dazzle and motley,
  In long bright waves,
Brushed by the palm-fronds
  Grapple and whirl
Ox-eyed matron,
  And slim white girl.

Fat wet bodies
  Go waddling by,
Girdled with satin,
  Though God knows why;
Gripped by satyrs
  In white and black,
With a fat wet hand
  On the fat wet back.

See, there is one child
  Fresh from school,
Learning the ropes
  As the old hands rule.
God, how the dead men
  Chuckle again,
As she begs for a dose
  Of the best cocaine.

"What did you think
  We should find," said a shade,
"When the last shot echoed
  And the peace was made?"
"Christ," laughed the fleshless
  Jaws of his friend,
"I thought that they'd be praying
  For worlds to mend,

"Making earth better,
  Or something silly,
Like whitewashing hell
  Or Picadilly
They've a sense of humor,

These women of ours,
These exquisite lilies,
  These fresh young flowers!"

"Pish," said a statesman
  Standing near,
"I'm glad that they can busy
  Their thoughts elsewhere!
We mustn't reproach 'em,
  They're young, you see."
"Ah," said the dead men,
  "So were we!"

Victory! Victory!
  On with the dance!
Back to the jungle
  The new beasts prance!
Gee, how the dead men
  Grin by the wall,
Watching the fun
  Of the Victory Ball.

ALFRED NOYES

GRASS

Pile the bodies high at Austerlitz and Waterloo.
Shovel them under and let me work—
  I am the grass; I cover all.

And pile them high at Gettysburg
And pile them high at Ypres and Verdun.
Shovel them under and let me work.
Two years, ten years, and passengers ask the conductor:
  What place is this?
  Where are we now?

  I am the grass.
  Let me work.

CARL SANDBURG

HERE DEAD LIE WE

Here dead lie we because we did not choose
    To live and shame the land from which we sprung.
Life, to be sure, is nothing much to lose;
    But young men think it is, and we were young.

A. E. HOUSMAN

WHISPERIN' BILL

So ye're runnin' fer Congress, mister? Le' me tell ye 'bout my son—
    Might make you fellers carefuller down there in Washington—
He clings to his rifle an' uniform—folks call him Whisperin' Bill;
    An' I tell ye the war ain't over yit up here on Bouman's Hill.

This dooryard is his battlefield—le's see, he was nigh sixteen
    When Sumter fell, an' as likely a boy as ever this world has seen;
An' what with the news o' battles lost, the speeches an' all the noise,
    I guess ev'ry farm in the neighborhood lost a part of its crop o'
    boys.

'Twas harvest time when Bill left home: ev'ry stalk in the fields o'
    rye
    Seemed to stan' tiptoe to see him off an' wave him a fond good-
    bye;
His sweetheart was here with some other gals—the sassy little miss!
    An' purtendin' she wanted to whisper'n his ear, she gave him a
    rousin' kiss.

Oh, he was a han'some feller! an' tender an' brave an' smart,
    An' though he was bigger'n I was, the boy had a woman's heart.
I couldn't control my feelin's, but I tried with all my might,
    An' his mother an' me stood a-cryin' till Bill was out o' sight.

His mother she often tol' him, when she knew he was goin' away,
    That God would take care o' him, maybe, if he didn't fergit to
    pray;
An' on the bloodiest battlefields, when bullets whizzed in the air,
    An' Bill was a-fightin' desperit, he used to whisper a prayer.

Oh, his comrades has often told me that Bill never flinched a bit
  When every second a gap in the ranks tol' where a ball had hit.
An' one night when the field was covered with the awful harvest o'
    war,
  They found my boy 'mongst the martyrs o' the cause he was
    fightin' for.

His fingers was clutched in the dewy grass—oh, no, sir, he wasn't
    dead,
  But he lay kind o' helpless an' crazy with a rifle-ball in his head;
An' he trembled with the battle-fear as he lay there in the dew;
  An' he whispered as he tried to rise: "God'll take care o' you."

An officer wrote an' tol' us how the boy had been hurt in the fight,
  But he said that the doctors reckoned they could bring him around
    all right.
An' then we heard from a neighbor, disabled at Malvern Hill,
  That he thought in the course of a week or so he'd be comin'
    home with Bill.

We was that anxious t' see him we'd set up an' talk o' nights
  'Till the break o' day had dimmed the stars an' put out the north-
    ern lights,
We waited an' watched fer a month or more, the summer was nearly
    past,
  When a letter came one day that said they'd started fer home at
    last.

I'll never fergit the day Bill come—'twas harvest time again—
  An the air blown over the yeller fields was sweet with the scent o'
    the grain;
The dooryard was full o' the neighbors, who had come to share our
    joy,
  An' all of us sent up a mighty cheer at the sight o' that soldier boy.

An' all of a sudden somebody said; "My God! don't the boy know
    his mother?"
  An' Bill stood a-whisperin', fearful like, an' a-starin' from one to
    another;
"Don't be afraid, Bill," said he to himself, as he stood in his coat o'
    blue,
  "Why, God'll take care o' you, Bill, God'll take care o' you."

He seemed to be loadin' an' firin' a gun, an' to act like a man who hears
  The awful roar o' the battlefield a-soundin' in his ears;
Ten thousan' ghosts o' that bloody day was marchin' through his brain
  An' his feet they kind o' picked their way as if they felt the slain.

An' I grabbed his hand, an' says I to Bill, "Don't ye 'member me?
  I'm yer father—don't ye know me? How frightened ye seem to be!"
But the boy kep' a-whisperin' to himself, as if 'twas all he knew,
  "God'll take care o' you, Bill, God'll take care o' you."

He's never known us since that day, nor his sweetheart, an' never will;
  Father an' Mother an' sweetheart are all the same to Bill.
An' he groans like a wounded soldier, sometimes the whole night through,
  An' we smooth his head an' say: "Yes, Bill, He'll surely take care o' you."

Ye can stop a war in a minute, but when can ye stop the groans?
  Fer ye've broke our hearts an' sapped our blood an' plucked away our bones.
An' ye've filled our souls with bitterness that goes from sire to son,
  So ye best be kind o' careful down there in Washington.

IRVING BACHELLER

AMERICA

My country, 'tis of thee,
Sweet land of liberty,
    Of thee I sing;
Land where my fathers died,
Land of the pilgrims' pride,
From every mountain-side
    Let Freedom ring.

My native country, thee,
Land of the noble free,—
    Thy name I love;

I love thy rocks and rills,
Thy woods and templed hills;
My heart with rapture thrills
    Like that above.

Let music swell the breeze,
And ring from all the trees
    Sweet Freedom's song;
Let mortal tongues awake,
Let all that breathe partake,
Let rocks their silence break,
    The sound prolong.

Our fathers' God, to Thee,
Author of liberty,
    To Thee we sing;
Long may our land be bright
With Freedom's holy light;
Protect us by Thy might,
    Great God, our King.
        SAMUEL FRANCIS SMITH

I, TOO, SING AMERICA

I am the darker brother.
They send me to eat in the kitchen
When company comes,
But I laugh,
And eat well,
And grow strong.

Tomorrow,
I'll sit at the table
When company comes.
Nobody'll dare
Say to me,
"Eat in the kitchen,"
Then.

Besides,
They'll see how beautiful I am
And be ashamed—

I, too, am America.

LANGSTON HUGHES

A TOAST TO THE FLAG

Here's to the Red of it!
There's not a thread of it,
No, not a shred of it,
In all the spread of it
    From foot to head,
But heroes bled for it,
Faced steel and lead for it,
Precious blood shed for it,
    Bathing it Red.

Here's to the White of it!
Thrilled by the sight of it,
Who knows the right of it,
But feels the might of it,
    Through day and night.
Womanhood's care of it
Made manhood's dare for it;
Purity's prayer for it;
    Keeps it so White.

Here's to the Blue of it!
Heavenly view of it,
Star-spangled hue of it,
Honesty's due of it,
    Constant and true.
Here's to the whole of it,
Stars, stripes and pole of it,
Here's to the Soul of it,
Red, White, and Blue!

JOHN DALY

INTERNATIONAL HYMN

Two empires by the sea,
Two nations great and free,
  One anthem raise.
One race of ancient fame,
One tongue, one faith, we claim,
One God, whose glorious name
  We love and praise.

What deeds our fathers wrought
What battles we have fought,
  Let fame record.
Now, vengeful passion, cease,
Come, victories of peace,
Nor hate, nor pride's caprice
  Unsheath the sword.

Though deep the sea and wide,
'Twixt realm and realm, its tide
  Binds strand to strand.
So be the gulf between
Gray coasts and islands green,
With bonds of peace serene
  And friendship spanned.

Now, may the God above
Guard the dear land we love,
  Both East and West.
Let love more fervent glow,
As peaceful ages go,
And strength yet stronger grow,
  Blessing and blest.

GEORGE HUNTINGTON

I AM AN AMERICAN

I am an American.
My father belongs to the Sons of the Revolution;
My mother, to the Colonial Dames.
One of my ancestors pitched tea overboard in Boston Harbor;
Another stood his ground with Warren;
Another hungered with Washington at Valley Forge.
My forefathers were America in the making:
They spoke in her council halls;
They died on her battle-fields;
They commanded her ships;
They cleared her forests.
Dawns reddened and paled.
Stanch hearts of mine beat fast at each new star
In the nation's flag.
Keen eyes of mine foresaw her greater glory:
The sweep of her seas.
The plenty of her plains
The man-hives in her billion-wired cities.
Every drop of blood in me holds a heritage of patriotism.
I am proud of my past.
I am an American.

I am an American.
My father was an atom of dust,
My mother a straw in the wind,
To His Serene Majesty.
One of my ancestors died in the mines of Siberia;
Another was crippled for life by twenty blows of the knout;
Another was killed defending his home during the massacres.
The history of my ancestors is a trail of blood
To the palace-gate of the Great White Czar.
But then the dream came—
The dream of America.
In the light of the Liberty torch
The atom of the dust became a man
And the straw in the wind became a woman
For the first time.
"See," said my father, pointing to the flag that fluttered near,

"That flag of stars and stripes is yours;
It is the emblem of the promised land.
It means, my son, the hope of humanity.
Live for it—die for it!"
Under the open sky of my new country I swore to do so;
And every drop of blood in me will keep that vow.
I am proud of my future.
I am an American.

                                        ELIAS LIEBERMAN

THE KID HAS GONE TO THE COLORS

The Kid has gone to the Colors
    And we don't know what to say;
The Kid we have loved and cuddled
    Stepped out for the Flag to-day.
We thought him a child, a baby
    With never a care at all,
But his country called him man-size
    And the Kid has heard the call.

He paused to watch the recruiting,
    Where, fired by the fife and drum,
He bowed his head to Old Glory
    And thought that it whispered: "Come!"
The Kid, not being a slacker,
    Stood forth with patriot-joy
To add his name to the roster,
    And God, we're proud of the boy!

The Kid has gone to the Colors
    It seems but a little while
Since he drilled a school-boy army
    In a truly martial style.
But now he's a man, a soldier,
    And we lend him a listening ear,
For his heart is a heart all loyal,
    Unscourged by the curse of fear.

His dad, when he told him, shuddered,
　His mother—God bless her!—cried;
Yet, blest with a mother-nature,
　She wept with a mother-pride.
But he whose old shoulders straightened
　Was Granddad—for memory ran
To years when he, too, a youngster,
　Was changed by the Flag to a man!

W. M. HERSCHELL

EMILY GEIGER

'Twas in the days of the Revolution,—
　Dark days were they and drear,—
And by Carolina firesides
　The women sat in fear;
For the men were away at the fighting,
　And sad was the news that came,
That the battle was lost; and the death-list
　Held many a loved one's name.

When as heart-sore they sat round the camp-fires,
　"What, ho! Who'll volunteer
To carry a message to Sumter?"
　A voice rang loud and clear.
There was a sudden silence,
　But not a man replied;
They knew too well of the peril
　Of one who dared that ride.

Outspoke then Emily Geiger
　With a rich flush on her cheek,—
"Give me the message to be sent;
　I am the one you seek.
For I am a Southern woman;
　And I'd rather do and dare
Than sit by a lonely fireside,
　My heart gnawed through with care."

They gave her the precious missive;
    And on her own good steed
She rode away, 'mid the cheers of the men,
    Upon her daring deed.
And away through the lonely forests,
    Steadily galloping on,
She saw the sun sink low in the sky,
    And in the west go down.

"Halt!—or I fire!" On a sudden
    A rifle clicked close by.
"Let you pass? Not we, till we know you are
    No messenger or spy."
"She's a Whig,—from her face,—I will wager,"
    Swore the officer of the day.
"To the guard-house, and send for a woman
    To search her without delay."

No time did she lose in bewailing;
    As the bolt creaked in the lock,
She quickly drew the precious note
    That was hidden in her frock.
And she read it through with hurried care,
    Then ate it piece by piece,
And calmly sat her down to wait
    Till time should bring release.

They brought her out in a little,
    And set her on her steed,
With many a rude apology,
    For his discourteous deed.
On, on, once more through the forest black,
    The good horse panting strains,
Till the sentry's challenge: "Who comes there?"
    Tells that the end she gains.

Ere an hour, in the camp of Sumter
    There was hurrying to and fro.
"Saddle and mount, saddle and mount,"
    The bugles shrilly blow.

"Forward trot!" and the long ranks wheel,
    And into the darkness glides:
Long shall the British rue that march
    And Emily Geiger's ride.

UNKNOWN

TO THE MEMORY OF THE BRAVE AMERICANS

under General Greene, in South Carolina, who fell in the action of September 8, 1781.

At Eutaw Springs the valiant died;
    Their limbs with dust are covered o'er—
Weep on, ye springs, your tearful tide;
    How many heroes are no more!

If in this wreck of ruin, they
    Can yet be thought to claim a tear,
O smite your gentle breast, and say
    The friends of freedom slumber here!

Thou, who shalt trace this bloody plain,
    If goodness rules thy generous breast,
Sigh for the wasted rural reign;
    Sigh for the shepherds, sunk to rest!

Stranger, their humble graves adorn;
    You too may fall, and ask a tear;
'Tis not the beauty of the morn
    That proves the evening shall be clear.—

They saw their injured country's woe;
    The flaming town, the wasted field;
Then rushed to meet the insulting foe;
    They took the spear—but left the shield.

Led by thy conquering genius, Greene,
    The Britons they compelled to fly;
None distant viewed the fatal plain,
    None grieved, in such a cause to die—

But, like the Parthian, famed of old,
  Who, flying, still their arrows threw,
These routed Britons, full as bold,
  Retreated, and retreating slew.

Now rest in peace, our patriot band;
  Though far from nature's limits thrown,
We trust they find a happier land,
  A brighter sunshine of their own.

                              PHILIP FRENEAU

IN AN AGE OF FOPS AND TOYS

(from *Voluntaries*)

In an age of fops and toys,
Wanting wisdom, void of right,
Who shall nerve heroic boys
To hazard all in Freedom's fight,—
Break sharply off their jolly games,
Forsake their comrades gay
And quit proud homes and youthful dames
For famine, toil and fray?
Yet on the nimble air benign
Speed nimbler messages,
That waft the breath of grace divine
To hearts in sloth and ease.
So nigh is grandeur to our dust,
So near is God to man,
When Duty whispers low, *Thou must,*
The youth replies, *I can.*

                        RALPH WALDO EMERSON

BARBARA FRIETCHIE

Up from the meadows rich with corn,
Clear in the cool September morn,

The clustered spires of Frederick stand
Green-walled by the hills of Maryland.

Round about them orchards sweep,
Apple and peach tree fruited deep,

Fair as the garden of the Lord
To the eyes of the famished rebel horde,

On that pleasant morn of the early fall
When Lee marched over the mountain-wall;

Over the mountains winding down,
Horse and foot, into Frederick town.

Forty flags with their silver stars,
Forty flags with their crimson bars,

Flapped in the morning wind: the sun
Of noon looked down, and saw not one.

Up rose old Barbara Frietchie then,
Bowed with her fourscore years and ten;

Bravest of all in Frederick town,
She took up the flag the men hauled down;

In her attic window the staff she set,
To show that one heart was loyal yet.

Up the street came the rebel tread,
Stonewall Jackson riding ahead.

Under his slouched hat left and right
He glanced; the old flag met his sight.

"Halt!"—the dust-brown ranks stood fast.
"Fire!"—out blazed the rifle-blast.

It shivered the window, pane and sash;
It rent the banner with seam and gash.

Quick as it fell, from the broken staff
Dame Barbara snatched the silken scarf.

She leaned far out on the window-sill,
And shook it forth with a royal will.

"Shoot, if you must, this old gray head,
But spare your country's flag," she said.

A shade of sadness, a blush of shame,
Over the face of the leader came;

The nobler nature within him stirred
To life at that woman's deed and word;

"Who touches a hair of yon gray head
Dies like a dog! March on!" he said.

All day long through Frederick street
Sounded the tread of marching feet:

All day long that free flag tossed
Over the heads of the rebel host.

Ever its torn folds rose and fell
On the loyal winds that loved it well;

And through the hill-gaps sunset light
Shone over it with a warm good-night.

Barbara Frietchie's work is o'er,
And the Rebel rides on his raids no more.

Honor to her! and let a tear
Fall, for her sake, on Stonewall's bier.

Over Barbara Frietchie's grave,
Flag of Freedom and Union, wave!

Peace and order and beauty draw
Round thy symbol of light and law;

And ever the stars above look down
On thy stars below in Frederick town!

JOHN GREENLEAF WHITTIER

BEAT! BEAT! DRUMS!

Beat! beat! drums!—blow! bugles! blow!
Through the windows—through doors—burst like a ruthless force,
Into the solemn church, and scatter the congregation,
Into the school where the scholar is studying;
Leave not the bridegroom quiet—no happiness must he have now
    with his bride,
Nor the peaceful farmer any peace, ploughing his field or gathering
    his grain,
So fierce you whirr and pound you drums—so shrill you bugles blow.

Beat! beat! drums!—blow! bugles! blow!
Over the traffic of cities—over the rumble of wheels in the streets;
Are beds prepared for sleepers at night in the houses? no sleepers
    must sleep in those beds,
No bargainers' bargains by day—no brokers or speculators—would
    they continue?
Would the talkers be talking? would the singer attempt to sing?
Would the lawyer rise in the court to state his case before the judge?
Then rattle quicker, heavier drums—you bugles wilder blow.

Beat! beat! drums!—blow! bugles! blow!
Make no parley—stop for no expostulation,
Mind not the timid—mind not the weeper or prayer,
Mind not the old man beseeching the young man,
Let not the child's voice be heard, nor the mother's entreaties,
Make even the trestles to shake the dead where they lie awaiting
    the hearses,
So strong you thump O terrible drums—so loud you bugles blow.
                     WALT WHITMAN

BIVOUAC ON A MOUNTAIN SIDE

I see before me now a traveling army halting,
Below a fertile valley spread, with barns and the orchards of summer,
Behind, the terraced sides of a mountain, abrupt, in places rising
    high,
Broken, with rocks, with clinging cedars, with tall shapes dingily
    seen,
The numerous camp-fires scatter'd near and far, some away up on
    the mountain,

The shadowy forms of men and horses, looming, large-sized, flicker-
ing,
And over all the sky—the sky! far, far out of reach, studded, break-
ing out, the eternal stars.

WALT WHITMAN

AN ARMY CORPS ON THE MARCH

With its cloud of skirmishers in advance,
With now the sound of a single shot snapping like a whip, and now
an irregular volley,
The swarming ranks press on and on, the dense brigades press on,
Glittering dimly, toiling under the sun—the dust-cover'd men,
In columns rise and fall to the undulations of the ground,
With artillery interspers'd—the wheels rumble, the horses sweat,
As the army corps advances.

WALT WHITMAN

O CAPTAIN! MY CAPTAIN!

O Captain! my Captain! our fearful trip is done,
The ship has weathered every rack, the prize we sought is won,
The port is near, the bells I hear, the people all exulting,
While follow eyes the steady keel, the vessel grim and daring
  But O heart! heart! heart!
    O the bleeding drops of red,
  Where on the deck my Captain lies,
    Fallen cold and dead.

O Captain! my Captain! rise up and hear the bells;
Rise up—for you the flag is flung—for you the bugle trills,
For you bouquets and ribboned wreaths—for you the shores a-crowd-
ing,
For you they call, the swaying mass, their eager faces turning;
  Here Captain! dear father!
    This arm beneath your head!
  It is some dream that on the deck
    You've fallen cold and dead.

My Captain does not answer, his lips are pale and still,
My father does not feel my arm, he has no pulse nor will,
The ship is anchored safe and sound, its voyage closed and done,
From fearful trip the victor ship comes in with object won;

Exult O shores, and ring O bells!
　But I with mournful tread,
Walk the deck my Captain lies,
　Fallen cold and dead.

WALT WHITMAN

JACK ELLYAT HEARD THE GUNS

(from *John Brown's Body*)

Jack Ellyat heard the guns with a knock at his heart
When he first heard them. They were going to be in it, soon.
He wondered how it would feel. They would win, of course,
But how would it feel? He'd never killed anything much.
Ducks and rabbits, but ducks and rabbits weren't men.
He'd never seen a man killed, a man die,
Except Uncle Amos, and Uncle Amos was old.
He saw a red sop spreading across the close
Feathers of a duck's breast—it had been all right,
But now it made him feel sick for a while, somehow.
Then they were down on the ground, and they were firing,
And that was all right—just fire as you fired at drill.
Was anyone firing at them? He couldn't tell.
There was a stone bridge. Were there rebels beyond the bridge?
The shot he was firing now might go and kill rebels
But it didn't feel like it.
　　　　　　　A man down the line
Fell and rolled flat, with a minor coughing sound
And then was quiet. Ellyat felt the cough
In the pit of his stomach a minute.
But, after that, it was just like a man falling down.
It was all so calm except for their guns and the distant
Shake in the air of cannon. No more men were hit,
And, after a while, they all got up and marched on.
If Rebels had been by the bridge, the rebels were gone,
And they were going on somewhere, you couldn't say where,
Just marching along the way that they always did.
The only funny thing was, leaving the man
Who had made that cough, back there in the trampled grass
With the red stain sopping through the blue of his coat
Like the stain on a duck's breast. He hardly knew the man
But it felt funny to leave him just lying there.

STEPHEN VINCENT BENÉT

CUSTER'S LAST CHARGE

(JUNE 25, 1876)

Dead! Is it possible? He, the bold rider,
  Custer, our hero, the first in the fight,
Charming the bullets of yore to fly wider,
  Far from our battle-king's ringlets of light!
Dead, our young chieftain, and dead, all forsaken!
  No one to tell us the way of his fall!
Slain in the desert, and never to waken,
  Never, not even to victory's call!

Proud for his fame that last day that he met them!
  All the night long he had been on their track,
Scorning their traps and the men that had set them,
  Wild for a charge that should never give back.
There on the hilltop he halted and saw them.—
  Lodges all loosened and ready to fly;
Hurrying scouts with the tidings to awe them,
  Told of his coming before he was nigh.

All the wide valley was full of their forces,
  Gathered to cover the lodges' retreat!—
Warriors running in haste to their horses,
  Thousands of enemies close to his feet!
Down in the valleys the ages had hollowed,
  There lay the Sitting Bull's camp for a prey!
Numbers! What recked he? What recked those who followed—
  Men who had fought ten to one ere that day?

Out swept the squadrons, the fated three hundred,
  Into the battle-line steady and full;
Then down the hillside exultingly thundered,
  Into the hordes of the old Sitting Bull!
Wild Ogalallah, Arapahoe, Cheyenne,
  Wild Horse's braves, and the rest of their crew,
Shrank from that charge like a herd from a lion,—
  Then closed around, the grim horde of wild Sioux!

Right to their centre he charged, and then facing—
  Hark to those yells! and around them, O see!

Over the hilltops the Indians come racing,
    Coming as fast as the waves of the sea!
Red was the circle of fire around them;
    No hope of victory, no ray of light,
Shot through that terrible black cloud without them,
    Brooding in death over Custer's last fight.

Then did he blench? Did he die like a craven,
    Begging those torturing fiends for his life?
Was there a soldier who carried the Seven
    Flinched like a coward or fled from the strife?
No, by the blood of our Custer, no quailing!
    There in the midst of the Indians they close,
Hemmed in by thousands, but ever assailing,
    Fighting like tigers, all bayed amid foes!

Thicker and thicker the bullets came singing;
    Down go the horses and riders and all;
Swiftly the warriors round them were ringing,
    Circling like buzzards awaiting their fall.
See the wild steeds of the mountain and prairie,
    Savage eyes gleaming from forests of mane;
Quivering lances with pennons so airy,
    War-painted warriors charging amain.

Backward, again and again, they were driven,
    Shrinking to close with the lost little band;
Never a cap that had worn the bright Seven
    Bowed till its wearer was dead on the strand.
Closer and closer the death-circle growing,
    Ever the leader's voice, clarion clear,
Rang out his words of encouragement glowing,
    "We can but die once, boys,—we'll sell our lives dear!"

Dearly they sold them like Berserkers raging,
    Facing the death that encircled them round;
Death's bitter pangs by their vengeance assuaging,
    Marking their tracks by their dead on the ground.
Comrades, our children shall yet tell their story,—
    Custer's last charge on the old Sitting Bull;
And ages shall swear that the cup of his glory
    Needed but that death to render it full.

                                    FREDERICK WHITTAKER

DO NOT WEEP, MAIDEN, FOR WAR IS KIND

(from *War Is Kind*)

Do not weep, maiden, for war is kind.
Because your lover threw wild hands toward the sky
And the affrighted steed ran on alone,
Do not weep.
War is kind.

    Hoarse, booming drums of the regiment,
    Little souls who thirst for fight—
    These men were born to drill and die.
    The unexplained glory flies above them;
    Great is the battle-god, great—and his kingdom
    A field where a thousand corpses lie.

Do not weep, babe, for war is kind.
Because your father tumbled in the yellow trenches,
Raged at his breast, gulped and died,
Do not weep.
War is kind.

    Swift-blazing flag of the regiment,
    Eagle with crest of red and gold,
    These men were born to drill and die.
    Point for them the virtue of slaughter,
    Make plain to them the excellence of killing,
    And a field where a thousand corpses lie.

Mother whose heart hung humble as a button
On the bright splendid shroud of your son,
Do not weep.
War is kind.

STEPHEN CRANE

THE BATTLE-FIELD

Once this soft turf, this rivulet's sands,
   Were trampled by a hurrying crowd,
And fiery hearts and armed hands
   Encountered in the battle-cloud.

Ah! never shall the land forget
   How gushed the life-blood of her brave—
Gushed, warm with hope and courage yet,
   Upon the soil they fought to save.

Now all is calm, and fresh, and still;
   Alone the chirp of flitting bird,
And talk of children on the hill,
   And bell of wandering kine, are heard.

No solemn host goes trailing by
   The black-mouthed gun and staggering wain;
Men start not at the battle-cry,
   Oh, be it never heard again!

Soon rested those who fought; but thou
   Who minglest in the harder strife
For truths which men receive not now,
   Thy warfare only ends with life.

A friendless warfare! lingering long
   Through weary day and weary year;
A wild and many-weaponed throng
   Hang on thy front, and flank, and rear.
Yet nerve thy spirit to the proof,
   And blench not at thy chosen lot,
The timid good may stand aloof,
   The sage may frown—yet faint thou not.

Nor heed the shaft too surely cast,
   The foul and hissing bolt of scorn;
For with thy side shall dwell, at last,
   The victory of endurance born.

Truth, crushed to earth, shall rise again;
  Th' eternal years of God are hers;
But Error, wounded, writhes in pain,
  And dies among his worshippers.

Yea, though thou lie upon the dust,
  When they who helped thee flee in fear,
Die full of hope and manly trust,
  Like those who fell in battle here.

Another hand thy sword shall wield,
  Another hand the standard wave,
Till from the trumpet's mouth is pealed
  The blast of triumph o'er thy grave.

WILLIAM CULLEN BRYANT

THE HARP THAT ONCE THROUGH TARA'S HALLS

The harp that once through Tara's halls
  The soul of music shed,
Now hangs as mute on Tara's walls
  As if that soul were fled.
So sleeps the pride of former days,
  So glory's thrill is o'er,
And hearts that once beat high for praise
  Now feel that pulse no more!
No more to chiefs and ladies bright
  The harp of Tara swells;
The chord alone that breaks at night
  Its tale of ruin tells.
Thus Freedom now so seldom wakes,
  The only throb she gives
Is when some heart indignant breaks,
  To show that still she lives.

THOMAS MOORE

WHEN A MAN HATH NO FREEDOM
TO FIGHT FOR AT HOME

When a man hath no freedom to fight for at home,
 Let him combat for that of his neighbors;
Let him think of the glories of Greece and of Rome,
 And get knocked on the head for his labors.

To do good to Mankind is the chivalrous plan,
 And is always as nobly requited;
Then battle for Freedom wherever you can,
 And, if not shot or hanged, you'll get knighted.
      GEORGE GORDON BYRON

THE SPIRES OF OXFORD

(AS SEEN FROM THE TRAIN)

I saw the spires of Oxford
 As I was passing by,
The gray spires of Oxford
 Against a pearl-gray sky.
My heart was with the Oxford men
 Who went abroad to die.

The years go fast in Oxford,
 The golden years and gay,
The hoary Colleges look down
 On careless boys at play.
But when the bugles sounded war
 They put their games away.

They left the peaceful river,
 The cricket-field, the quad,
The shaven lawns of Oxford
 To seek a bloody sod—
They gave their merry youth away
 For country and for God.

God rest you, happy gentlemen,
  Who laid your good lives down,
Who took the khaki and the gun
  Instead of cap and gown.
God bring you to a fairer place
  Than even Oxford town.

WINIFRED M. LETTS

THE SOLDIER

(from 1914)

If I should die, think only this of me:
That there's some corner of a foreign field
That is forever England. There shall be
In that rich earth a richer dust concealed;
A dust whom England bore, shaped, made aware,
Gave, once, her flowers to love, her ways to roam;
A body of England's, breathing English air,
Washed by the rivers, blest by suns of home.
And think, this heart, all evil shed away,
A pulse in the eternal mind, no less
Gives somewhere back the thoughts by England given;
Her sights and sounds; dreams happy as her day;
And laughter, learnt of friends; and gentleness,
In hearts at peace, under an English heaven.

RUPERT BROOKE

ENGLAND, MY ENGLAND

What have I done for you,
  England, my England?
What is there I would not do,
  England, my own?
With your glorious eyes austere,
As the Lord were walking near,
Whispering terrible things and dear
  As the Song on your bugles blown,
    England—
  Round the world on your bugles blown!

Where shall the watchful Sun,
    England, my England,
Match the master-work you've done,
    England, my own?
When shall he rejoice agen
Such a breed of mighty men
As come forward, one to ten,
    To the Song on your bugles blown,
        England—
    Down the years on your bugles blown?

Ever the faith endures,
    England, my England:—
"Take and break us: we are yours,
    England, my own!
Life is good, and joy runs high
Between English earth and sky:
Death is death; but we shall die
    To the Song on your bugles blown,
        England—
    To the stars on your bugles blown!"

They call you proud and hard,
    England, my England:
You with worlds to watch and ward,
    England, my own!
You whose mailed hand keeps the keys
Of such teeming destinies,
You could know nor dread nor ease
    Were the Song on your bugles blown,
        England,
    Round the Pit on your bugles blown!

Mother of Ships whose might
    England, my England,
Is the fierce old Sea's delight,
    England, my own,
Chosen daughter of the Lord,
Spouse-in-Chief of the ancient Sword,

There's the menace of the Word
  In the Song on your bugles blown,
    England—
  Out of heaven on your bugles blown!
                    WILLIAM ERNEST HENLEY

I HAVE LOVED ENGLAND

(from *The White Cliffs*)

I have loved England, dearly and deeply,
Since the first morning, shining and pure,
The white cliffs, of Dover, I saw rising steeply,
Out of the sea that once made her secure.

I had no thought then of husband or lover,
I was a traveler, the guest of a week;
Yet when they pointed "the white cliffs of Dover"
Startled I found there were tears on my cheek.

I have loved England, and still as a stranger,
Here is my home, and I still am alone.
Now in her hour of trial and danger,
Only the English are really her own.
                    ALICE DUER MILLER

PEACE IN THE WORLD

(Message for the Livre d'Orde la Paix, Geneva)

  God send us wit to banish far
  The incense and the reeking breath,
  The lances and the fame of war,
  And all the devilments of death.
  Let there be wisdom and increase,
  The harvest reconcilement brings,
  So shall we see the eyes of Peace,
  And feel the wafting of Her wings.
                    JOHN GALSWORTHY

THE BATTLE OF BLENHEIM

(AUGUST 13, 1704)

It was a summer evening;
  Old Kaspar's work was done,
And he before his cottage-door
  Was sitting in the sun;
And by him sported on the green
His little grandchild, Wilhelmine.

She saw her brother Peterkin
  Roll something large and round,
That he beside the rivulet,
  In playing there, had found:
She ran to ask what he had found,
That was so large and smooth and round.

Old Kaspar took it from the boy,
  Who stood expectant by;
And then the old man shook his head,
  And with a natural sigh,
" 'Tis some poor fellow's skull," said he,
"Who fell in the great victory.

"I find them in my garden,
  For there's many here about;
And often, when I go to plough,
  The ploughshare turns them out;
For many thousand men," said he,
"Were slain in that great victory."

"Now tell us what 'twas all about,"
  Young Peterkin, he cries;
And little Wilhelmine looks up
  With wonder-waiting eyes;
"Now tell us all about the war,
  And what they fought each other for."

"It was the English," Kaspar cried,
  "Who put the French to rout;
But what they fought each other for
  I could not well make out;
But everybody said," quoth he,
"That 'twas a famous victory.

"My father lived at Blenheim then,
  Yon little stream hard by;
They burned his dwelling to the ground,
  And he was forced to fly;
So with his wife and child he fled,
Nor had he where to rest his head.

"With fire and sword the country round
  Was wasted far and wide,
And many a childing mother then,
  And new-born baby, died;
But things like that, you know, must be
At every famous victory.

"They say it was a shocking sight
  After the field was won;
For many thousand bodies here
  Lay rotting in the sun:
But things like that, you know, must be
After a famous victory.

"Great praise the Duke of Marlborough won
  And our good Prince Eugene."
"Why, 'twas a very wicked thing!"
  Said little Wilhelmine.
"Nay, nay, my little girl," quoth he,
"It was a famous victory.

"And everybody praised the Duke,
  Who this great fight did win."
"But what good came of it at last?"
  Quoth little Peterkin.
"Why, that I cannot tell," said he;
"But 'twas a famous victory."

                              ROBERT SOUTHEY

VI. *Humor, Nonsense, and Whimsey*

THE GOAT

There was a man, now please take note,
There was a man, who had a goat.
He lov'd that goat, indeed he did,
He lov'd that goat, just like a kid.

One day that goat felt frisk and fine,
Ate three red shirts from off the line.
The man he grabbed him by the back,
And tied him to a railroad track.

But when the train hove into sight,
That goat grew pale and green with fright.
He heaved a sigh, as if in pain,
Coughed up those shirts and flagged the train.

UNKNOWN

THE MIGHTY HUNTER

He riseth up early in the morning
And disturbeth the whole household.
   He stampeth down the hall in his heavy boots
   And shouteth, "Where are my shells?"
He consumeth much toast and hot coffee
And partaketh of eggs and of bacon.
   He goeth forth with great expectations
   And boasteth loud of his marksmanship.
He knoweth the flight of the mallard,
The widgeon, the sprig, and the red head,
   The spoonie, the "can," the green-winged teel;
   The call of the brant and the honker.
He baggeth the quail, dove, and pigeon,
The rabbit, the grouse, and the pheasant.
   He knoweth the haunts of the grizzly,
   The caribou, moose, and the mountain sheep;
The wild boar, the wolf, and the cougar,

And the range where the furtive deer feedeth.
   He promiseth his friends much venison
   And inviteth his lodge to a barbecue.
He packeth a heavy knap-sack, a shell-vest,
A rifle, a shot-gun, a kodak, tobacco,
   A canteen, skinning knife, and field glasses,
   Rubber boots, rations, first aid kit.
He trampeth miles in the mountains
And wadeth in streams to his waist-line.
   He chaseth the fleet-footed deer,
   The wolf, and the nimble mountain goat.
He hunteth the fierce grizzly bear.
He waiteth patiently for the elusive snipe
   He returneth home late in the evening,
   Sore of foot, of back, and of temper.
He bringeth no game on his shoulders
Nor game hath he in his knap-sack.
   He devoureth much food from the ice-box
   And the spirit of truth is not in him,
For he braggeth thus to his comrades,
"Boys, I got the limit."

                         MRS. J. B. WORLEY

WHEN FATHER CARVES THE DUCK

We all look on with anxious eyes,
   When father carves the duck,
And mother almost always sighs,
   When father carves the duck.
Then all of us prepare to rise,
And hold our bibs before our eyes,
And be prepared for some surprise,
   When father carves the duck.

He braces up and grabs a fork
   Whene'er he carves a duck,
And won't allow a soul to talk,
   Until he's carved the duck.
The fork is jabbed into the sides,
Across the breast the knife he slides,

While every careful person hides
    From flying chips of duck.

The platter's always sure to slip
    When father carves a duck,
And how it makes the dishes skip!
    Potatoes fly amuck!
The squash and cabbage leap in space,
We get some gravy in our face,
And father mutters Hindu grace
    Whene'er he carves a duck.

We then have learned to walk around
    The dining-room and pluck
From off the window-sills and walls
    Our share of father's duck.
While father growls and blows and jaws,
And swears the knife was full of flaws,
And mother jeers at him because
    He couldn't carve a duck.

ERNEST VINCENT WRIGHT

JOHNNY'S HIST'RY LESSON

I think of all the things at school
    A boy has got to do,
That studyin' hist'ry, as a rule,
    Is worst of all, don't you?
Of dates there are an awful sight,
An' though I study day an' night,
There's only one I've got just right—
    That's fourteen ninety-two.

Columbus crossed the Delaware
    In fourteen ninety-two;
We whipped the British, fair an' square,
    In fourteen ninety-two.
At Concord an' at Lexington
We kept the redcoats on the run
While the band played "Johnny Get Your Gun,"
    In fourteen ninety-two.

Pat Henry, with his dyin' breath—
    In fourteen ninety-two—
Said "Gimme liberty or death!"
    In fourteen ninety-two.
An' Barbara Fritchie, so 'tis said,
Cried, "Shoot if you must this old gray head,
But I'd rather 'twould be your own instead!"
    In fourteen ninety-two.

The Pilgrims came to Plymouth Rock
    In fourteen ninety-two,
An' the Indians standin' on the dock
    Asked, "What are you goin' to do?"
An' they said, "We seek your harbor drear
That our children's children's children dear
May boast that their forefathers landed here
    In fourteen ninety-two."

Miss Pocahontas saved the life,
    In fourteen ninety-two,
Of John Smith, an' became his wife
    In fourteen ninety-two.
An' the Smith tribe started then an' there,
An' now there are John Smiths everywhere,
But they didn't have any Smiths to spare
    In fourteen ninety-two.

Kentucky was settled by Daniel Boone
    In fourteen ninety-two,
An' I think the cow jumped over the moon
    In fourteen ninety-two.
Ben Franklin flew his kite so high
He drew the lightnin' from the sky,
An' Washington couldn't tell a lie,
    In fourteen ninety-two.

NIXON WATERMAN

SIMILAR CASES

There was once a little animal,
  No bigger than a fox,
And on five toes he scampered
  Over Tertiary rocks.
They called him Eohippus,
  And they called him very small,
And they thought him of no value—
  When they thought of him at all;
For the lumpish old Dinoceras
  And Coryphodon so slow
Were the heavy aristocracy
  In days of long ago.

Said the little Eohippus,
  "I am going to be a horse!
And on my middle finger-nails
  To run my earthly course!
I'm going to have a flowing tail!
  I'm going to have a mane!
I'm going to stand fourteen hands high
  On the psychozoic plain!"

The Coryphodon was horrified,
  The Dinoceras was shocked;
And they chased young Eohippus,
  But he skipped away and mocked.
And they laughed enormous laughter,
  And they groaned enormous groans,
And they bade young Eohippus
  Go view his father's bones.
Said they, "You always were as small
  And mean as now we see,
And that's conclusive evidence
  That you're always going to be.
What! Be a great, tall, handsome beast,
  With hoofs to gallop on?
Why! You'd have to change your nature!"
  Said the Loxolophodon.

They considered him disposed of,
　　And retired with gait serene;
That was the way they argued
　　In "the early Eocene."

There was once an Anthropoidal Ape,
　　Far smarter than the rest,
And everything that they could do
　　He always did the best;
So they naturally disliked him,
　　And they gave him shoulders cool,
And when they had to mention him
　　They said he was a fool.

Cried this pretentious Ape one day,
　　"I'm going to be a Man!
And stand upright, and hunt, and fight,
　　And conquer all I can!
I'm going to cut down forest trees,
　　To make my houses higher!
I'm going to kill the Mastodon!
　　I'm going to make a fire!"

Loud screamed the Anthropoidal Apes
　　With laughter wild and gay;
They tried to catch that boastful one,
　　But he always got away.
So they yelled at him in chorus,
　　Which he minded not a whit;
And they pelted him with cocoanuts,
　　Which didn't seem to hit.
And then they gave him reasons
　　Which they thought of much avail,
To prove how his preposterous
　　Attempt was sure to fail.
Said the sages, "In the first place,
　　The thing cannot be done!
And, second, if it could be,
　　It would not be any fun!
And, third, and most conclusive,
　　And admitting no reply,
You would have to change your nature!

We should like to see you try!"
They chuckled then triumphantly,
    These lean and hairy shapes,
For these things passed as arguments
    With the Anthropoidal Apes.

There was once a Neolithic Man,
    An enterprising wight,
Who made his chopping implements
    Unusually bright.
Unusually clever he,
    Unusually brave,
And he drew delightful Mammoths
    On the borders of his cave.
To his Neolithic neighbors,
    Who were startled and surprised,
Said he, "My friends, in course of time,
    We shall be civilized!
We are going to live in cities!
    We are going to fight in wars!
We are going to eat three times a day
    Without the natural cause!
We are going to turn life upside down
    About a thing called gold!
We are going to want the earth, and take
    As much as we can hold!
We are going to wear great piles of stuff
    Outside our proper skins!
We are going to have diseases!
    And Accomplishments!! And Sins!!!"

Then they all rose up in fury
    Against their boastful friend,
For prehistoric patience
    Cometh quickly to an end.
Said one, "This is chimerical!
    Utopian! Absurd!"
Said another, "What a stupid life!
    Too dull, upon my word!"
Cried all, "Before such things can come,
    You idiotic child,

You must alter Human Nature!"
  And they all sat back and smiled.
Thought they, "An answer to that last
  It will be hard to find!"
It was a clinching argument
  To the Neolithic Mind!
           CHARLOTTE PERKINS STETSON GILMAN

REVERIE

(Of a Gentleman of Sensibility at an Italian Table d'Hôte)

I

'Twas in a basement tobble d'hote
I met a sad sardine;
It was the saddest thing, I trow,
That I have ever seen,
With eyes so wan and lusterless
And frame so worn and lean.

II

I gazed into its mournful eye,
Its eye gazed back at me;
I could not bear to eat a fish
That looked so mournfully.
"You, too, have suffered," I remarked,
And sighed with sympathy.

III

I am a staid, reflective man,
Of meditations grave;
The barber tells me all his griefs
When I go in to shave—
I wondered what this fish's life
Had been beneath the wave.

IV

Sometimes a very little thing
Will make my tears to flow—
"What was your life," I asked the fish,
"In those damp depths below?"
He did not answer me; words were
Too weak to bear his woe.

V

I am not always understood:
A dead bird on a hat
Moved me, one time, to weep upon
My hostess' neck—for that,
Although I only kissed her twice,
They kicked me from their flat.

VI

They did not realize I crave
Affection in my grief—
My bleeding heart oft yearns for love
As mustard yearns for beef—
"Poor fish," I said, "you lie so mute
Upon your lettuce leaf!"

VII

"If you could only speak, perhaps
The words might ease your pain!"
He looked at me as dull as look
The slag-heaps after rain
When one goes into Pittsburg town
Upon a railroad train.

VIII

"Perhaps from some great vessel's deck,
In mournful years long syne,
I've dropped into the moaning deep
A tear that mixed with thine—
What was your history before
We twain met here to dine?"

IX

Not one sign did he give to me
That showed he might have heard;
He only held me with his gaze,
He did not speak a word—
Did he withhold his confidence,
Or was it but deferred?

X

In either case, it made me mourn—
Though I am used to it;
Too often people stand aloof
From my more melting fit,
Too oft they fling and pierce me with
Their darts of cruel wit!

XI

I do recall a dream I had
In which I was full fed,
And when I woke at dawn I found
I'd eaten up my bed—
O gods! the bitter, witty words
That my landlady said!

XII

I do not care to write them down;
After the lapse of years
They still have power to trouble me;
They burn within my ears
As the harsh oaths of the Bedouins burn
Which the sad camel hears.

XIII

And what so sad as camels are
When through the desert dawn
A Pharaoh's mummy they descry
Lying his bier upon
With sand in his esophagus
And his ambition gone?

XIV

In the Smithsonian Institute
I knew a mummy mum
Who stared forever at the roof
All written and all glum,
As if he had four thousand years
Of colic in his tum;

XV

And I would stand as twilight fell
Beside his carven tomb
And strive to lighten with my songs
His long dyspeptic doom,
While skeletons of dinosaurs
Draw nearer in the gloom.

XVI

I never see a dinosaur
So patient and so mute
But that a song of pity springs
Unbidden to my lute—
He stayed a lizard, but he wished
To be a bird, poor brute!

XVII

I am so seldom understood!
Once, as my teardrops fell,
Upon a little lizard's head
Hard by a sylvan well
Coarse villagers came out in force
And haled me to a cell.

XVIII

I've never seen a lizard crawl
Along a rustic fence
But that I've thought, "Poor helpless thing!
Some child may pluck you hence,
Thinking that you are edible—
They have so little sense!"

XIX

O little sad sardine, I find
This grief where'er I go!
And you have suffered likewise, for
Your manner tells me so—
O little sad sardine, I fear
Our world is full of woe!

DON MARQUIS

NOAH AN' JONAH AN' CAP'N JOHN SMITH

Noah an' Jonah an' Cap'n John Smith,
Mariners, travelers, magazines of myth,
Settin' up in Heaven, chewin' and a-chawin',
Eatin' their terbaccy, talkin' and a-jawin';
Settin' by a crick, spittin' in the worter,
Talkin' tall an' tactless, as saints hadn't orter,
Lollin' in the shade, baitin' hooks and anglin',
Occasionally friendly, occasionally wranglin'.

Noah took his halo from his old bald head
An' swatted of a hoppergrass an' knocked it dead,
An' he baited of his hook, an' he spoke an' said:
"When I was the Skipper of the tight leetle Ark
I useter fish fer porpus, useter fish for shark,
Often I have ketched in a single hour on Monday
Sharks enough to feed the fambly till Sunday—
To feed all the sarpints, the tigers an' donkeys,
To feed all the zebras, the insects an' monkeys,
To feed all the varmints, bears an' gorillars,
To feed all the camels, cats an' armadillers,
To give all the pelicans stews for their gizzards,
To feed all the owls an' catamounts an' lizards,
To feed all the humans, their babies an' their nusses,
To feed all the houn' dawgs an' hippopotamusses,
To feed all the oxen, feed all the asses,
Feed all the bison an' leetle hoppergrasses—
Always I ketched, in half a hour on Monday
All that the fambly could gormandize till Sunday!"

Jonah took his harp, to strum and to string her,
An' Cap'n John Smith teched his nose with his finger.
Cap'n John Smith, he hemmed some an' hawed some,
An' he bit off a chaw, an' he chewed some and chawed some:—
"When I was to China, when I was to Guinea,
When I was to Java, an' also in Verginney,
I teached all the natives how to be ambitious,
I learned 'em my trick of ketchin' devilfishes.
I've fitten tigers, I've fitten bears,
I have fitten sarpints an' wolves in their lairs,
I have fit with wild men, an' hippopotamusses,
But the perilousest varmints is the bloody octopusses!
I'd rub my forehead with phosphorescent light
An' plunge into the ocean an' seek 'em out at night!
I ketched 'em in grottoes, I ketched 'em in caves,
I used fer to strangle 'em underneath the waves!
When they seen the bright light blazin' on my forehead
They used ter to rush at me, screamin' something horrid!
Tentacles wavin', teeth white an' gnashin',
Hollerin' an' bellerin', wallerin' an' splashin'!
I useter grab 'em as they rushed from their grots,
Ketch all their legs an' tie 'em into knots!"

Noah looked at Jonah, an' said not a word,
But if winks made noises, a wink had been heard.
Jonah took the hook from a mudcat's middle
An' strummed on the strings of his hallelujah fiddle;
Jonah give his whiskers a backhand wipe
An' cut some plug terbaccer an' crammed it in his pipe!
—(Noah an' Jonah an' Cap'n John Smith,
Fishermen an' travelers, narreratin' myth,
Settin' up in Heaven all eternity,
Fishin' in the shade, contented as could be!
Spittin' their terbaccer in the little shaded creek,
Stoppin' of their yarns fer ter hear the ripples speak!
I hope fer Heaven, when I think of this—
You folks bound hellward, a lot of fun you'll miss!)

Jonah, he decapitates that mudcat's head,
An' gets his pipe ter drawin'; an' this is what he said:
"Excuse me ef your stories don't excite me much!
Excuse me ef I seldom agitate fer such!
You think yer fishermen! I won't argue none!

I won't even tell yer the half o' what I done!
You has careers dangerous an' checkered!
All as I will say is: Go and read my record!
You think yer fishermen! You think yer great!
All I asks is this: Has one of ye been *bait*?
Cap'n Noah, Cap'n John, I heerd when ye hollered;
What I asks is this: Has one of ye been *swallered*?
It's mighty purty fishin' with little hooks and reels.
It's mighty easy fishin' with little rods an' creels,
It's mighty pleasant ketchin' mudcats fer yer dinners.
But this here is my challenge fer saints an' fer sinners,
Which one of ye has v'yaged in a varmint's inners?
When I seen a big fish, tough as Methooslum,
I used for to dive into his oozly-goozlum!
When I seen the strong fish, wallopin' like a lummicks,
I useter foller 'em, dive into their stummicks!
I could v'yage an' steer 'em, I could understand 'em,
I useter navigate 'em, I useter land 'em!
Don't you pester *me* with any more narration!
Go git famous! Git a reputation!"

—Cap'n John he grinned his hat brim beneath,
Clicked his tongue of silver on his golden teeth:
Noah an' Jonah an' Cap'n John Smith,
Strummin' golden harps, narreratin' myth!
Settin' by the shallows forever an' forever,
Swappin' yarns an' fishin' in a little river.

DON MARQUIS

THE COMPLACENT CLIFF-DWELLER

I have a little home amidst the city's din
With kitchenette and shower bath and tub thrown in,
With fresh milk and vegetables and taxis close at hand—
The country can't beat that though Nature is grand.

The garbage is collected and I am not concerned
With where the men take it to be drowned or burned.
There are lots of different places that I can go for lunch
And autumn leaves are selling at fifty cents a bunch.

MARGARET FISHBACK

SITTING PRETTY

How nice to be a local swan
With quarters in the Park upon
That pond close to the Plaza where,
Despite the lack of rural air,
And sun, there's such a lovely view
It gives a bird plenty to do
Just lolling back and looking . . .
     That's
A program for aristocrats!
MARGARET FISHBACK

JEST 'FORE CHRISTMAS

Father calls me William, sister calls me Will,
Mother calls me Willie, but the fellers call me Bill!
Mighty glad I ain't a girl—ruther be a boy,
Without them sashes, curls, an' things that's worn by Fauntleroy!
Love to chawnk green apples an' go swimmin' in the lake—
Hate to take the castor-ile they give for belly-ache!
'Most all the time, the whole year round, there ain't no flies on me,
But jest 'fore Christmas I'm as good as I kin be!

Got a yeller dog named Sport, sick him on the cat;
First thing she knows she doesn't know where she is at!
Got a clipper sled, an' when us kids goes out to slide,
'Long comes the grocery cart, an' we all hook a ride!
But sometimes when the grocery man is worrited an' cross,
He reaches at us with his whip, an' larrups up his hoss,
An' then I laff an' holler, "Oh, ye never teched *me!*"
But jest 'fore Christmas I'm as good as I kin be!

Gran'ma says she hopes that when I git to be a man,
I'll be a missionarer like her oldest brother, Dan,
As was et up by the cannibuls that lives in Ceylon's Isle,
Where every prospeck pleases, an' only man is vile!

But gran'ma she has never been to see a Wild West show,
Nor read the Life of Daniel Boone, or else I guess she'd know
That Buff'lo Bill and cow-boys is good enough for me!
Excep' jest 'fore Christmas, when I'm good as I kin be!

And then old Sport he hangs around, so solemn-like an' still,
His eyes they keep a-sayin': "What's the matter, little Bill?"
The old cat sneaks down off her perch an' wonders what's become
Of them two enemies of hern that used to make things hum!
But I am so perlite an' 'tend so earnestly to biz,
That mother says to father: "How improved our Willie is!"
But father, havin' been a boy hisself, suspicions me
When jest 'fore Christmas, I'm as good as I kin be!

For Christmas, with its lots an' lots of candies, cakes an' toys,
Was made, they say, for proper kids an' not for naughty boys;
So wash yer face an' bresh yer hair, an' mind yer p's an' q's,
An' don't bust out yer pantaloons, an' don't wear out yer shoes;
Say "Yessum" to the ladies, an' "Yessur" to the men,
An' when they's company, don't pass yer plate for pie again;
But, thinking of the things yer'd like to see upon that tree,
Jest 'fore Christmas be as good as yer kin be!

                                                    EUGENE FIELD

THE DUEL

The gingham dog and the calico cat
Side by side on the table sat;
'Twas half past twelve, and (what do you think!)
Nor one nor t'other had slept a wink!
   The old Dutch clock and the Chinese plate
   Appeared to know as sure as fate
There was going to be a terrible spat.
      (I *wasn't there: I simply state*
      What was told to me by the Chinese plate!)

The gingham dog went, "Bow-wow-wow!"
And the calico cat replied, "Mee-ow!"
The air was littered, an hour or so,
With bits of gingham and calico,
   While the old Dutch clock in the chimney-place
   Up with its hands before its face,

For it always dreaded a family row!
  (*Now mind; I'm only telling you*
  What the old Dutch clock declares is true!)

The Chinese plate looked very blue,
And wailed, "Oh, dear! what shall we do!"
But the gingham dog and the calico cat
Wallowed this way and tumbled that,
  Employing every tooth and claw
  In the awfullest way you ever saw—
And, oh! how the gingham and calico flew!
  (*Don't fancy I exaggerate—*
  I got my news from the Chinese plate!)

Next morning, where the two had sat
They found no trace of dog or cat:
And some folks think unto this day
That burglars stole that pair away!
  But the truth about the cat and pup
  Is this: they ate each other up!
Now what do you really think of that!
  (*The old Dutch clock it told me so,*
  And that is how I came to know.)

EUGENE FIELD

THE PURPLE COW

Reflections on a Mythic Beast,
Who's Quite Remarkable, at Least.

I never saw a Purple Cow;
  I never Hope to See One;
But I can Tell you, Anyhow,
  I'd rather See than Be One.

GELETT BURGESS

DARIUS GREEN AND HIS FLYING-MACHINE

If ever there lived a Yankee lad,
Wise or otherwise, good or bad,
Who, seeing the birds fly, didn't jump
With flapping arms from stake or stump,
Or, spreading the tail of his coat for a sail,
Take a soaring leap from post or rail,
And wonder why *he* couldn't fly,
And flap and flutter and wish and try,—
If ever you knew a country dunce
Who didn't try that as often as once,
All I can say is, that's a sign
He never would do for a hero of mine.

An aspiring genius was D. Green:
The son of a farmer,—age fourteen;
His body was long and lank and lean,—
Just right for flying, as will be seen;
He had two eyes as bright as a bean,
And a freckled nose that grew between,
A little awry;—for I must mention
That he had riveted his attention
Upon his wonderful invention,
Twisting his tongue as he twisted the strings,
And working his face as he worked the wings,
And with every turn of gimlet and screw
Turning and screwing his mouth round too,
Till his nose seemed bent to catch the scent,
Around some corner, of new-baked pies,
And his wrinkled cheeks and his squinting eyes
Grew puckered into a queer grimace,
That made him look very droll in the face,
      And also very wise.

And wise he must have been, to do more
Than ever a genius did before,
Excepting Daedalus of yore
And his son Icarus, who wore
Upon their backs those wings of wax

He had read of in the old almanacs.
Darius was clearly of the opinion,
That the air was also man's dominion,
And that, with paddle or fin or pinion,
We soon or late should navigate
The azure as now we sail the sea.
The thing looks simple enough to me;
    And, if you doubt it,
Hear how Darius reasoned about it:

"The birds can fly, an' why can't I?
  Must we give in," says he with a grin,
"'T the bluebird an' phoebe are smarter'n we be?
Jest fold our hands, an' see the swaller
An' blackbird an' catbird beat us holler?
Does the leetle chatterin', sassy wren,
No bigger'n my thumb, know more than men?
Jest show me that! er prove 't the bat
Hez got more brains than's in my hat,
An' I'll back down, an' not till then!"

He argued further: "Ner I can't see
What's th' use o' wings to a bumble-bee,
Fer to git a livin' with, more'n to me;—
Ain't my business importanter'n his'n is?
That Icarus was a silly cuss,—
Him an' his daddy Daedalus;
They might 'a' knowed wings made o' wax
Wouldn't stan' sun-heat an' hard whacks:
I'll make mine o' luther, er suthin' er other."

And he said to himself, as he tinkered and planned:
"But I ain't goin' to show my hand
To nummies that never can understand
The fust idee that's big an' grand.
They'd 'a' laft an' made fun
O' Creation itself afore 'twas done!"
So he kept his secret from all the rest,
Safely buttoned within his vest;
And in the loft above the shed
Himself he locks, with thimble and thread
And wax and hammer and buckles and screws,

And all such things as geniuses use;—
Two bats for patterns, curious fellows!
A charcoal-pot and a pair of bellows;
An old hoop-skirt or two, as well as
Some wire, and several old umbrellas;
A carriage-cover, for tail and wings;
A piece of harness; and straps and strings;
And a big strong box, in which he locks
These and a hundred other things.

His grinning brothers, Reuben and Burke
And Nathan and Jotham and Solomon, lurk
Around the corner to see him work,—
Sitting cross-legged, like a Turk,
Drawing the waxed-end through with a jerk,
And boring the holes with a comical quirk
Of his wise old head, and a knowing smirk.
But vainly they mounted each other's backs,
And poked through knot-holes and pried through cracks;
With wood from the pile and straw from the stacks
He plugged the knot-holes and calked the cracks;
And a bucket of water, which one would think
He had brought up into the loft to drink
When he chanced to be dry,
Stood always nigh, for Darius was sly!
And, whenever at work he happened to spy
At chink or crevice a blinking eye,
He let a dipper of water fly:

"Take that! an', ef ever ye git a peep,
Guess ye'll ketch a weasel asleep!"
And he sings as he locks his big strong box:
"The weasel's head is small an' trim,
An' he is leetle an' long an' slim,
An' quick of motion an' nimble of limb,
An', ef yeou'll be advised by me,
Keep wide awake when ye're ketchin' him!"

      So day after day
He stitched and tinkered and hammered away,
      Till at last 'twas done,—
The greatest invention under the sun!
"An' now," says Darius, "hooray fer some fun!"

'Twas the Fourth of July, and the weather was dry,
And not a cloud was on all the sky,
Save a few light fleeces, which here and there,
    Half mist, half air,
Like foam on the ocean went floating by,—
Just as lovely a morning as ever was seen
For a nice little trip in a flying-machine.

Thought cunning Darius, "Now I shan't go
Along 'ith the fellers to see the show:
I'll say I've got sich a terrible cough!
An' then, when the folks 'ave all gone off,
I'll hev full swing fer to try the thing,
An' practyse a little on the wing."

"Ain't goin' to see the celebration?"
Says brother Nate. "No; botheration!
I've got sich a cold—a toothache—I—
My gracious!—feel's though I should fly!"
Said Jotham, " 'Sho! guess ye better go."
    But Darius said, "No!
Shouldn't wonder 'f yeou might see me, though,
'Long 'bout noon, ef I git red
O' this jumpin', thumpin' pain 'n my head."
For all the while to himself he said,—
    "I tell ye what!
I'll fly a few times around the lot,
To see how 't seems, then soon's I've got
The hang o' the thing, ez likely's not,
I'll astonish the nation, an' all creation,
By flyin' over the celebration!
Over their heads I'll sail like an eagle;
I'll balance myself on my wings like a sea-gull;
I'll dance on the chimbleys; I'll stan' on the steeple;
I'll flop up to winders an' scare the people!
I'll light on the libbe'ty-pole, an' crow;
An' I'll say to the gawpin' fools below,
'What world's this 'ere that I've come near?'
Fer I'll make 'em b'lieve I'm a chap f'm the moon;
An' I'll try a race 'ith their ol' balloon!"

He crept from his bed;
And, seeing the others were gone, he said,
"I'm a-gittin' over the cold 'n my head."
       And away he sped,
To open the wonderful box in the shed.

His brothers had walked but a little way,
When Jotham to Nathan chanced to say,
"What on airth is he up to, hey?"
"Don'o',—the' 's suthin' er other to pay,
Er he wouldn't 'a' stayed to hum to-day."
Says Burke, "His toothache's all 'n his eye!
He never'd miss a Fo'th-o'-July,
Ef he hedn't got some machine to try."
Then Sol, the little one, spoke: "By darn!
Le's hurry back, an' hide 'n the barn,
An' pay him fer tellin' us that yarn!"
"Agreed!" Through the orchard they creep back,
Along by the fences, behind the stack,
And one by one, through a hole in the wall,
In under the dusty barn they crawl,
Dressed in their Sunday garments all;
And a very astonishing sight was that,
When each in his cobwebbed coat and hat
Came up through the floor like an ancient rat.

And there they hid; and Reuben slid
The fastenings back, and the door undid.
       "Keep dark!" said he,
"While I squint an' see what the' is to see."

As knights of old put on their mail,—
From head to foot an iron suit,
Iron jacket and iron boot,
Iron breeches, and on the head
No hat, but an iron pot instead,
And under the chin the bail,—
(I believe they called the thing a helm,)—
And, thus accoutred, they took the field,
Sallying forth to overwhelm
The dragons and pagans that plagued the realm;
So this modern knight prepared for flight,

Put on his wings and strapped them tight,—
Jointed and jaunty, strong and light,—
Buckled them fast to shoulder and hip,—
Ten feet they measured from tip to tip!
And a helm had he, but that he wore,
Not on his head, like those of yore,
 But more like the helm of a ship.

"Hush!" Reuben said, "he's up in the shed!
He's opened the winder,—I see his head!
He stretches it out, an' pokes it about,
Lookin' to see 'f the coast is clear,
 An' nobody near;—
Guess he don'o' who's hid in here!
He's riggin' a spring-board over the sill!
Stop laffin', Solomon! Burke, keep still!
He's a climbin' out now—Of all the things!
What's he got on? I van, it's wings!
An' that t'other thing? I vum, it's a tail!
An' there he sets like a hawk on a rail!
Steppin' careful, he travels the length
Of his spring-board, and teeters to try its strength.
Now he stretches his wings, like a monstrous bat;
Peeks over his shoulder, this way an' that,
Fer to see 'f the' 's any one passin' by;
But the' 's on'y a ca'f an' a goslin' nigh.
They turn up at him a wonderin' eye,
To see—The dragon! he's goin' to fly!
Away he goes! Jimminy! what a jump!
Flop—flop—an' plump to the ground with a thump!
Flutt'rin' an' flound'rin', all 'n a lump!"

As a demon is hurled by an angel's spear,
Heels over head, to his proper sphere,—
Heels over head, and head over heels,
Dizzily down the abyss he wheels,—
So fell Darius. Upon his crown,
In the midst of the barn-yard, he came down,
In a wonderful whirl of tangled strings,
Broken braces and broken springs,
Broken tail and broken wings,
Shooting-stars, and various things,—

Barn-yard litter of straw and chaff,
And much that wasn't so sweet by half.
Away with a bellow fled the calf,
And what was that? Did the gosling laugh?
'Tis a merry roar from the old barn-door,
And he hears the voice of Jotham crying;
"Say, D'rius! how de yeou like flyin'?"

Slowly, ruefully, where he lay,
Darius just turned and looked that way,
As he stanched his sorrowful nose with his cuff,
"Wal, I like flyin' well enough,"
He said; "but the' ain't sich a thunderin' sight
O' fun in 't when ye come to light."

I just have room for the MORAL here:
And this is the moral,—Stick to your sphere;
Or, if you insist, as you have the right,
On spreading your wings for a loftier flight,
The moral is,—Take care how you light.

JOHN TOWNSEND TROWBRIDGE

IF I SHOULD DIE TO-NIGHT

After Arabella Eugenia Smith

If I should die to-night
And you should come to my cold corpse and say,
Weeping and heartsick o'er my lifeless clay—
If I should die to-night,
And you should come in deepest grief and woe—
And say: "Here's that ten dollars that I owe,"
I might arise in my large white cravat
And say, "What's that?"

If I should die to-night
And you should come to my cold corpse and kneel,
Clasping my bier to show the grief you feel,
I say, if I should die to-night

And you should come to me, and there and then
Just even hint at paying me that ten,
    I might arise the while,
    But I'd drop dead again.

BEN KING

MY FACE

As a beauty I am not a star.
There are others more handsome by far;
    But my face I don't mind it
    For I am behind it;
It's the people in front get the jar.

ANTHONY EUWER

TOBACCO

Tobacco is a dirty weed:
    I like it.
It satisfies no normal need:
    I like it.
It makes you thin, it makes you lean,
It takes the hair right off your bean,
It's the worst darn stuff I've ever seen:
    I like it.

GRAHAM LEE HEMMINGER

VERY LIKE A WHALE

One thing that literature would be greatly the better for
Would be a more restricted employment by authors of simile and
    metaphor.
Authors of all races, be they Greeks, Romans, Teutons or Celts,
Can't seem just to say that anything is the thing it is but have to go
    out of their way to say that it is like something else.
What does it mean when we are told
That the Assyrian came down like a wolf on the fold?

In the first place, George Gordon Byron had had enough experience
To know that it probably wasn't just one Assyrian, it was a lot of
Assyrians.
However, as too many arguments are apt to induce apoplexy and thus
hinder longevity,
We'll let it pass as one Assyrian for the sake of brevity.
Now then, this particular Assyrian, the one whose cohorts were
gleaming in purple and gold,
Just what does the poet mean when he says he came down like a
wolf on the fold?
In heaven and earth more than is dreamed of in our philosophy there
are a great many things,
But I don't imagine that among them there is a wolf with purple
and gold cohorts or purple and gold anythings.
No, no, Lord Byron, before I'll believe that this Assyrian was actually
like a wolf I must have some kind of proof;
Did he run on all fours and did he have a hairy tail and a big red
mouth and big white teeth and did he say Woof woof?
Frankly I think it very unlikely, and all you were entitled to say, at
the very most,
Was that the Assyrian cohorts came down like a lot of Assyrian
cohorts about to destroy the Hebrew host.
But that wasn't fancy enough for Lord Byron, oh dear me no, he had
to invent a lot of figures of speech and then interpolate them,
With the result that whenever you mention Old Testament soldiers
to people they say Oh yes, they're the ones that a lot of wolves
dressed up in gold and purple ate them.
That's the kind of thing that's being done all the time by poets, from
Homer to Tennyson;
They're always comparing ladies to lilies and veal to venison,
And they always say things like that the snow is a white blanket after
a winter storm.
Oh it is, is it, all right then, you sleep under a six-inch blanket of
snow and I'll sleep under a half-inch blanket of unpoetical blanket
material and we'll see which one keeps warm,
And after that maybe you'll begin to comprehend dimly
What I mean by too much metaphor and simile.

OGDEN NASH

I NEVER EVEN SUGGESTED IT

I know lots of men who are in love and lots of men who are married
    and lots of men who are both,
And to fall out with their loved ones is what all of them are most
    loth.
They are conciliatory at every opportunity,
Because all they want is serenity and a certain amount of impunity.
Yes, many the swain who has finally admitted that the earth is flat
Simply to sidestep a spat,
Many the masculine Positively or Absolutely which has been diluted
    to an If
Simply to avert a tiff,
Many the two-fisted executive whose domestic conversation is limited
    to a tactfully interpolated Yes,
And then he is amazed to find that he is being raked backwards over
    a bed of coals nevertheless.
These misguided fellows are under the impression that it takes two
    to make a quarrel, that you can sidestep a crisis by nonaggression
    and nonresistance,
Instead of removing yourself to a discreet distance.
Passivity can be a provoking *modus operandi*;
Consider the Empire and Gandhi.
Silence is golden, but sometimes invisibility is golder,
Because loved ones may not be able to make bricks without straw
    but often they don't need any straw to manufacture a bone to pick
    or blood in their eye or a chip for their soft white shoulder.
It is my duty, gentlemen, to inform you that women are dictators all,
    and I recommend to you this moral:
In real life it takes only one to make a quarrel.

OGDEN NASH

SO THAT'S WHO I REMIND ME OF

When I consider men of golden talents,
I'm delighted, in my introverted way,
To discover, as I'm drawing up the balance,
How much we have in common, I and they.

Like Burns, I have a weakness for the bottle,
Like Shakespeare, little Latin and less Greek;
I bite my fingernails like Aristotle;
Like Thackeray, I have a snobbish streak.

I'm afflicted with the vanity of Byron,
I've inherited the spitefulness of Pope;
Like Petrarch, I'm a sucker for a siren,
Like Milton, I've a tendency to mope.

My spelling is suggestive of a Chaucer;
Like Johnson, well, I do not wish to die
(I also drink my coffee from the saucer);
And if Goldsmith was a parrot, so am I.

Like Villon, I have debits by the carload,
Like Swinburne, I'm afraid I need a nurse;
By my dicing is Christopher out-Marlowed,
And I dream as much as Coleridge, only worse.

In comparison with men of golden talents,
I am all a man of talent ought to be;
I resemble every genius in his vice, however heinous—
Yet I write so much like me.

OGDEN NASH

O'GRADY'S GOAT

O'Grady lived in Shanty row;
   The neighbors often said
They wished that he would move away
   Or that his goat was dead.
He kept the neighborhood in fear,
   And the children always vexed;
They couldn't tell just when or where
   The goat would pop up next.

Ould widow Casey stood wan day
   The dirty clothes to rub
Upon the washboard, when she dived
   Head foremost o'er the tub;

She lit upon her back and yelled,
    As she was lying flat:
"Go git your goon an' shoot thot baste,
    O'Grady's goat doon that."

Pat Doolan's woife hung out the wash
    Upon the line to dry;
She wint to take it in at night,
    But stopped to have a cry.
The sleeves av two red flannel shirts,
    That once were worn by Pat,
Were chewed off almost to the neck—
    O'Grady's goat doon that.

They had a party at McCune's,
    An' they were having foon,
Whin suddinly ther was a crash
    An' ivirybody roon.
The iseter soup fell on the floor,
    An' nearly drowned the cat;
The stove was knocked to smithereens—
    O'Grady's goat doon that.

Moike D'yle was courtin' Biddy Shea,
    Both standin' at the gate,
An' they wor jist about to kiss
    Aich oother sly and shwate.
They coom togither like two rams,
    An' mashed their noses flat.
They niver shpake whin they goes by,
    O'Grady's goat doon that.

Folks in O'Grady's neighborhood
    All live in fear or fright;
They think it's certain death to go
    Around there after night.
An' in their shlape they sees a ghost
    Upon the air afloat,
An' wake thimselves by shoutin' out:
    "Luck out for Grady's goat."

One winter morning whin the shnow
    Was deep upon the ground,
Men, women, children—in a crowd—
    Were sad an' shtandin' 'round
The form of wan, cold, stiff an' dead,
    An' shtickin' down his throat
Was Mag McGinty's bushtlefast,
    That inded Grady's goat.

                 WILL S. HAYS

SOAP, THE OPPRESSOR

The folks at home half the time are thinkin' about dirt;
It sort of gives 'em horrors an' they act as if it hurt;
The sight of just a little makes 'em daffy as can be—
They're always washin' somethin', and half the time it's me.
It ain't because I wet my feet that gives me colds and such;
'Tain't runnin' round that keeps me thin—it's cause I'm washed too
    much.
It does no good to tell 'em, they're so stubborn, but I hope
That some day they'll discover what deceitful stuff is soap.
I tell you very often when my hands was clean and white
I've gone along to wash 'em 'cause it did no good to fight.
When I stuck 'em in the basin, it was plain enough to see
The soap would make the water as dirty as could be.
If folks would give me half a chance with soap that didn't cheat,
I guess they'd be surprised to find I'm nacherally neat;
I'd take on flesh and leave off havin' colds an' such, I know.
And no one would complain about the parts of me that show.

                 BURGES JOHNSON

HE AND SHE

When I am dead you'll find it hard,
    Said he,
To ever find another man
    Like me.

What makes you think, as I suppose
    You do,
I'd ever want another man
    Like you?   EUGENE FITCH WARE

A BALLAD IN "G"

I

A man with a marvelous mug
 Rode out of Fort Scott on a nag;
He carried a jug in a bag,
 And many and many a swig
Reposed in that corpulent jug;
 And a cob fitted in for a plug
As snug as a snag in a bog.

The nag had a wigglety jig
 Which churned up the jag in the jug;
And along by its side went a dog
 Which jiggled along in a jog,
With narrative shaggy and sag,
 Which he wearily, warily wug.

Oh! That jig, and that jog and that jag;—
 O! that jog, and that jag, and that jug.

II

The man shouted "Whoa"—to the nag,
 Then took out the jug from the bag,
Then took out the plug from the jug,
 And then from the jug took a jag,—
A terrible, horrible jag
 Which acted as quick as a drug.

He shouted "Yip-yip" to the nag,
 And dug in his heels with a dig,
And the nag who would never renig
 Sprang off with the speed of a stag.
Then the man with the marvelous mug
 Began a vociferous brag:

"Whoo-pee—I'm a bird on a crag,
 I'm a thief, and a wolf, and a thug,

I'm a bug-eater hunting a bug,
  O, I can hold more than a kag,
And I have got boodle and swag
  That says that my grave don't get dug."

III

To the front with a yelp went the dog—
  And—shouting "Yip-yip!" to the nag—
Pell-mell with the jug and the bag
  Went the man with the marvelous mug.
And there in the road lay a hog
  As still as a bump on the log.

Then down in a pile went the nag,
  And the dog and the hog and the jug,
And that was the end of the hog,
  And that was the end of the dog,
And vain were his efforts to wag
  The narrative previously wug.
And limber and limp as a rag
  In a wad on his lug lay the nag.

IV

And the man with the marvelous mug
  Rolled up like a cavalry flag,
Done up like a family rug,
  Lay there with his head in the bag.
And twenty feet off stood the jug—
  The opulent, corpulent jug—
Unharmed, while the loyal cob plub—
  Held down what was left of the jag.

And this is the song of the jag,
  And the jug, and the jog, and the jig.
And this is the song of the nag,
  Of the nag that would never renig,
And the dog and the hog and the bag—
  A song of the swag and the swig.

EUGENE FITCH WARE

THE INVENTOR'S WIFE

It's easy to talk of the patience of Job. Humph! Job hed nothin' to
try him!
Ef *he'd* been married to 'Bijah Brown, folks wouldn't have dared
come nigh him.
Trials, indeed! Now I'll tell you what—eh you want to be sick of
your life,
Jest come and change places with me a spell—for I'm an inventor's
wife.
And sech inventions! I'm never sure, when I take up my coffee-pot,
That 'Bijah hain't ben "improvin" it, and it mayn't go off like a shot.
Why, didn't he make me a cradle once, that would keep itself
a-rockin';
And didn't it pitch the baby out, and wasn't his head bruised shockin'?
And there was his "Patent Peeler," too—a wonderful thing, I'll say;
But it hed one fault,—it never stopped till the apple was peeled away.
As for locks, and clocks, and mowin' machines, and reapers, and all
sech trash,
Why 'Bijah's invented heaps of 'em, but they don't bring in no *cash*.
Law! That don't worry him—not at all; he's the aggravatin'est man—
He'll set in his little workshop there, and whistle, and think, and
plan,
Inventin' a Jew's-harp to go by steam, or a new-fangled powder-horn,
While the children goin' barefoot to school and the weeds is chokin'
our corn.
When 'Bijah and me kep' company, he warn't like this, you know;
Our folks all thought he was dreadful smart—but that was years ago.
He was handsome as any pictur then, and he had such a glib, bright
way—
I never thought that a time would come when I'd rue my weddin' day;
But when I've been forced to chop the wood, and tend to the farm
beside,
And look at 'Bijah a-settin' there, I've jest dropped down and cried.
We lost the hull of our turnip crop while he was inventin' a gun;
But I counted it one of my marcies when it bust before 'twas done.
So he turned it into a "burglar alarm." It ought to give thieves a
fright—
'Twould scare an honest man out of his wits ef he sot it off at night.
Sometimes I wonder ef 'Bijah's crazy, he does sech cur'ous things.

Hev I told about his bedstead yit?—'twas full of wheels and springs;
It hed a key to wind it up, and a clock face at the head;
All you did was to turn them hands, and at any hour you said,
That bed got up and shook itself, and bounced you on the floor,
And then shet up, jest like a box, so you couldn't sleep no more.
Wa'al, 'Bijah he fixed it all complete, and he sot it at half-past five,
But he hadn't more'n got into it when—dear me! sakes alive!
Them wheels began to whizz and whirr. I heerd a fearful snap!
And there was that bedstead, with 'Bijah inside, shet up jest like a trap!
I screamed, of course, but 'twan't no use, then I worked that hull
   long night
A-tryin' to open the pesky thing. At last I got in a fright;
I couldn't hear his voice inside, and I thought he might be dyin';
So I took a crowbar and smashed it in.—There was 'Bijah, peace-
   fully lyin',
Inventin' a way to git out agin. That was all very well to say,
But I don't b'lieve he'd have found it out if I'd left him in all day.
Now, sence I've told you my story, do you wonder I'm tired of life?
Or think it strange I often wish I warn't an inventor's wife?

MRS. E. R. CORBETT

THANKS JUST THE SAME

I hate to spend the night
In someone else's home,
When I have no tooth brush,
And didn't bring my comb;
I hate to wake up mornings
And not know where I am,
Then have to eat a breakfast
Of scrambled eggs, and ham;
I feel so lousy, later,
Without a change of clothes,
And no clean folded hanky
On which to blow my nose;
I'm fond of people evenings,
But in the morning—well,
Staying places overnight
Is my idea of hell.

My friends are of the finest,
Their beds are of the best,
But just give me an army cot
At home when I need rest.

UNKNOWN

NOTHING TO WEAR

AN EPISODE OF CITY LIFE

Miss Flora McFlimsey, of Madison Square,
Has made three separate journeys to Paris,
And her father assures me, each time she was there,
That she and her friend Mrs. Harris
(Not the lady whose name is so famous in history,
But plain Mrs. H., without romance or mystery)
Spent six consecutive weeks without stopping
In one continuous round of shopping,—
Shopping alone, and shopping together,
At all hours of the day, and in all sorts of weather,—
For all manner of things that a woman can put
On the crown of her head or the sole of her foot,
Or wrap round her shoulders or fit round her waist,
Or that can be sewed on, or pinned on, or laced,
Or tied on with a string, or stitched on with a bow,
In front or behind, above or below;
For bonnets, mantillas, capes, collars, and shawls;
Dresses for breakfasts and dinners and balls;
Dresses to sit in and stand in and walk in;
Dresses to dance in and flirt in and talk in;
Dresses in which to do nothing at all;
Dresses for winter, spring, summer, and fall;
All of them different in color and pattern,
Silk, muslin, and lace, crape, velvet, and satin,
Brocade, and broadcloth, and other material,
Quite as expensive and much more ethereal;
In short, for all things that could ever be thought of,
Or milliner, *modiste*, or tradesman be bought of,
   From ten-thousand-francs robes to twenty-sous frills;
In all quarters of Paris, and to every store,

While McFlimsey in vain stormed, scolded, and swore,
  They footed the streets, and he footed the bills.

The last trip, their goods shipped by the steamer Arago,
Formed, McFlimsey declares, the bulk of her cargo,
Not to mention a quantity kept from the rest,
Sufficient to fill the largest-sized chest,
Which did not appear on the ship's manifest,
But for which the ladies themselves manifested
Such particular interest, that they invested
Their own proper persons in layers and rows
Of muslins, embroideries, worked under-clothes,
Gloves, handkerchiefs, scarfs, and such trifles as those;
Then, wrapped in great shawls, like Circassian beauties,
Gave *good-by* to the ship, and *go-by* to the duties.
Her relations at home all marvelled, no doubt,
Miss Flora had grown so enormously stout
  For an actual belle and a possible bride;
But the miracle ceased when she turned inside out,
  And the truth came to light, and the dry-goods beside,
Which, in spite of collector and custom-house sentry,
Had entered the port without any entry.

And yet, though scarce three months have passed since the day
This merchandise went, on twelve carts, up Broadway,
This same Miss McFlimsey, of Madison Square,
The last time we met was in utter despair,
Because she had nothing whatever to wear!

Nothing to Wear! Now, as this is a true ditty,
  I do not assert—this, you know, is between us—
That she's in a state of absolute nudity,
  Like Powers' Greek Slave, or the Medici Venus;
But I do mean to say, I have heard her declare,
  When, at the same moment, she had on a dress
  Which cost five hundred dollars, and not a cent less
  And jewelry worth ten times more, I should guess,
That she had not a thing in the wide world to wear!

I should mention just here, that out of Miss Flora's
Two hundred and fifty or sixty adorers,

I had just been selected as he who should throw all
The rest in the shade, by the gracious bestowal
On myself, after twenty or thirty rejections,
Of those fossil remains which she called her "affections,"
And that rather decayed, but well-known work of art,
Which Miss Flora persisted in styling "her heart."
So we were engaged. Our troth had been plighted,
Not by moonbeam or starbeam, by fountain or grove,
But in a front parlor, most brilliantly lighted,
Beneath the gas-fixtures we whispered our love.
Without any romance or raptures or sighs,
Without any tears in Miss Flora's blue eyes,
Or blushes, or transports, or such silly actions,
It was one of the quietest business transactions,
With a very small sprinkling of sentiment, if any,
And a very large diamond imported by Tiffany.
On her virginal lips while I printed a kiss,
She exclaimed, as a sort of parenthesis,
And by way of putting me quite at my ease,
"You know, I'm to polka as much as I please,
And flirt when I like,—now, stop, don't you speak,—
And you must not come here more than twice in the week,
Or talk to me either at party or ball,
But always be ready to come when I call;
So don't prose to me about duty and stuff,
If we don't break this off, there will be time enough
For that sort of thing; but the bargain must be
That, as long as I choose, I am perfectly free,
For this is a sort of engagement, you see,
Which is binding on you but not binding on me."

Well, having thus wooed Miss McFlimsey and gained her,
With the silks, crinolines, and hoops that contained her,
I had, as I thought, a contingent remainder
At least in the property, and the best right
To appear as its escort by day and by night;
And it being the week of the Stuckups' grand ball,—
    Their cards had been out for a fortnight or so,
    And set all the Avenue on the tiptoe,—
I considered it only my duty to call,
    And see if Miss Flora intended to go.
I found her,—as ladies are apt to be found,

When the time intervening between the first sound
Of the bell and the visitor's entry is shorter
Than usual,—I found—I won't say, I caught her,—
Intent on the pier-glass, undoubtedly meaning
To see if perhaps it didn't need cleaning.
She turned as I entered,—"Why, Harry, you sinner,
I thought that you went to the Flashers' to dinner!"
"So I did," I replied; "but the dinner is swallowed
    And digested, I trust, for 'tis now nine and more,
So being relieved from that duty, I followed
    Inclination, which led me, you see, to your door;
And now will your ladyship so condescend
As just to inform me if you intend
Your beauty and graces and presence to lend
(All of which, when I own, I hope no one will borrow)
To the Stuckups', whose party, you know, is to-morrow?"

The fair Flora looked up with a pitiful air,
And answered quite promptly, "Why, Harry, *mon cher*,
I should like above all things to go with you there;
But really and truly—I've nothing to wear."

"Nothing to wear! go just as you are;
Wear the dress you have on, and you'll be by far,
I engage, the most bright and particular star
    On the Stuckup horizon"—I stopped—for her eye,
Notwithstanding this delicate onset of flattery,
Opened on me at once a most terrible battery
    Of scorn and amazement. She made no reply,
But gave a slight turn to the end of her nose
    (That pure Grecian feature), as much as to say,
"How absurd that any sane man should suppose
That a lady would go to a ball in the clothes,
    No matter how fine, that she wears every day!"

So I ventured again: "Wear your crimson brocade,"
    (Second turn-up of nose)—"That's too dark by a shade."
"Your blue silk"—"That's too heavy." "Your pink"—
    "That's too light."
"Wear tulle over satin"—"I can't endure white."
"Your rose-colored, then, the best of the batch"—

"I haven't a thread of point lace to match."
"Your brown *moire antique*"—"Yes, and look like a
    Quaker."
"The pearl-colored"—"I would, but that plaguey dressmaker
Has had it a week." "Then that exquisite lilac
In which you would melt the heart of a Shylock."
(Here the nose took again the same elevation)—
"I wouldn't wear that for the whole of creation."
  "Why not? It's my fancy, there's nothing could strike it
As more *comme il faut*"—"Yes, but, dear me! that lean
  Sophronia Stuckup has got one just like it,
And I won't appear dressed like a chit of sixteen."
"Then that splendid purple, that sweet Mazarine,
That superb *point d'aiguille*, that imperial green,
That zephyr-like tarlatan, that rich *grenadine*"—
"Not one of all which is fit to be seen,"
Said the lady, becoming excited and flushed.
"Then wear," I exclaimed, in a tone which quite crushed
  Opposition, "that gorgeous *toilette* which you sported
In Paris last spring, at the grand presentation,
When you quite turned the head of the head of the nation;
  And by all the grand court were so very much courted."
The end of the nose was portentously tipped up,
And both the bright eyes shot forth indignation,
As she burst upon me with the fierce exclamation,
"I have worn it three times at the least calculation,
  And that and the most of my dresses are ripped up!"
Here I ripped *out* something, perhaps rather rash,
  Quite innocent, though; but, to use an expression
More striking than classic, it "settled my hash,"
  And proved very soon the last act of our session.
"Fiddlesticks, it is, sir? I wonder the ceiling
Doesn't fall down and crush you—oh! you men have no feeling;
You selfish, unnatural, illiberal creatures,
Who set yourselves up as patterns and preachers,
Your silly pretense,—why, what a mere guess it is!
Pray, what do you know of a woman's necessities!
I have told you and shown you I've nothing to wear,
And it's perfectly plain you not only don't care,
But you do not believe me" (here the nose went still higher).
"I suppose, if you dared, you would call me a liar.
Our engagement is ended, sir—yes, on the spot;

You're a brute and a monster, and—I don't know what."
I mildly suggested the words—Hottentot,
Pickpocket, and cannibal, Tartar, and thief,
As gentle expletives which might give relief;
But this only proved as spark to the powder,
And the storm I had raised came faster and louder;
It blew and it rained, thundered, lightened, and hailed
Interjections, verbs, pronouns, till language quite failed
To express the abusive, and then its arrears
Were brought up all at once by a torrent of tears,
And my last faint, despairing attempt at an obs-
Ervation was lost in a tempest of sobs.

Well, I felt for the lady, and felt for my hat, too,
Improvised on the crown of the latter a tattoo,
In lieu of expressing the feelings which lay
Quite too deep for words, as Wordsworth would say;
Then, without going through the form of a bow,
Found myself in the entry—I hardly knew how,—
On doorstep and sidewalk, past lamp-post and square,
At home and up stairs, in my own easy-chair;
  Poked my feet into slippers, my fire into blaze,
And said to myself, as I lit my cigar,
Supposing a man had the wealth of the Czar
  Of the Russias to boot, for the rest of his days,
On the whole, do you think he would have much to spare,
If he married a woman with nothing to wear?

Since that night, taking pains that it should not be bruited
Abroad in society, I've instituted
A course of inquiry, extensive and thorough,
On this vital subject, and find, to my horror,
That the fair Flora's case is by no means surprising,
  But that there exists the greatest distress
In our female community, solely arising
  From this unsupplied destitution of dress,
Whose unfortunate victims are filling the air
With the pitiful wail of "Nothing to wear."
Researches in some of the "Upper Ten" districts
Reveal the most painful and startling statistics,
Of which let me mention only a few:
In one single house, on Fifth Avenue,

Three young ladies were found, all below twenty-two,
Who have been three whole weeks without anything new
In the way of flounced silks, and, thus left in the lurch,
Are unable to go to ball, concert, or church.
In another large mansion, near the same place,
Was found a deplorable, heartrending case
Of entire destitution of Brussels point lace.
In a neighboring block there was found, in three calls,
Total want, long continued, of camel's-hair shawls;
And a suffering family, whose case exhibits
The most pressing need of real ermine tippets;
One deserving young lady almost unable
To survive for the want of a new Russian sable;
Another confined to the house, when it's windier
Than usual, because her shawl isn't India.
Still another, whose tortures have been most terrific
Ever since the sad loss of the steamer Pacific,
In which were engulfed, not friend or relation
(For whose fate she perhaps might have found consolation
Or borne it, at least, with serene resignation),
But the choicest assortment of French sleeves and collars
Ever sent out from Paris, worth thousands of dollars,
And all as to style most *recherche* and rare,
The want of which leaves her with nothing to wear,
And renders her life so drear and dyspeptic
That she's quite a recluse, and almost a sceptic;
For she touchingly says that this sort of grief
Cannot find in Religion the slightest relief,
And Philosophy has not a maxim to spare
For the victims of such overwhelming despair.
But the saddest by far of all these sad features
Is the cruelty practised upon the poor creatures
By husbands and fathers, real Bluebeards and Timons,
Who resist the most touching appeals made for diamonds
By their wives and their daughters, and leave them for days
Unsupplied with new jewelry, fans, or bouquets,
Even laugh at their miseries whenever they have a chance,
And deride their demands as useless extravagance;
One case of a bride was brought to my view,
Too sad for belief, but, alas! 'twas too true,
Whose husband refused, as savage as Charon,

To permit her to take more than ten trunks to Sharon.
The consequence was, that when she got there,
At the end of three weeks she had nothing to wear,
And when she proposed to finish the season
    At Newport, the monster refused out and out,
For his infamous conduct alleging no reason,
    Except that the waters were good for his gout.
Such treatment as this was too shocking, of course,
And proceedings are now going on for divorce.

But why harrow the feelings by lifting the curtain
From these scenes of woe? Enough, it is certain,
Has here been disclosed to stir up the pity
Of every benevolent heart in the city,
And spur up Humanity into a canter
To rush and relieve these sad cases instanter.
Won't somebody, moved by this touching description,
Come forward to-morrow and head a subscription?
Won't some kind philanthropist, seeing that aid is
So needed at once by these indigent ladies,
Take charge of the matter? Or won't Peter Cooper
The corner-stone lay of some splendid super-
Structure, like that which to-day links his name
In the Union unending of honor and fame;
And found a new charity just for the care
Of these unhappy women with nothing to wear,
Which, in view of the cash which would daily be claimed,
The *Laying-out* Hospital well might be named?
Won't Stewart, or some of our dry-goods importers,
Take a contract for clothing our wives and our daughters?
Or, to furnish the cash to supply these distresses,
And life's pathway strew with shawls, collars, and dresses,
Ere the want of them makes it much rougher and thornier,
Won't someone discover a new California?

Oh ladies, dear ladies, the next sunny day
Please trundle your hoops just out of Broadway,
From its whirl and its bustle, its fashion and pride,
And the temples of Trade which tower on each side,
To the alleys and lanes, where Misfortune and Guilt
Their children have gathered, their city have built;

Where Hunger and Vice, like twin beasts of prey,
  Have hunted their victims to gloom and despair;
Raise the rich, dainty dress, and the fine broidered skirt,
Pick your delicate way through the dampness and dirt,
  Grope through the dark dens, climb the rickety stair
To the garret, where wretches, the young and the old,
Half-starved, and half-naked, lie crouched from the cold.
  See those skeleton limbs, those frost-bitten feet,
All bleeding and bruised by the stones of the street;
Hear the sharp cry of childhood, the deep groans that swell
  From the poor dying creature who writhes on the floor,
Hear the curses that sound like the echoes of Hell,
  As you sicken and shudder and fly from the door;
Then home to your wardrobes, and say, if you dare,—
Spoiled children of Fashion,—you've nothing to wear!

And oh, if perchance there should be a sphere
Where all is made right which so puzzles us here,
Where the glare and the glitter and tinsel of Time
Fade and die in the light of that region sublime,
Where the soul, disenchanted of flesh and of sense,
Unscreened by its trappings and shows and pretense,
Must be clothed for the life and the service above,
With purity, truth, faith, meekness and love;
O daughters of Earth! foolish virgins, beware!
Lest in that upper realm you have nothing to wear!

WILLIAM ALLEN BUTLER

TROUBLE

Better never trouble Trouble
Until Trouble troubles you;
For you only make your trouble
Double-trouble when you do;
And the trouble—like a bubble—
That you're troubling about,
May be nothing but a cipher
With its rim rubbed out.

DAVID KEPPEL

THE GREAT PANJANDRUM HIMSELF

So she went into the garden
to cut a cabbage leaf
to make an apple pie;
and at the same time
a great she-bear, coming down the street,
pops its head into the shop.
What! No soap?
So he died,
and she very imprudently married the Barber.
and there were present
the Picninnies,
and the Joblillies,
and the Garyulies,
and the great Panjandrum himself,
with the little round button at top;
and they all fell to playing the game
of catch-as-catch-can,
till the gunpowder ran out at the heels of their boots.

UNKNOWN

SOME LITTLE BUG

In these days of indigestion
It is oftentimes a question
    As to what to eat and what to leave alone;
For each microbe and bacillus
Has a different way to kill us,
    And in time they always claim us for their own.
There are germs of every kind
In any food that you can find
    In the market or upon the bill of fare.
Drinking water's just as risky
As the so-called deadly whiskey,
    And it's often a mistake to breathe the air.

Some little bug is going to find you some day,
Some little bug will creep behind you some day,

Then he'll send for his bug friends
And all your earthly trouble ends;
Some little bug is going to find you some day.
The inviting green cucumber
Gets most everybody's number,
    While the green corn has a system of its own;
Though a radish seems nutritious
Its behaviour is quite vicious,
    And a doctor will be coming to your home.
Eating lobster cooked or plain
Is only flirting with ptomaine,
    While an oyster sometimes has a lot to say,
But the clams we eat in chowder
Make the angels chant the louder,
    For they know that we'll be with them right away.

Take a slice of nice fried onion
And you're fit for Dr. Munyon,
    Apple dumplings kill you quicker than a train.
Chew a cheesy midnight "rabbit"
And a grave you'll soon inhabit—
    Ah, to eat at all is such a foolish game.
Eating huckleberry pie
Is a pleasing way to die.
    While sauerkraut brings on softening of the brain.
When you eat banana fritters
Every undertaker titters,
    And the casket makers nearly go insane.

Some little bug is going to find you some day,
Some little bug will creep behind you some day,
    With a nervous little quiver
    He'll give cirrhosis of the liver;
Some little bug is going to find you some day.
When cold storage vaults I visit
I can only say what is it
    Makes poor mortals fill their systems with such stuff?
Now, for breakfast, prunes are dandy
If a stomach pump is handy
    And your doctor can be found quite soon enough.
Eat a plate of fine pigs' knuckles

And the headstone cutter chuckles,
    While the grave digger makes a note upon his cuff.
Eat that lovely red bologna
And you'll wear a wooden kimona,
    As your relatives start scrappin' 'bout your stuff.

Some little bug is going to find you some day,
Some little bug will creep behind you some day,
    Eating juicy sliced pineapple
    Makes the sexton dust the chapel;
Some little bug is going to find you some day.

All those crazy foods they mix
Will float us 'cross the River Styx,
    Or they'll start us climbing up the milky way.
And the meals we eat in courses
Mean a hearse and two black horses
    So before a meal some people always pray.
Luscious grapes breed 'pendicitis,
And the juice leads to gastritis,
    So there's only death to greet us either way;
And fried liver's nice, but, mind you,
Friends will soon ride slow behind you
    And the papers then will have nice things to say.

Some little bug is going to find you some day,
Some little bug will creep behind you some day
    Eat some sauce, they call it chili,
    On your breast they'll place a lily;
Some little bug is going to find you some day.

                                        ROY ATWELL

ANTIGONISH

    As I was going up the stair
        I met a man who wasn't there!
    He wasn't there again today!
    I wish, I *wish* he'd stay away!

                            HUGHES MEARNS

THE NEW CHURCH ORGAN

They've got a brand-new organ, Sue,
    For all their fuss and search;
They've done just as they said they'd do,
    And fetched it into church.
They're bound the critter shall be seen,
    And on the preacher's right
They've hoisted up their new machine,
    In every body's sight.
They've got a chorister and choir,
    Ag'in' *my* voice and vote;
For it was never *my* desire
    To praise the Lord by note!

I've been a sister good an' true
    For five-an'-thirty year;
I've done what seemed my part to do,
    An' prayed my duty clear;
I've sung the hymns both slow and quick,
    Just as the preacher read,
And twice, when Deacon Tubbs was sick,
    I took the fork an' led!
And now, their bold, new-fangled ways
    Is comin' all about;
And I, right in my latter days,
    Am fairly crowded out!

To-day the preacher, good old dear,
    With tears all in his eyes,
Reads, "I can read my title clear
    To mansions in the skies."
I al'ays liked that blessed hymn—
    I s'pose I al'ays will;
It somehow gratifies *my* whim,
    In good old Ortonville;
But when that choir got up to sing,
    I couldn't catch a word;
They sung the most dog-gondest thing
    A body ever heard!

Some worldly chaps was standin' near;
   An' when I see them grin,
I bid farewell to every fear,
   And boldly waded in.
I thought I'd chase their tune along,
   An' tried with all my might;
But though my voice is good an' strong,
   I couldn't steer it right;
When they was high, then I was low,
   An' also contrawise;
An' I too fast, or they too slow,
   To "mansions in the skies."

An' after every verse, you know,
   They play a little tune;
I didn't understand, and so
   I started in too soon.
I pitched it pretty middlin' high,
   I fetched a lusty tone,
But, oh, alas! I found that I
   Was singin' there alone!
They laughed a little, I am told;
   But I had done my best;
And not a wave of trouble rolled
   Across my peaceful breast.

And Sister Brown—I could but look—
   She sits right front of me;
She never was no singin'-book,
   An' never went to be;
But then she al'ays tried to do
   The best she could, she said;
She understood the time right through,
   An' kep' it with her head;
But when she tried this morning, oh,
   I had to laugh, or cough!
It kep' her head a-bobbin' so,
   It e'en a'most came off!

An' Deacon Tubbs—he all broke down,
   As one might well suppose;

He took one look at Sister Brown,
 And meekly scratched his nose.
He looked his hymn-book through and through,
 And laid it on the seat,
And then a pensive sigh he drew,
 And looked completely beat.
And when they took another bout,
 He didn't even rise;
But drawed his red bandanner out,
 An' wiped his weepin' eyes.

I've been a sister, good an' true,
 For five-an'-thirty year;
I've done what seemed my part to do,
 An' prayed my duty clear;
But Death will stop my voice, I know,
 For he is on my track;
And some day I to church will go,
 And never more come back;
And when the folks gets up to sing—
 Whene'er that time shall be—
I do not want no *patent* thing
 A-squealin' over me!

      WILL CARLETON

JOHN GRUMLIE

John Grumlie swore by the light o' the moon
 And the green leaves on the tree,
That he could do more work in a day
 Than his wife could do in three.
His wife rose up in the morning
 Wi' cares and troubles enow—
John Grumlie bide at hame, John,
 And I'll go haud the plow.

First ye maun dress your children fair,
 And put them a' in their gear;
And ye maun turn the malt, John,
 Or else ye'll spoil the beer;
And ye maun reel the tweel, John,

That I span yesterday;
And ye maun ca' in the hens, John,
  Else they'll all lay away.

O he did dress his children fair,
  And put them a' in their gear;
But he forgot to turn the malt,
  And so he spoiled the beer:
And he sang loud as he reeled the tweel
  That his wife span yesterday;
But he forgot to put up the hens,
    And the hens all layed away.

The hawket crummie loot down nae milk;
  He kirned, nor butter gat;
And a' gade wrang, and naught gade right;
  He danced wi' rage, and grat;
Then up he ran to the head o' the knowe
  Wi' mony a wave and shout—
She heard him as she heard him not,
  And steered the stots about.

John Grumlie's wife cam hame at e'en,
  A weary wife and sad,
And burst into a laughter loud,
  And laughed as she'd been mad:
While John Grumlie swore by the light o' the moon
  And the green leaves on the tree,
If my wife should na win a penny a day
  She's aye her will for me.

                    ALLAN CUNNINGHAM

THE JANITOR'S BOY

Oh I'm in love with the janitor's boy,
  And the janitor's boy loves me;
He's going to hunt for a desert isle
  In our geography.

A desert isle with spicy trees
  Somewhere near Sheepshead Bay;

A right nice place, just fit for two
  Where we can live alway.

Oh I'm in love with the janitor's boy,
  He's busy as he can be;
And down in the cellar he's making a raft
  Out of an old settee.

He'll carry me off, I know that he will,
  For his hair is exceedingly red;
And the only thing that seems to me
  Is to dutifully shiver in bed.

The day that we sail, I shall leave this brief note,
  For my parents I hate to annoy:
"I have flown away to an isle in the bay
  With the janitor's red-haired boy."

NATHALIA CRANE

THE OWL AND THE PUSSY-CAT

The Owl and the Pussy-cat went to sea
  In a beautiful pea-green boat:
They took some honey, and plenty of money
  Wrapped up in a five-pound note.
The Owl looked up to the stars above,
  And sang to a small guitar,
"O lovely Pussy, O Pussy, my love,
  What a beautiful Pussy you are,
      You are,
      You are!
  What a beautiful Pussy you are!"

Pussy said to the Owl, "You elegant fowl,
  How charmingly sweet you sing!
Oh! let us be married; too long we have tarried:
  But what shall we do for a ring?"
They sailed away, for a year and a day,
  To the land where the bong-tree grows;
And there in a wood a Piggy-wig stood,

With a ring at the end of his nose,
   His nose,
   His nose,
With a ring at the end of his nose.

"Dear Pig, are you willing to sell for one shilling
   Your ring?" Said the Piggy, "I will."
So they took it away, and were married next day
   By the Turkey who lives on the hill.
They dined on mince and slices of quince,
   Which they ate with a runcible spoon;
And hand in hand, on the edge of the sand,
   They danced by the light of the moon,
     The moon,
     The moon,
   They danced by the light of the moon.

                        EDWARD LEAR

THE NUTCRACKERS AND THE SUGAR-TONGS

I

The Nutcrackers sate by a plate on the table;
   The Sugar-tongs sate by a plate at his side;
And the Nutcrackers said, "Don't you wish we were able
   Along the blue hills and green meadows to ride?
Must we drag on this stupid existence forever,
   So idle and weary, so full of remorse,
While every one else takes his pleasure, and never
   Seems happy unless he is riding a horse?

II

"Don't you think we could ride without being instructed?
   Without any saddle or bridle or spur?
Our legs are so long, and so aptly constructed,
   I'm sure that an accident could not occur.

Let us all of a sudden hop down from the table,
  And hustle downstairs, and each jump on a horse!
Shall we try? Shall we go? Do you think we are able?"
  The Sugar-tongs answered distinctly, "Of course!"

III

So down the long staircase they hopped in a minute;
  The Sugar-tongs snapped, and the Crackers said "Crack!"
The stable was open; the horses were in it:
  Each took out a pony, and jumped on his back.
The Cat in a fright scrambled out of the doorway;
  The Mice tumbled out of a bundle of hay;
The brown and white Rats, and the black ones from Norway,
  Screamed out, "They are taking the horses away!"

IV

The whole of the household was filled with amazement:
  The Cups and the Saucers danced madly about;
The Plates and the Dishes looked out of the casement;
  The Saltcellar stood on his head with a shout;
The Spoons, with a chatter, looked out of the lattice;
  The Mustard-pot climbed up the gooseberry-pies;
The Soup-ladle peeped through a heap of veal-patties,
  And squeaked with a ladle-like scream of surprise.

V

The Frying-pan said, "It's an awful delusion!"
  The Tea-kettle hissed and grew black in the face;
And they all rushed down stairs in the wildest confusion,
  To see the great Nutcracker-Sugar-tong race.
And out of the stable, with screamings and laughter,
  (Their ponies were cream-coloured, speckled with brown,)
The Nutcrackers first, and the Sugar-tongs after,
  Rode all round the yard, and then all round the town.

VI

They rode through the street, and they rode by the station;
 They galloped away to the beautiful shore;
In silence they rode, and "made no observation,"
 Save this: "We will never go back any more!"
And still you might hear, till they rode out of hearing,
 The Sugar-tongs snap, and the Crackers say "Crack!"
Till, far in the distance their forms disappearing,
 They faded away; and they never came back!

EDWARD LEAR

FATHER WILLIAM

(from *Alice in Wonderland*)

After Southey

"You are old, Father William," the young man said,
 "And your hair has become very white;
And yet you incessantly stand on your head—
 Do you think, at your age, it is right?"

"In my youth," Father William replied to his son,
 "I feared it might injure the brain;
But, now that I'm perfectly sure I have none,
 Why, I do it again and again."

"You are old," said the youth, "as I mentioned before,
 And have grown most uncommonly fat;
Yet you turned a back-somersault in at the door—
 Pray, what is the reason of that?"

"In my youth," said the sage, as he shook his gray locks,
 "I kept all my limbs very supple
By the use of this ointment—one shilling the box—
 Allow me to sell you a couple?"

"You are old," said the youth, "and your jaws are too weak
  For anything tougher than suet;
Yet you finished the goose, with the bones and the beak—
  Pray, how did you manage to do it?"

"In my youth," said his father, "I took to the law,
  And argued each case with my wife;
And the muscular strength which it gave to my jaw,
  Has lasted the rest of my life."

"You are old," said the youth, "one would hardly suppose
  That your eye was as steady as ever;
Yet you balanced an eel on the end of your nose—
  What made you so awfully clever?"

"I have answered three questions and that is enough,"
  Said his father; "don't give yourself airs!
Do you think I can listen all day to such stuff?
  Be off, or I'll kick you downstairs!"

LEWIS CARROLL

VII. The Ages of Man

LULLABY

(from The Princess)

Sweet and low, sweet and low,
   Wind of the western sea,
Low, low, breathe and blow,
   Wind of the western sea!
Over the rolling waters go,
Come from the dying moon, and blow,
   Blow him again to me;
While my little one, while my pretty one, sleeps.

Sleep and rest, sleep and rest,
   Father will come to thee soon;
Rest, rest, on mother's breast,
   Father will come to thee soon;
Father will come to his babe in the nest,
Silver sails all out of the west
   Under the silver moon:
Sleep, my little one, sleep, my pretty one, sleep.

ALFRED TENNYSON

INFANT JOY

"I have no name;
I am but two days old."
What shall I call thee?
"I happy am,
Joy is my name."
Sweet joy befall thee!

Pretty joy!
Sweet joy, but two days old.
Sweet joy I call thee;
Thou dost smile,
I sing the while;
Sweet joy befall thee!

CRADLE SONG

Sleep, sleep, beauty bright,
Dreaming in the joys of night;
Sleep, sleep; in thy sleep
Little sorrows sit and weep.

Sweet babe, in thy face
Soft desires I can trace,
Secret joys and secret smiles,
Little pretty infant wiles.

As thy softest limbs I feel
Smiles as of the morning steal
O'er thy cheek, and o'er thy breast
Where thy little heart doth rest.

O the cunning wiles that creep
In thy little heart asleep!
When thy little heart doth wake,
Then the dreadful night shall break.

WILLIAM BLAKE

A CHILD'S LAUGHTER

All the bells of heaven may ring,
All the birds of heaven may sing,
All the wells on earth may spring,
All the winds on earth may bring
  All sweet sounds together;
Sweeter far than all things heard,
Hand of harper, tone of bird,
Sound of woods at sundawn stirred,
Welling water's winsome word,
  Wind in warm wan weather,

One thing yet there is, that none
Hearing ere its chime be done
Knows not well the sweetest one

Heard of man beneath the sun,
  Hoped in heaven hereafter;
Soft and strong and loud and light—
Very sound of very light
Heard from morning's rosiest height—
When the soul of all delight
  Fills a child's clear laughter.

Golden bells of welcome rolled
Never forth such notes, nor told
Hours so blithe in tones so bold,
As the radiant mouth of gold
  Here that rings forth heaven.
If the golden-crested wren
Were a nightingale—why, then,
Something seen and heard of men
Might be half as sweet as when
  Laughs a child of seven.

ALGERNON CHARLES SWINBURNE

A LIFE-LESSON

There! little girl, don't cry!
  They have broken your doll, I know;
    And your tea-set blue,
    And your play-house, too,
  Are things of the long ago;
    But childish troubles will soon pass by.—
      There! little girl, don't cry!

There! little girl, don't cry!
  They have broken your slate, I know;
    And the glad, wild ways
    Of your school-girl days
  Are things of the long ago;
    But life and love will soon come by.—
      There! little girl, don't cry!

There! little girl, don't cry!
  They have broken your heart, I know;

And the rainbow gleams
Of your youthful dreams
Are things of the long ago;
But Heaven holds all for which you sigh.—
There! little girl, don't cry!

JAMES WHITCOMB RILEY

LITTLE BOY BLUE

The little toy dog is covered with dust,
  But sturdy and stanch he stands;
And the little toy soldier is red with rust,
  And his musket moulds in his hands.
Time was when the little toy dog was new,
  And the soldier was passing fair;
And that was the time when our Little Boy Blue
  Kissed them and put them there.

"Now, don't you go till I come," he said,
  "And don't you make any noise!"
So, toddling off to his trundle-bed,
  He dreamt of the pretty toys;
And, as he was dreaming, an angel song
  Awakened our Little Boy Blue—
Oh! the years are many, the years are long,
  But the little toy friends are true!

Ay, faithful to Little Boy Blue they stand,
  Each in the same old place,
Awaiting the touch of a little hand,
  The smile of a little face;
And they wonder, as waiting the long years through
  In the dust of that little chair,
What has become of our Little Boy Blue,
  Since he kissed them and put them there.

EUGENE FIELD

THE BAREFOOT BOY

Blessings on thee, little man,
Barefoot boy, with cheek of tan!
With thy turned-up pantaloons,
And thy merry whistled tunes;
With thy red lip, redder still
Kissed by strawberries on the hill;
With the sunshine on thy face,
Through thy torn brim's jaunty grace;
From my heart I give thee joy,—
I was once a barefoot boy!
Prince thou art,—the grown-up man
Only is republican.
Let the million-dollared ride!
Barefoot, trudging at his side,
Thou hast more than he can buy
In the reach of ear and eye,—
Outward sunshine, inward joy:
Blessings on thee, barefoot boy!

Oh for boyhood's painless play,
Sleep that wakes in laughing day,
Health that mocks the doctor's rules,
Knowledge never learned of schools,
Of the wild bee's morning chase,
Of the wild flower's time and place,
Flight of fowl and habitude
Of the tenants of the wood;
How the tortoise bears his shell,
How the woodchuck digs his cell,
And the ground-mole sinks his well;
How the robin feeds her young,
How the oriole's nest is hung;
Where the whitest lilies blow,
Where the freshest berries grow,
Where the ground-nut trails its vine,
Where the wood-grape's clusters shine;
Of the black wasp's cunning way,
Mason of his walls of clay,

And the architectural plans
Of gray hornet artisans!
For, eschewing books and tasks,
Nature answers all he asks;
Hand in hand with her he walks,
Face to face with her he talks,
Part and parcel of her joy,—
Blessings on the barefoot boy!

Oh for boyhood's time of June,
Crowding years in one brief moon,
When all things I heard or saw,
Me, their master, waited for.
I was rich in flowers and trees,
Humming-birds and honey-bees;
For my sport the squirrel played,
Plied the snouted mole his spade;
For my taste the blackberry cone
Purpled over hedge and stone;
Laughed the brook for my delight
Through the day and through the night,
Whispering at the garden wall,
Talked with me from fall to fall;
Mine the sand-rimmed pickerel pond
Mine the walnut slopes beyond,
Mine, on bending orchard trees,
Apples of Hesperides!
Still as my horizon grew,
Larger grew my riches too;
All the world I saw or knew
Seemed a complex Chinese toy,
Fashioned for a barefoot boy!

Oh for festal dainties spread,
Like my bowl of milk and bread;
Pewter spoon and bowl of wood,
On the door-stone, gray and rude!
O'er me, like a regal tent,
Cloudy-ribbed, the sunset bent,
Purple-curtained, fringed with gold,
Looped in many a wind-swung fold;
While for music came the play

Of the pied frogs' orchestra;
And, to light the noisy choir,
Lit the fly his lamp of fire.
I was monarch: pomp and joy
Waited on the barefoot boy!

Cheerily, then, my little man,
Live and laugh, as boyhood can!
Though the flinty slopes be hard,
Stubble-speared the new-mown sward,
Every morn shall lead thee through
Fresh baptisms of the dew;
Every evening from thy feet
Shall the cool wind kiss the heat:
All too soon these feet must hide
In the prison cells of pride,
Lose the freedom of the sod,
Like a colt's for work be shod,
Made to tread the mills of toil,
Up and down in ceaseless moil:
Happy if their track be found
Never on forbidden ground;
Happy if they sink not in
Quick and treacherous sands of sin.
Ah! that thou couldst know thy joy,
Ere it passes, barefoot boy!

JOHN GREENLEAF WHITTIER

FERN HILL

Now as I was young and easy under the apple boughs
About the lilting house and happy as the grass was green,
   The night above the dingle starry,
     Time let me hail and climb
   Golden in the heydays of his eyes,
And honoured among wagons I was prince of the apple towns
And once below a time I lordly had the trees and leaves
     Trail with daisies and barley
   Down the rivers of the windfall light.

And as I was green and carefree, famous among the barns
About the happy yard and singing as the farm was home,
  In the sun that is young once only,
    Time let me play and be
  Golden in the mercy of his means,
And green and golden I was huntsman and herdsman, the calves
Sang to my horn, the foxes on the hills barked clear and cold,
    And the sabbath rang slowly
  In the pebbles of the holy streams.

All the sun long it was running, it was lovely, the hay-
Fields high as the house, the tunes from the chimneys, it was air
  And playing, lovely and watery
    And fire green as grass.
  And nightly under the simple stars
As I rode to sleep the owls were bearing the farm away,
All the moon long I heard, blessed among stables, the nightjars
  Flying with the ricks, and the horses
    Flashing into the dark.

And then to awake, and the farm, like a wanderer white
With the dew, come back, the cock on his shoulder: it was all
  Shining, it was Adam and maiden,
    The sky gathered again
  And the sun grew round that very day.
So it must have been after the birth of the simple light
In the first, spinning place, the spellbound horses walking warm
  Out of the whinnying green stable
    On to the fields of praise.

And honoured among foxes and pheasants by the gay house
Under the new made clouds and happy as the heart was long,
  In the sun born over and over,
    I ran my heedless ways,
  My wishes raced through the house-high hay
And nothing I cared, at my sky blue trades, that time allows
In all his tuneful turning so few and such morning songs
  Before the children green and golden
    Follow him out of grace,

Nothing I cared, in the lamb white days, that time would take me
Up to the swallow thronged loft by the shadow of my hand,
In the moon that is always rising,
Nor that riding to sleep
I should hear him fly with the high fields
And wake to the farm forever fled from the childless land.
Oh as I was young and easy in the mercy of his means,
Time held me green and dying
Though I sang in my chains like the sea.

DYLAN THOMAS

YOUNG AND OLD

(from *The Water Babies*)

When all the world is young, lad,
And all the trees are green;
And every goose a swan, lad,
And every lass a queen;
Then hey for boot and horse, lad,
And round the world away;
Young blood must have its course, lad,
And every dog his day.

When all the world is old, lad,
And all the trees are brown;
And all the sport is stale, lad,
And all the wheels run down:
Creep home, and take your place there,
The spent and maimed among:
God grant you find one face there
You loved when all was young.

CHARLES KINGSLEY

MY LOST YOUTH

Often I think of the beautiful town
That is seated by the sea;
Often in thought go up and down
The pleasant streets of that dear old town,

And my youth comes back to me.
 And a verse of a Lapland song
 Is haunting my memory still:
 "A boy's will is the wind's will,
And the thoughts of youth are long, long thoughts."

I can see the shadowy lines of its trees,
 And catch, in sudden gleams,
The sheen of the far-surrounding seas,
And islands that were the Hesperides
 Of all my boyish dreams.
  And the burden of that old song,
  It murmurs and whispers still:
  "A boy's will is the wind's will,
And the thoughts of youth are long, long thoughts."

I remember the black wharves and the slips,
 And the sea-tides tossing free;
And Spanish sailors with bearded lips,
And the beauty and mystery of the ships,
 And the magic of the sea.
  And the voice of that wayward song
  Is singing and saying still:
  "A boy's will is the wind's will,
And the thoughts of youth are long, long thoughts."

I remember the bulwarks by the shore,
 And the fort upon the hill;
The sunrise gun, with its hollow roar,
The drum-beat repeated o'er and o'er,
 And the bugle wild and shrill.
  And the music of that old song
  Throbs in my memory still:
  "A boy's will is the wind's will,
And the thoughts of youth are long, long thoughts."

I remember the sea-fight far away,
 How it thundered o'er the tide!
And the dead captains, as they lay
In their graves, o'erlooking the tranquil bay
 Where they in battle died.
  And the sound of that mournful song
  Goes through me with a thrill:

"A boy's will is the wind's will,
And the thoughts of youth are long, long thoughts."

I can see the breezy dome of groves,
    The shadows of Deering's Woods;
And the friendships old and the early loves
Come back with a Sabbath sound, as of doves
    In quiet neighborhoods.
        And the verse of that sweet old song,
        It flutters and murmurs still:
        "A boy's will is the wind's will,
And the thoughts of youth are long, long thoughts."

I remember the gleams and glooms that dart
    Across the school-boy's brain;
The song and the silence in the heart,
That in part are prophecies, and in part
        Are longings wild and vain.
        And the voice of that fitful song
        Sings on, and is never still:
        "A boy's will is the wind's will,
And the thoughts of youth are long, long thoughts."

There are things of which I may not speak;
    There are dreams that cannot die;
There are thoughts that make the strong heart weak,
And bring a pallor into the cheek,
    And a mist before the eye.
        And the words of that fatal song
        Come over me like a chill:
        "A boy's will is the wind's will,
And the thoughts of youth are long, long thoughts."

Strange to me are the forms I meet
    When I visit the dear old town;
But the native air is pure and sweet,
And the trees that o'ershadow each well-known street,
    As they balance up and down,
        Are singing the beautiful song,
        Are sighing and whispering still:
        "A boy's will is the wind's will,
And the thoughts of youth are long, long thoughts."

And Deering's Woods are fresh and fair,
    And with joy that is almost pain
My heart goes back to wander there,
And among the dreams of the days that were
    I find my lost youth again.
        And the strange and beautiful song,
        The groves are repeating it still:
        "A boy's will is the wind's will,
And the thoughts of youth are long, long thoughts."
                HENRY WADSWORTH LONGFELLOW

YOUTH AND AGE

Verse, a breeze 'mid blossoms straying,
Where Hope clung feeding like a bee,—
Both were mine! Life went a-maying
With Nature, Hope, and Poesy
                When I was young!

When I was young?—Ah, woful When!
Ah, for the change 'twixt Now and Then!
This breathing house not built with hands,
This body that does me grievous wrong,
O'er aery cliffs and glittering sands,
How lightly *then* it flashed along:—
Like those trim skiffs, unknown of yore,
On winding lakes and rivers wide,
That ask no aid of sail or oar,
That fear no spite of wind or tide!
Naught cared this body for wind or weather
When Youth and I lived in't together.
Flowers are lovely; Love is flower-like;
Friendship is a sheltering tree;
Oh! the joys that came down shower-like,
Of Friendship, Love, and Liberty
                Ere I was old!

Ere I was old? Ah, woful Ere,
Which tells me, Youth's no longer here!
O Youth! for years so many and sweet,
'Tis known that Thou and I were one.

I'll think it but a fond conceit—
It cannot be that Thou art gone!
Thy vesper-bell hath not yet tolled:—
And thou wert aye a masker bold!
What strange disguise hast now put on
To make believe that thou art gone?
I see these locks in silvery slips,
This drooping gait, this altered size:
But Springtide blossoms on thy lips,
And tears take sunshine from thine eyes!
Life is but thought: so think I will
That Youth and I are house-mates still.

Dewdrops are the gems of morning,
But the tears of mournful eve!
Where no hope is, life's a warning
That only serves to make us grieve
                    When we are old:
That only serves to make us grieve
With oft and tedious taking-leave,
Like some poor nigh-related guest,
That may not rudely be dismissed,
Yet hath outstayed his welcome while,
And tells the jest without the smile.

SAMUEL TAYLOR COLERIDGE

ALL THE WORLD'S A STAGE

(from *As You Like It*)

                    All the world's a stage,
And all the men and women merely players.
They have their exits and their entrances,
And one man in his time plays many parts,
His acts being seven ages. At first, the infant,
Mewling and puking in the nurse's arms.
Then the whining schoolboy, with his satchel
And shining morning face, creeping like a snail
Unwillingly to school. And then the lover,
Sighing like a furnace, with a woful ballad

Made to his mistress' eyebrow. Then a soldier,
Full of strange oaths and bearded like the pard,
Jealous in honour, sudden and quick in quarrel,
Seeking the bubble reputation
Even in the cannon's mouth. And then the justice,
In fair round belly with good capon lin'd,
With eyes severe and beard of formal cut,
Full of wise saws and modern instances;
And so he plays his part. The sixth age shifts
Into the lean and slipper'd pantaloon,
With spectacles on nose and pouch on side;
His youthful hose, well sav'd, a world too wide
For his shrunk shank, and his big manly voice,
Turning again toward childish treble, pipes
And whistles in his sound. Last scene of all,
That ends this strange eventful history,
Is second childishness and mere oblivion,
Sans teeth, sans eyes, sans taste, sans everything.

WILLIAM SHAKESPEARE

YOUTH SINGS A SONG OF ROSEBUDS

(TO ROBERTA)

Since men grow diffident at last,
And care no whit at all,
If spring be come, or the fall be past,
Or how the cool rains fall,

I come to no flower but I pluck,
I raise no cup but I sip,
For a mouth is the best of sweets to suck;
The oldest wine's on the lip.

If I grow old in a year or two,
And come to the querulous song
Of "Alack and aday" and "This was true,
And that, when I was young,"

I must have sweets to remember by,
Some blossom saved from the mire,
Some death-rebellious ember I
Can fan into a fire.

COUNTEE CULLEN

HOW OLD ARE YOU?

Age is a quality of mind.
If you have left your dreams behind,
If hope is cold,
If you no longer look ahead,
If your ambitions' fires are dead—
Then you are old.
But if from life you take the best,
If in life you keep the jest,
If love you hold;
No matter how the years go by,
No matter how the birthdays fly—
You are not old.

H. S. FRITSCH

YOUTH

Youth is not a time of life—it is a state of mind. It is not a matter of red cheeks, red lips and supple knees. It is a temper of the will; a quality of the imagination; a vigor of the emotions; it is a freshness of the deep springs of life. Youth means a temperamental predominance of courage over timidity, of the appetite for adventure over a life of ease. This often exists in a man of fifty, more than in a boy of twenty. Nobody grows old by merely living a number of years; people grow old by deserting their ideals.

Years may wrinkle the skin, but to give up enthusiasm wrinkles the soul. Worry, doubt, self-distrust, fear and despair—these are the long, long years that bow the head and turn the growing spirit back to dust.

Whether seventy or sixteen, there is in every being's heart a love of wonder; the sweet amazement at the stars and starlike things and thoughts; the undaunted challenge of events, the unfailing, childlike appetite for what comes next, and the joy in the game of life.

You are as young as your faith, as old as your doubt; as young as your self-confidence, as old as your fear; as young as your hope, as old as your despair.

In the central place of your heart there is a wireless station. So long as it receives message of beauty, hope, cheer, grandeur, courage and power from the earth, from men and from the Infinite—so long are you young. When the wires are all down and the central places of your heart are covered with the snows of pessimism and the ice of cynicism, then you are grown old, indeed!

SAMUEL ULLMAN

PEEKABOO, I ALMOST SEE YOU

Middle-aged life is merry, and I love to lead it,
But there comes a day when your eyes are all right but your arm isn't
    long enough to hold the telephone book where you can read it,
And your friends get jocular, so you go to the oculist,
And of all your friends he is the joculist,
So over his facetiousness let us skim,
Only noting that he has been waiting for you ever since you said
    Good evening to his grandfather clock under the impression that
    it was him,
And you look at his chart and it says SHRDLU QWERTYOP, and
    you say Well, why SHRDNTLU QWERTYOP? and he says
    one set of glasses won't do.
You need two,
One for reading Erle Stanley Gardner's Perry Mason and Keats's
    "Endymion" with,
And the other for walking around without saying Hello to strange
    wymion with.
So you spend your time taking off your seeing glasses to put on your
    reading glasses, and then remembering that your reading glasses
    are upstairs or in the car,
And then you can't find your seeing glasses again because without
    them you can't see where they are.
Enough of such mishaps, they would try the patience of an ox,
I prefer to forget both pairs of glasses and pass my declining years
    saluting strange women and grandfather clocks.

OGDEN NASH

WHOM THE GODS LOVE

"Whom the gods love die young," I used to quote
Glibly, but in the rather thoughtless way,
One says a thing that he has learned by rote,
Nor knows the meaning which the words convey.

For then I thought it meant they died when young
In years, and this no doubt is often true;
But now with time a clearer note has rung
New meaning to the words; there are a few

Whom time can never age—not even with years;
These keep a dream, nor let its flame burn low . . .
They look ahead, beyond regrets and tears—
Old age is something they can never know.

MARGARET E. BRUNER

TOO LATE

"Ah! si la jeunesse savait,—si la viellesse pouvait!"

There sat an old man on a rock,
  And unceasing bewailed him of Fate,—
That concern where we all must take stock,
  Though our vote has no hearing or weight;
    And the old man sang him an old, old song,—
    Never sang voice so clear and strong
  That it could drown the old man's long,
      For he sang the song "Too late! Too late!

"When we want, we have for our pains
  The promise that if we but wait
Till the want has burned out of our brains,
  Every means shall be present to sate;
    While we send for the napkin the soup gets cold,
    While the bonnet is trimming the face grows old,
    When we've matched our buttons the pattern is sold,
      And everything comes too late—too late!

"When strawberries seemed like red heavens,
   Terrapin stew a wild dream,
When my brain was at sixes and sevens,
   If my mother had 'folks' and ice-cream,
     Then I gazed with a lickerish hunger
     At the restaurant man and fruit-monger—
     But, O, how I wished I were younger
       When the goodies all came in a stream—in a stream!

"I've a splendid bloodhorse—and a liver
   That it jars into torture to trot;
My row-boat's the gem of the river,—
   Gout makes every knuckle a knot!
     I can buy boundless credits on Paris and Rome,
     But no palate for *menus*, no eyes for a dome—
     Those belonged to the youth who must tarry at home,
       When no home but an attic he'd got—he'd got!

"How I longed, in that lonest of garrets,
   Where the tiles baked my brains all July,
For ground to grow two pecks of carrots,
   Two pigs of my own in a sty,
     A rosebush—a little thatched cottage—
     Two spoons—love—a basin of pottage!
     Now in freestone I sit—and my dotage—
       With a woman's chair empty close by—close by!—

"Ah! now, though I sit on a rock,
   I have shared one seat with the great;
I have sat, knowing naught of the clock—
   On Love's high throne of state;
     But the lips that kissed, and the arms that caressed,
     To a mouth grown stern with delay were pressed,
     And circled a breast that their clasp had blessed
       Had they only not come too late—too late!"

                        FITZ HUGH LUDLOW

ON GROWING OLD

Be with me, Beauty, for the fire is dying;
My dog and I are old, too old for roving.
Man, whose young passion sets the spindrift flying,
Is soon too lame to march, too cold for loving.
I take the book and gather to the fire,
Turning old yellow leaves; minute by minute
The clock ticks to my heart. A withered wire
Moves a thin ghost of music in the spinet.
I cannot sail your seas, I cannot wander
Your cornland, nor your hill-land nor your valleys
Ever again, nor share the battle yonder
Where the young knight the broken squadron rallies.
Only stay quiet while my mind remembers
The beauty of fire from the beauty of embers.

Beauty, have pity! for the strong have power,
The rich their wealth, the beautiful their grace,
Summer of man its sunlight and its flower,
Spring-time of man all April in a face.
Only, as in the jostling in the Strand,
Where the mob thrusts or loiters or is loud
The beggar with the saucer in his hand
Asks only a penny from the passing crowd,
So, from this glittering world with all its fashion,
Its fire, and play of men, its stir, its march,
Let me have wisdom, Beauty, wisdom and passion,
Bread to the soul, rain where the summers parch.
Give me but these, and, though the darkness close
Even the night will blossom as the rose.

JOHN MASEFIELD

THE OLD MAN DREAMS

Oh for one hour of youthful joy!
　Give back my twentieth spring!
I'd rather laugh, a bright-haired boy,
　Than reign, a gray-beard king.

Off with the spoils of wrinkled age!
　Away with Learning's crown!
Tear out life's Wisdom-written page,
　And dash its trophies down!

One moment let my life-blood stream
　From boyhood's fount of flame!
Give me one giddy, reeling dream
　Of life all love and fame!

My listening angel heard the prayer,
　And, calmly smiling, said,
"If I but touch thy silvered hair,
　Thy hasty wish hath sped.

"But is there nothing in thy track
　To bid thee fondly stay,
While the swift seasons hurry back
　To find the wished-for day?"

"Ah, truest soul of womankind!
　Without thee what were life?
One bliss I cannot leave behind:
　I'll take—my—precious—wife!"

The angel took a sapphire pen
　And wrote in rainbow dew,
The man would be a boy again,
　And be a husband, too!

"And is there nothing yet unsaid,
　Before the change appears?
Remember, all their gifts have fled
　With those dissolving years."

"Why, yes;" for memory would recall
  My fond paternal joys;
"I could not bear to leave them all—
  I'll take—my—girl—and—boys."

The smiling angel dropped his pen,—
  "Why, this will never do;
The man would be a boy again,
  And be a father, too!"

———

And so I laughed,—my laughter woke
  The household with its noise,—
And wrote my dream, when morning broke,
  To please the gray-haired boys.
        OLIVER WENDELL HOLMES

THE LAST LEAF

I saw him once before,
As he passed by the door,
    And again
The pavement stones resound,
As he totters o'er the ground
    With his cane.

They say that in his prime,
Ere the pruning-knife of Time
    Cut him down,
Not a better man was found
By the Crier on his round
    Through the town.

But now he walks the streets,
And he looks at all he meets
    Sad and wan,
And he shakes his feeble head,
That it seems as if he said,
    "They are gone."

The mossy marbles rest
On the lips that he has pressed
    In their bloom,
And the names he loved to hear
Have been carved for many a year
    On the tomb.

My grandmamma has said,—
Poor old lady, she is dead
    Long ago,—
That he had a Roman nose,
And his cheek was like a rose
    In the snow;

But now his nose is thin,
And it rests upon his chin
    Like a staff,
And a crook is in his back,
And a melancholy crack
    In his laugh.

I know it is a sin
For me to sit and grin
    At him here;
But the old three-cornered hat,
And the breeches, and all that,
    Are so queer!

And if I should live to be
The last leaf upon the tree
    In the spring,
Let them smile, as I do now,
At the old forsaken bough
    Where I cling.

                OLIVER WENDELL HOLMES

TERMINUS

It is time to be old,
To take in sail:—
The god of bounds,

Who sets to seas a shore,
Came to me in his fatal rounds,
And said: "No more!
No farther shoot
Thy broad ambitious branches, and thy root.
Fancy departs: no more invent;
Contract thy firmament
To compass of a tent.
There's not enough for this and that,
Make thy option which of two;
Economize the failing river,
Not the less revere the Giver,
Leave the many and hold the few.
Timely wise accept the terms,
Soften the fall with wary foot;
A little while
Still plan and smile,
And,—fault of novel germs,—
Mature the unfallen fruit.
Curse, if thou wilt, thy sires,
Bad husbands of their fires,
Who, when they gave thee breath,
Failed to bequeath
The needful sinew stark as once,
The Baresark marrow to thy bones,
But left a legacy of ebbing veins,
Inconstant heat and nerveless reins,—
Amid the Muses, left thee deaf and dumb,
Amid the Gladiators, halt and numb."

As the bird trims her to the gale,
I trim myself to the storm of time,
I man the rudder, reef the sail,
Obey the voice at eve obeyed at prime:
"Lowly faithful, banish fear,
Right onward drive unharmed;
The port, well worth the cruise, is near,
And every wave is charmed."

RALPH WALDO EMERSON

AUTUMN

RESIGNATION

Come! let us draw the curtains,
    heap up the fire, and sit
hunched by the flame together,
    and make a friend of it.

Listen! the wind is rising,
    and the air is wild with leaves,
we have had our summer evenings:
    now for October eves!

The great beech-trees lean forward,
    and strip like a diver. We
had better turn to the fire,
    and shut our minds to the sea,

Where the ships of youth are running
    close-hauled on the edge of the wind,
with all adventure before them,
    and only the old behind.

Love and youth and the seabirds
    meet in the stormy weather,
and with one bright flash of laughter
    clasp into the dark together.

Come! let us draw the curtains,
    and talk of other things;
and presently all will be quiet—
    love, youth, and the sound of wings.

HUMBERT WOLFE

VIII. Death

AND YOU AS WELL MUST DIE, BELOVED DUST

And you as well must die, beloved dust,
And all your beauty stand you in no stead;
This flawless, vital hand, this perfect head,
This body of flame and steel, before the gust
Of Death, or under his autumnal frost,
Shall be as any leaf, be no less dead
Than the first leaf that fell,—this wonder fled,
Altered, estranged, disintegrated, lost.
Nor shall my love avail you in your hour.
In spite of all my love, you will arise
Upon that day and wander down the air
Obscurely as the unattended flower,
It mattering not how beautiful you were,
Or how beloved above all else that dies.

EDNA ST. VINCENT MILLAY

THE DEATH OF THE FLOWERS

The melancholy days are come, the saddest of the year,
Of wailing winds, and naked woods, and meadows brown and sere.
Heaped in the hollows of the grove, the autumn leaves lie dead;
They rustle to the eddying gust, and to the rabbit's tread;
The robin and the wren are flown, and from the shrubs the jay,
And from the wood-top calls the crow through all the gloomy day.

Where are the flowers, the fair young flowers, that lately sprang and
    stood
In brighter light and softer airs, a beauteous sisterhood?
Alas! they all are in their graves, the gentle race of flowers
Are lying in their lowly beds, with the fair and good of ours.
The rain is falling where they lie, but the cold November rain
Calls not from out the gloomy earth the lovely ones again.

The wind-flower and the violet, they perished long ago,
And the brier-rose and the orchis died amid the summer glow;

But on the hill the golden-rod, and the aster in the wood,
And the yellow sun-flower by the brook, in autumn beauty stood,
Till fell the frost from the clear cold heaven, as falls the plague on
　　men,
And the brightness of their smile was gone, from upland, glade, and
　　glen.

And now, when comes the calm mild day, as still such days will
　　come,
To call the squirrel and the bee from out their winter home;
When the sound of dropping nuts is heard, though all the trees are
　　still,
And twinkle in the smoky light the waters of the rill,
The south wind searches for the flowers whose fragrance late he bore,
And sighs to find them in the wood and by the stream no more.

And then I think of one who in her youthful beauty died,
The fair meek blossom that grew up and faded by my side.
In the cold moist earth we laid her, when the forest cast the leaf,
And we wept that one so lovely should have a life so brief:
Yet not unmeet it was that one like that young friend of ours,
So gentle and so beautiful, should perish with the flowers.

WILLIAM CULLEN BRYANT

TO THE FRINGED GENTIAN

Thou blossom bright with autumn dew,
And colored with the heaven's own blue,
That openest when the quiet light
Succeeds the keen and frosty night,

Thou comest not when violets lean
O'er wandering brooks and springs unseen,
Or columbines, in purple dressed,
Nod o'er the ground-bird's hidden nest.

Thou waitest late and com'st alone,
When woods are bare and birds are flown,
And frost and shortening days portend
The aged year is near his end.

Then doth thy sweet and quiet eye
Look through its fringes to the sky,
Blue—blue—as if that sky let fall
A flower from its cerulean wall.

I would that thus, when I shall see
The hour of death draw near to me,
Hope, blossoming within my heart,
May look to heaven as I depart.

WILLIAM CULLEN BRYANT

GRIEF

I tell you, hopeless grief is passionless;
  That only men incredulous of despair,
  Half-taught in anguish, through the midnight air
Beat upward to God's throne in loud access
Of shrieking and reproach. Full desertness,
  In souls as countries, lieth silent-bare
  Under the blanching, vertical eye-glare
Of the absolute Heavens. Deep-hearted man, express
Grief for thy Dead in silence like to death—
  Most like a monumental statue set
In everlasting watch and moveless woe
Till itself crumble to the dust beneath.
  Touch it; the marble eyelids are not wet:
If it could weep, it could arise and go.

ELIZABETH BARRETT BROWNING

SOME TIME AT EVE

Some time at eve when the tide is low,
  I shall slip my mooring and sail away,
With no response to the friendly hail
  Of kindred craft in the busy bay.
In the silent hush of the twilight pale,
  When the night stoops down to embrace the day,
And the voices call in the waters' flow—
Some time at eve when the tide is low,
  I shall slip my mooring and sail away.

Through the purpling shadows that darkly trail
  O'er the ebbing tide of the Unknown Sea,
I shall fare me away, with a dip of sail
And a ripple of waters to tell the tale
  Of a lonely voyager, sailing away
  To the Mystic Isles where at anchor lay
The crafts of those who have sailed before
O'er the Unknown Sea to the Unseen Shore.

A few who have watched me sail away
Will miss my craft from the busy bay;
  Some friendly barks that were anchored near,
  Some loving souls that my heart held dear,
  In silent sorrow will drop a tear—

But I shall have peacefully furled my sail
In moorings sheltered from storm or gale,
  And greeted the friends who have sailed before
  O'er the Unknown Sea to the Unseen Shore.

ELIZABETH CLARK HARDY

A DEATH SONG

Lay me down beneaf de willers in de grass,
Whah de branch'll go a-singin' as it pass.
    An' w'en I's a-layin' low,
    I kin hyeah it as it go
Singin', "Sleep, my hone, tek yo' res' at las'."

Lay me nigh to whah hit meks a little pool,
An' de watah stan's so quiet lak an' cool,
    Whah de little birds in spring,
    Ust to come an' drink an' sing,
An' de chillen waded on dey way to school.

Let me settle w'en my shouldahs draps dey load
Nigh enough to hyeah de noises in de road;
    Fu' I t'ink de las' long res'
    Gwine to soothe my sperrit bes'
Ef I's layin' 'mong de t'ings I's allus knowed.

PAUL LAURENCE DUNBAR

WHEN I AM DEAD

I do not want a gaping crowd
To come with lamentations loud,
    When life has fled;
Nor would I have my words or ways
Rehearsed, perhaps 'mid tardy praise,
    When I am dead.

I do not want strange, curious eyes
To see my face when still it lies,
    In silence dread;
Nor do I want them, if they would,
To tell my deeds were ill or good,
    When I am dead.

I only want a chosen few
Who stood through good and evil, too,
    True friendship's test;
Just they who sought to find the good,
And then, as only true friends could,
    Forgave the rest.

They who, with sympathetic heart,
Sought hope and comfort to impart,
    Where there was life;
Not keeping all the tears and sighs
Till weary, worn-out nature dies,
    And ends the strife.

I'd have them come, "the friendly few,"
And drop, perhaps, a tear or two,
    By kindness led;
Not many tears I'd have them shed,
Nor do I want much sung or said,
    When I am dead.

To have them each come in alone,
And call me in the old, sweet tone,
    Would suit me best;

And then, without a sob or moan,
Go softly out and leave alone
    The dead to rest.

Just as I've lived, almost unknown,
A life unmarked, obscure and lone,
    So let me die;
Just one who lived, and loved, and died—
A mound of earth and naught beside,
    There let me lie.

JAMES EDWARD WILSON

COOL TOMBS

When Abraham Lincoln was shovelled into the tombs,
    he forgot the copperheads and the assassin . . .
    in the dust, in the cool tombs.

And Ulysses Grant lost all thought of con men and
    Wall Street, cash and collateral turned ashes . . .
    in the dust, in the cool tombs.

Pocahontas' body, lovely as a poplar, sweet as a
    red haw in November or a pawpaw in May, did she
    wonder? does she remember? . . .
    in the dust, in the cool tombs?

Take any streetful of people buying clothes and
    groceries, cheering a hero or throwing confetti
    and blowing tin horns . . . tell me if the lovers
    are losers . . . tell me if any get more than the
    lovers . . . in the dust . . . in the cool tombs.

CARL SANDBURG

SHOULD YOU GO FIRST

Should you go first and I remain
    To walk the road alone,
I'll live in memory's garden, dear,
    With happy days we've known.

In Spring I'll wait for roses red,
 When fades the lilac blue,
In early Fall, when brown leaves call
 I'll catch a glimpse of you.

Should you go first and I remain
 For battles to be fought,
Each thing you've touched along the way
 Will be a hallowed spot.
I'll hear your voice, I'll see your smile,
 Though blindly I may grope,
The memory of your helping hand
 Will buoy me on with hope.

Should you go first and I remain
 To finish with the scroll,
No length'ning shadows shall creep in
 To make this life seem droll.
We've known so much of happiness,
 We've had our cup of joy,
And memory is one gift of God
 That death cannot destroy.

Should you go first and I remain,
 One thing I'd have you do:
Walk slowly down that long, lone path,
 For soon I'll follow you.
I'll want to know each step you take
 That I may walk the same,
For some day down that lonely road
 You'll hear me call your name.

A. K. ROWSWELL

SO MIGHT IT BE

Death, when you come to me, tread with a footstep
 Light as the moon's on the grasses asleep,
So that I know not the moment of darkness,
 Know not the drag and the draw of the deep.

Death, when you come to me, let there be sunlight,
　Dogs and dear creatures about me at play,
Flowers in the fields and the song of the blackbird—
　Spring in the world when you fetch me away!
JOHN GALSWORTHY

THE HOUSE OF FALLING LEAVES WE ENTERED IN

(from *The House of Falling Leaves*)

The House of Falling Leaves we entered in—
He and I—we entered in and found it fair;
At midnight some one called him up the stair,
And closed him in the Room I could not win.
Now must I go alone out in the din
Of hurrying days: for forth he cannot fare;
I must go on with Time, and leave him there
In Autumn's house where dreams will soon grow thin.

When Time shall close the door unto the house
And open that of Winter's soon to be,
And dreams go moving through the ruined boughs—
He who went in comes out a Memory.
From his deep sleep no sound may e'er arouse,—
The moaning rain, nor wind-embattled sea.
WILLIAM STANLEY BRAITHWAITE

THE SHIP

I am standing upon the seashore. A ship at my side spreads her white sails to the morning breeze and starts for the blue ocean.

She is an object of beauty and strength, and I stand and watch her until at length she is only a speck of white cloud just where the sea and sky meet and mingle with each other. Then someone at my side exclaims, "There, she's gone!"

Gone where? Gone from my sight, that is all. She is just as large in hull and mast and spar as she was when she left my side, and just as able to bear her load of living freight to the place of her destination. Her diminished size is in me, not in her.

And just at the moment when someone at my side says, "She's gone," there are other eyes watching for her coming and other voices ready to take up the glad shout, "There, she comes!"

And that is dying.

UNKNOWN

THE INDIAN BURYING-GROUND

In spite of all the learned have said,
   I still my old opinion keep;
The posture that we give the dead
   Points out the soul's eternal sleep.

Not so the ancients of these lands;—
   The Indian, when from life released,
Again is seated with his friends,
   And shares again the joyous feast.

His imaged birds, and painted bowl,
   And venison, for a journey dressed,
Bespeak the nature of the soul,
   Activity, that wants no rest.

His bow for action ready bent,
   And arrows with a head of stone,
Can only mean that life is spent.
   And not the old ideas gone.

Thou, stranger, that shalt come this way,
   No fraud upon the dead commit,—
Observe the swelling turf, and say,
   They do not lie, but here they sit.

Here still a lofty rock remains,
   On which the curious eye may trace
(Now wasted half by wearing rains)
   The fancies of a ruder race.

Here still an aged elm aspires,
  Beneath whose far projecting shade
(And which the shepherd still admires)
  The children of the forest played.

There oft a restless Indian queen
  (Pale Shebah with her braided hair),
And many a barbarous form is seen
  To chide the man that lingers there.

By midnight moons, o'er moistening dews,
  In habit for the chase arrayed,
The hunter still the deer pursues,
  The hunter and the deer—a shade!

And long shall timorous Fancy see
  The painted chief, and pointed spear,
And Reason's self shall bow the knee
  To shadows and delusions here.

                PHILIP FRENEAU

NATURE

As a fond mother, when the day is o'er,
  Leads by the hand her little child to bed,
  Half willing, half reluctant to be led,
And leave his broken playthings on the floor,
Still gazing at them through the open door,
  Nor wholly reassured and comforted
  By promises of others in their stead,
Which, though more splendid, may not please him more;
So Nature deals with us, and takes away
  Our playthings one by one, and by the hand
  Leads us to rest so gently, that we go
Scarce knowing if we wish to go or stay,
  Being too full of sleep to understand
  How far the unknown transcends the what we know.

           HENRY WADSWORTH LONGFELLOW

ELEGY WRITTEN IN A COUNTRY
CHURCHYARD

The curfew tolls the knell of parting day,
   The lowing herd winds slowly o'er the lea,
The plowman homeward plods his weary way,
   And leaves the world to darkness and to me.

Now fades the glimmering landscape on the sight,
   And all the air a solemn stillness holds,
Save where the beetle wheels his droning flight,
   And drowsy tinklings lull the distant folds:

Save that from yonder ivy-mantled tower
   The moping owl does to the moon complain
Of such as, wandering near her secret bower,
   Molest her ancient solitary reign.

Beneath those rugged elms, that yew-tree's shade,
   Where heaves the turf in many a moldering heap,
Each in his narrow cell for ever laid,
   The rude forefathers of the hamlet sleep.

The breezy call of incense-breathing morn,
   The swallow twittering from the straw-built shed,
The cock's shrill clarion, or the echoing horn,
   No more shall rouse them from their lowly bed.

For them no more the blazing hearth shall burn,
   Or busy housewife ply her evening care:
No children run to lisp their sire's return,
   Or climb his knees the envied kiss to share.

Oft did the harvest to their sickle yield,
   Their furrow oft the stubborn glebe has broke:
How jocund did they drive their team afield!
   How bowed the woods beneath their sturdy stroke!

Let not Ambition mock their useful toil,
  Their homely joys, and destiny obscure;
Nor Grandeur hear with a disdainful smile
  The short and simple annals of the poor.

The boast of heraldry, the pomp of power,
  And all that beauty, all that wealth e'er gave,
Awaits alike the inevitable hour:
  The paths of glory lead but to the grave.

Nor you, ye proud, impute to these the fault
  If Memory o'er their tomb no trophies raise,
Where through the long-drawn aisle and fretted vault
  The pealing anthem swells the note of praise.

Can storied urn or animated bust
  Back to its mansion call the fleeting breath?
Can Honor's voice provoke the silent dust,
  Or Flattery soothe the dull cold ear of death?

Perhaps in this neglected spot is laid
  Some heart once pregnant with celestial fire;
Hands, that the rod of empire might have swayed
  Or waked to ecstasy the living lyre.

But Knowledge to their eyes her ample page
  Rich with the spoils of time did ne'er unroll;
Chill Penury repressed their noble rage,
  And froze the genial current of the soul.

Full many a gem of purest ray serene
  The dark unfathomed caves of ocean bear:
Full many a flower is born to blush unseen,
  And waste its sweetness on the desert air.

Some village Hampden that, with dauntless breast,
  The little tyrant of his fields withstood,
Some mute inglorious Milton here may rest,
  Some Cromwell guiltless of his country's blood.

The applause of listening senates to command,
  The threats of pain and ruin to despise,
To scatter plenty o'er a smiling land,
  And read their history in a nation's eyes,

Their lot forbade: nor circumscribed alone
  Their growing virtues, but their crimes confined;
Forbade to wade through slaughter to a throne,
  And shut the gates of mercy on mankind;

The struggling pangs of conscious truth to hide,
  To quench the blushes of ingenuous shame,
Or heap the shrine of Luxury and Pride
  With incense kindled at the Muse's flame.

Far from the madding crowd's ignoble strife,
  Their sober wishes never learned to stray;
Along the cool, sequestered vale of life
  They kept the noiseless tenor of their way.

Yet even these bones from insult to protect
  Some frail memorial still erected nigh,
With uncouth rhymes and shapeless sculpture decked,
  Implores the passing tribute of a sigh.

Their name, their years, spelt by the unlettered Muse,
  The place of fame and elegy supply:
And many a holy text around she strews,
  That teach the rustic moralist to die.

For who, to dumb Forgetfulness a prey,
  This pleasing anxious being e'er resigned,
Left the warm precincts of the cheerful day,
  Nor cast one longing lingering look behind?

On some fond breast the parting soul relies,
  Some pious drops the closing eye requires;
E'en from the tomb the voice of Nature cries,
  E'en in our ashes live their wonted fires.

For thee, who, mindful of the unhonored dead,
  Dost in these lines their artless tale relate;
If chance, by lonely contemplation led,
  Some kindred spirit shall inquire thy fate,—

Haply some hoary-headed swain may say,
  "Oft have we seen him at the peep of dawn
Brushing with hasty steps the dews away
  To meet the sun upon the upland lawn.

"There at the foot of yonder nodding beech
  That wreathes its old fantastic roots so high,
His listless length at noontide would he stretch,
  And pore upon the brook that babbles by.

"Hard by yon wood, now smiling as in scorn,
  Muttering his wayward fancies he would rove,
Now drooping, woeful-wan, like one forlorn,
  Or crazed with care, or crossed in hopeless love.

"One morn I missed him on the 'customed hill,
  Along the heath, and near his favorite tree;
Another came; nor yet beside the rill,
  Nor up the lawn, nor at the wood was he:

"The next, with dirges due in sad array,
  Slow through the church-way path we saw him borne
Approach and read (for thou canst read) the lay
  Graved on the stone beneath yon aged thorn:"

THE EPITAPH

Here rests his head upon the lap of Earth
  A Youth, to Fortune and to Fame unknown.
Fair Science frowned not on his humble birth,
  And Melancholy marked him for her own.

Large was his bounty, and his soul sincere,
  Heaven did a recompense as largely send:
He gave to Misery (all he had) a tear,
  He gained from Heaven ('twas all he wished) a friend.

No *farther seek his merits to disclose,*
  Or draw his frailties from their dread abode,
  (*There they alike in trembling hope repose,*)
  The bosom of his Father and his God.

THOMAS GRAY

THE MORNING AFTER DEATH

The bustle in a house
The morning after death
Is solemnest of industries
Enacted upon earth,—

The sweeping up the heart,
And putting love away
We shall not want to use again
Until eternity.

EMILY DICKINSON

I'VE SEEN A DYING EYE

I've seen a dying eye
Run round and round a room
In search of something, as it seemed,
Then cloudier become;
And then, obscure with fog,
And then be soldered down,
Without disclosing what it be,
'Twere blessed to have seen.

EMILY DICKINSON

EPITAPH

(Placed on the tomb of his daughter by Mark Twain)

Warm summer sun shine kindly here;
Warm southern wind blow softly here;
Green sod above lie light, lie light—
Goodnight, dear heart, goodnight, goodnight.

ROBERT RICHARDSON

REQUIEM

Under the wide and starry sky
Dig the grave and let me lie.
Glad did I live and gladly die,
  And I laid me down with a will.

This be the verse you grave for me:
Here he lies where he longed to be;
Home is the sailor, home from sea,
  And the hunter home from the hill.
                    ROBERT LOUIS STEVENSON

CROSSING THE BAR

Sunset and evening star,
  And one clear call for me!
And may there be no moaning of the bar,
  When I put out to sea,

But such a tide as moving seems asleep,
  Too full for sound and foam,
When that which drew from out the boundless deep
  Turns again home.

Twilight and evening bell,
  And after that the dark!
And may there be no sadness of farewell,
  When I embark;

For though from out our bourne of Time and Place
  The flood may bear me far,
I hope to see my Pilot face to face
  When I have crossed the bar.
                    ALFRED TENNYSON

PROSPICE

Fear death?—to feel the fog in my throat,
  The mist in my face,
When the snows begin, and the blasts denote
  I am nearing the place,
The power of the night, the press of the storm,
  The post of the foe;
Where he stands, the Arch Fear in a visible form,
  Yet the strong man must go:
For the journey is done and the summit attained,
  And the barriers fall,
Though a battle's to fight ere the guerdon be gained,
  The reward of it all.
I was ever a fighter, so—one fight more,
  The best and the last!
I would hate that death bandaged my eyes, and forbore
  And bade me creep past.
No! let me taste the whole of it, fare like my peers
  The heroes of old,
Bear the brunt, in a minute pay glad life's arrears
  Of pain, darkness and cold.
For sudden the worst turns the best to the brave,
  The black minute's at end,
And the elements' rage, the fiend-voices that rave,
  Shall dwindle, shall blend,
Shall change, shall become first a peace out of pain,
  Then a light, then thy breast,
O thou soul of my soul! I shall clasp thee again,
  And with God be the rest!

ROBERT BROWNING

IX. Reflection and Contemplation

SOLITUDE

Laugh, and the world laughs with you;
   Weep, and you weep alone,
For the sad old earth must borrow its mirth,
   But has trouble enough of its own.
Sing, and the hills will answer;
   Sigh, it is lost on the air,
The echoes bound to a joyful sound,
   But shrink from voicing care.

Rejoice, and men will seek you;
   Grieve, and they turn and go.
They want full measure of all your pleasure,
   But they do not need your woe.
Be glad, and your friends are many;
   Be sad, and you lose them all,—
There are none to decline your nectared wine,
   But alone you must drink life's gall.

Feast, and your halls are crowded;
   Fast, and the world goes by.
Succeed and give, and it helps you live,
   But no man can help you die.
There is room in the halls of pleasure
   For a long and lordly train,
But one by one we must all file on
   Through the narrow aisles of pain.

ELLA WHEELER WILCOX

FOUR THINGS

Four things a man must learn to do
If he would make his record true:
To think without confusion clearly;

To love his fellow-men sincerely;
To act from honest motives purely;
To trust in God and Heaven securely.

HENRY VAN DYKE

VERSES

SUPPOSED TO BE WRITTEN BY ALEXANDER SELKIRK DURING
HIS SOLITARY ABODE ON THE ISLAND OF JUAN FERNANDEZ

I am monarch of all I survey;
My right there is none to dispute;
From the center all round to the sea
I am lord of the fowl and the brute.
O Solitude! where are the charms
That sages have seen in thy face?
Better dwell in the midst of alarms,
Than reign in this horrible place.

I am out of humanity's reach,
I must finish my journey alone,
Never hear the sweet music of speech;
I start at the sound of my own.
The beasts that roam over the plain
My form with indifference see;
They are so unacquainted with man,
Their tameness is shocking to me.

Society, Friendship, and Love,
Divinely bestowed upon man,
O, had I the wings of a dove
How soon would I taste you again!
My sorrows I then might assuage
In the ways of religion and truth,
Might learn from the wisdom of age,
And be cheered by the sallies of youth.

Religion! what treasure untold
Resides in that heavenly word!
More precious than silver and gold,

Or all that this earth can afford.
But the sound of the church-going bell
These valleys and rocks never heard,
Nor sighed at the sound of a knell,
Or smiled when a Sabbath appeared.

Ye winds, that have made me your sport,
Convey to this desolate shore
Some cordial endearing report
Of a land I shall visit no more:
My friends,—do they now and then send
A wish or a thought after me?
O tell me I yet have a friend,
Though a friend I am never to see.

How fleet is a glance of the mind!
Compared with the speed of its flight,
The tempest itself lags behind,
And the swift-winged arrows of light.
When I think of my own native land,
In a moment I seem to be there;
But alas! recollection at hand
Soon hurries me back to despair.

But the sea-fowl is gone to her nest,
The beast is laid down in his lair;
Even here is a season of rest,
And I to my cabin repair.
There's mercy in every place,
And mercy, encouraging thought!
Gives even affliction a grace
And reconciles man to his lot.

WILLIAM COWPER

IN MEN WHOM MEN CONDEMN AS ILL

(from *Byron*)

In men whom men condemn as ill
I find so much of goodness still,
In men whom men pronounce divine

I find so much of sin and blot,
I do not dare to draw a line
Between the two, where God has not.
                              JOAQUIN MILLER

A LITTLE WORK

(from *Trilby*)

A little work, a little play
To keep us going—and so, good-day!

A little warmth, a little light
Of love's bestowing—and so, good-night!

A little fun, to match the sorrow
Of each day's growing—and so, good-morrow.

A little trust that when we die
We reap our sowing! And so—good-bye!
                              GEORGE DU MAURIER

FORGET IT

If you see a tall fellow ahead of the crowd,
A leader of music, marching fearless and proud,
And you know of a tale whose mere telling aloud
Would cause his proud head to in anguish be bowed,
      It's a pretty good plan to forget it.

If you know of a skeleton hidden away
In a closet, and guarded and kept from the day
In the dark; whose showing, whose sudden display
Would cause grief and sorrow and lifelong dismay,
      It's a pretty good plan to forget it.

If you know of a spot in the life of a friend
(We all have spots concealed, world without end)
Whose touching his heartstrings would sadden or rend,

Till the shame of its showing no grieving could mend,
    It's a pretty good plan to forget it.

If you know of a thing that will darken the joy
Of a man or a woman, a girl or a boy,
That will wipe out a smile or the least way annoy
A fellow, or cause any gladness to cloy,
    It's a pretty good plan to forget it.

UNKNOWN

BANKRUPT

One midnight, deep in starlight still,
I dreamed that I received this bill:
(—— in account with Life):
Five thousand breathless dawns all new;
Five thousand flowers fresh in dew;
Five thousand sunsets wrapped in gold;
One million snow-flakes served ice-cold;
Five quiet friends; one baby's love;
One white-mad sea with clouds above;
One hundred music-haunted dreams
Of moon-drenched roads and hurrying streams;
Of prophesying winds, and trees;
Of silent stars and browsing bees;
One June night in a fragrant wood;
One heart that loved and understood.
I wondered when I waked at day,
How—how in God's name—I could pay!

CORTLANDT W. SAYRES

A BUILDER'S LESSON

"How shall I a habit break?"
As you did that habit make.
As you gathered, you must lose;
As you yielded, now refuse.
Thread by thread the strands we twist

Till they bind us neck and wrist;
Thread by thread the patient hand
Must untwine ere free we stand.
As we builded, stone by stone,
We must toil unhelped, alone,
Till the wall is overthrown.

But remember, as we try,
Lighter every test goes by;
Wading in, the stream grows deep
Toward the center's downward sweep.
Backward turn, each step ashore
Shallower is than that before.

Ah! the precious years we waste
Levelling what we raised in haste;
Doing what must be undone
Ere content or love be won!
First across the gulf we cast
Kite-borne threads, till lines are passed,
And habit builds the bridge at last!

JOHN BOYLE O'REILLY

BREVITIES

I am that man who with a luminous look
Sits up at night to write a ruminant book.

I am that man who with furrowing frown
Thinks harshly of the world—and corks it down.

I am that man who loves to ride alone
When landscapes wear his mind's autumnal tone.

I am that man who, having lived his day,
Looks once on life and goes his wordless way.

SIEGFRIED SASSOON

THERE IS NO FRIGATE LIKE A BOOK

There is no frigate like a book
    To take us lands away,
Nor any coursers like a page
    Of prancing poetry.

This traverse may the poorest take
    Without oppress of toll;
How frugal is the chariot
    That bears a human soul!
                 EMILY DICKINSON

IF I CAN STOP ONE HEART FROM BREAKING

If I can stop one heart from breaking,
I shall not live in vain;
If I can ease one life the aching,
Or cool one pain,
Or help one fainting robin
Unto his nest again,
I shall not live in vain.
                 EMILY DICKINSON

THE CHAMBERED NAUTILUS

(from *The Autocrat of the Breakfast Table*)

This is the ship of pearl, which, poets feign,
    Sails the unshadowed main,—
    The venturous bark that flings
On the sweet summer wind its purpled wings
In gulfs enchanted, where the Siren sings,
    And coral reefs lie bare,
Where the cold sea-maids rise to sun their streaming hair.

Its webs of living gauze no more unfurl;
    Wrecked is the ship of pearl!
    And every chambered cell,
Where its dim dreaming life was wont to dwell,
As the frail tenant shaped his growing shell,
    Before thee lies revealed,—
Its irised ceiling rent, its sunless crypt unsealed!

Year after year beheld the silent toil
    That spread his lustrous coil;
    Still, as the spiral grew,
He left the past year's dwelling for the new,
Stole with soft step its shining archway through,
    Built up its idle door,
Stretched in his last-found home, and knew the old no more.

Thanks for the heavenly message brought by thee,
    Child of the wandering sea,
    Cast from her lap, forlorn!
From thy dead lips a clearer note is born
Than ever Triton blew from wreathed horn!
    While on mine ear it rings,
Through the deep caves of thought I hear a voice that sings—

Build thee more stately mansions, O my soul,
    As the swift seasons roll!
    Leave thy low-vaulted past!
Let each new temple, nobler than the last,
Shut thee from heaven with a dome more vast,
    Till thou at length art free,
Leaving thine outgrown shell by life's unresting sea!

                         OLIVER WENDELL HOLMES

THE WORLD IS TOO MUCH WITH US

The world is too much with us; late and soon,
Getting and spending, we lay waste our powers:
Little we see in Nature that is ours;
We have given our hearts away, a sordid boon!
This sea that bares her bosom to the moon,
The winds that will be howling at all hours,

And are up-gathered now like sleeping flowers;
For this, for everything, we are out of tune;
It moves us not.—Great God! I'd rather be
A Pagan suckled in a creed outworn;
So might I, standing on this pleasant lea,
Have glimpses that would make me less forlorn;
Have sight of Proteus rising from the sea;
Or hear old Triton blow his wreathed horn.

WILLIAM WORDSWORTH

WHICH ARE YOU?

I watched them tearing a building down,
A gang of men in a busy town;
With a ho-heave-ho and a lusty yell
They swung a beam and the sidewalk fell.
I asked the foreman: "Are these men skilled,
And the men you'd hire if you had to build?"
He gave a laugh and said: "No indeed!
Just common labor is all I need.
I can easily wreck in a day or two
What builders have taken a year to do!"

And I thought to myself as I went my way,
Which of these roles have I tried to play?
Am I a builder who works with care,
Measuring life by the rule and square?
Am I shaping my deeds to a well-made plan,
Patiently doing the best I can?
Or am I a wrecker, who walks the town,
Content with the labor of tearing down.

UNKNOWN

IT'S IN YOUR FACE

You don't have to tell how you live each day,
You don't have to say if you work or play,
A tried, true barometer serves in the place
However you live, it will show in your face.
The false, the deceit you bear in your heart

Will not stay inside, where it first got a start,
For sinew and blood are a thin veil of lace,
What you wear in your heart you wear in your face.
If your life is unselfish, if for others you live
For not what you get, but for how much you can give,
If you live close to God, in His infinite grace,
You don't have to tell it, it shows in your face.

UNKNOWN

FOR WHOM THE BELL TOLLS

(from *Devotions upon Emergent Occasions*)

No man is an island, entire of itself; every man is a piece of the
continent, a part of the main. If a clod be washed away by the sea,
Europe is the less, as well as if a promontory were, as well as if a
manor of thy friend's or of thine own were: any man's death dimin-
ishes me, because I am involved in mankind, and therefore never
send to know for whom the bell tolls; it tolls for thee.

JOHN DONNE

THE WAYS

To every man there openeth
A Way, and Ways and a Way.
And the High Soul climbs the High Way,
And the Low Soul gropes the Low,
And in between, on the misty flats,
The rest drift to and fro.
But to every man there openeth
A High Way, and a Low,
And every man decideth
The Way his soul shall go.

JOHN OXENHAM

VICTORY IN DEFEAT

Defeat may serve as well as victory
To shake the soul and let the glory out.
When the great oak is straining in the wind,
The boughs drink in new beauty, and the trunk
Sends down a deeper root on the windward side.
Only the soul that knows the mighty grief
Can know the mighty rapture. Sorrows come
To stretch out spaces in the heart for joy.

EDWIN MARKHAM

WHISTLING BOY

When the curtain of night, 'tween the dark and the light,
    Drops down from the set of the sun,
And the toilers who roam, to the loved ones come home,
    As they pass by my window is one
Whose coming I mark, for the song of the lark
    As it joyously soars in the sky
Is no dearer to me than the notes, glad and free,
    Of the boy who goes whistling by.

If a sense of unrest settles over my breast
    And my spirit is clouded with care,
It all flies away if he happens to stray
    Past my window a-whistling an air.
And I never shall know how much gladness I owe
    To this joy of the ear and the eye,
But I'm sure I'm in debt for much pleasure I get
    To the boy who goes whistling by.

And this music of his, how much better it is
    Than to burden his life with a frown,
For the toiler who sings to his purposes brings
    A hope his endeavor to crown.
And whenever I hear his glad notes, full and clear,
    I say to myself I will try
To make all of life with a joy to be rife,
    Like the boy who goes whistling by.

NIXON WATERMAN

TIME

Unfathomable Sea! whose waves are years,
  Ocean of Time, whose waters of deep woe
Are brackish with the salt of human tears!
  Thou shoreless flood, which in thy ebb and flow
Claspest the limits of mortality,
And sick of prey, yet howling on for more,
Vomitest thy wrecks on its inhospitable shore;
  Treacherous in calm, and terrible in storm,
    Who shall put forth on thee,
    Unfathomable Sea?

                 PERCY BYSSHE SHELLEY

A LITTLE LEARNING IS A DANGEROUS THING

(from *Essay on Criticism, II*)

A little learning is a dangerous thing;
Drink deep, or taste not the Pierian spring:
There shallow draughts intoxicate the brain,
And drinking largely sobers us again.
Fired at first sight with what the Muse imparts,
In fearless youth we tempt the heights of Arts,
While from the bounded level of our mind,
Short views we take, nor see the lengths behind;
But more advanced, behold with strange surprise
New distant scenes of endless science rise!
So pleased at first the towering Alps we try,
Mount o'er the vales, and seem to tread the sky,
Th' eternal snows appear already past,
And the first clouds and mountains seem the last;
But, those attained, we tremble to survey
The growing labors of the lengthened way,
Th' increasing prospect tires our wandering eyes,
Hills peep o'er hills, and Alps on Alps arise!

                 ALEXANDER POPE

THE RAINY DAY

The day is cold, and dark, and dreary;
It rains, and the wind is never weary;
The vine still clings to the moldering wall,
But at every gust the dead leaves fall,
  And the day is dark and dreary.

My life is cold, and dark, and dreary;
It rains, and the wind is never weary;
My thoughts still cling to the moldering Past,
But the hopes of youth fall thick in the blast
  And the days are dark and dreary.

Be still, sad heart! and cease repining;
Behind the clouds is the sun still shining;
  Thy fate is the common fate of all,
Into each life some rain must fall,
  Some days must be dark and dreary.

HENRY WADSWORTH LONGFELLOW

A PSALM OF LIFE

WHAT THE HEART OF THE YOUNG MAN SAID TO THE PSALMIST

Tell me not, in mournful numbers,
  Life is but an empty dream!—
For the soul is dead that slumbers,
  And things are not what they seem.

Life is real! Life is earnest!
  And the grave is not its goal;
Dust thou art, to dust returnest,
  Was not spoken of the soul.

Not enjoyment, and not sorrow,
  Is our destined end or way;
But to act, that each to-morrow
  Find us farther than to-day.

Art is long, and Time is fleeting,
  And our hearts, though stout and brave,
Still, like muffled drums, are beating
  Funeral marches to the grave.

In the world's broad field of battle,
  In the bivouac of Life,
Be not like dumb, driven cattle!
  Be a hero in the strife!

Trust no Future, howe'er pleasant!
  Let the dead Past bury its dead!
Act,—act in the living Present!
  Heart within, and God o'erhead!

Lives of great men all remind us
  We can make our lives sublime,
And, departing, leave behind us
  Footprints on the sands of time;

Footprints, that perhaps another,
  Sailing o'er life's solemn main,
A forlorn and shipwrecked brother,
  Seeing, shall take heart again.

Let us, then, be up and doing,
  With a heart for any fate;
Still achieving, still pursuing,
  Learn to labor and to wait.

HENRY WADSWORTH LONGFELLOW

IT IS TOO LATE!

(from *Morituri Salutamus*)

It is too late! Ah, nothing is too late
Till the tired heart shall cease to palpitate.
Cato learned Greek at eighty; Sophocles
Wrote his grand Oedipus, and Simonides
Bore off the prize of verse from his compeers,

When each had numbered more than fourscore years,
And Theophrastus, at fourscore and ten,
Had but begun his "Characters of Men."
Chaucer, at Woodstock with the nightingales,
At sixty wrote the Canterbury Tales;
Goethe at Weimar, toiling to the last,
Completed Faust when eighty years were past.

HENRY WADSWORTH LONGFELLOW

FOR THIS IS WISDOM

(from *The Teak Forest*)

For this is Wisdom; to love, to live,
To take what Fate, or the Gods, may give,
To ask no question, to make no prayer,
To kiss the lips and caress the hair,
Speed passion's ebb as you greet its flow,—
To have,—to hold,—and,—in time,—let go!

LAURENCE HOPE

DREAMER OF DREAMS

We are all of us dreamers of dreams;
   On visions our childhood is fed;
And the heart of the child is unhaunted, it seems,
   By the ghosts of dreams that are dead.

From childhood to youth's but a span
   And the years of our youth are soon sped;
Yet the youth is no longer a youth, but a man,
   When the first of his dreams is dead.

There's no sadder sight this side the grave
   Than the shroud o'er a fond dream spread,
And the heart should be stern and the eyes be brave
   To gaze on a dream that is dead.

'Tis a cup as of wormwood and gall
   When the doom of a great dream is said,
And the best of a man is under the pall
   When the best of his dreams is dead.

He may live on by compact and plan
   When the fine bloom of living is shed,
But God pity the little that's left of a man
   When the last of his dreams is dead.

Let him show a brave face if he can,
   Let him woo fame or fortune instead,
Yet there's not much to do but bury a man
   When the last of his dreams is dead.

                  WILLIAM HERBERT CARRUTH

ILICET

A.G.

I think the gentle soul of him
   Goes softly in some garden place,
With the old smile time may not dim
   Upon his face.

He who was lover of the Spring,
   With love that never quite forgets,
Surely sees roses blossoming
   And violets.

Now that his day of toil is through,
   I love to think he sits at ease,
With some old volume that he knew
   Upon his knees.

Watching, perhaps, with quiet eyes
   The white clouds' drifting argosy;
Or twilight opening flower-wise
   On land and sea.

He who so loved companionship
    I may not think walks quite alone,
Failing some friendly hand to slip
    Within his own.

Those whom he loved aforetime, still,
    I doubt not, bear him company;
Yea, even laughter yet may thrill
    Where he may be.

A thought, a fancy—who may tell?
    Yet I who ever pray it so,
Feel through my tears that all is well;
    And this I know,—

That God is gentle to his guest,
    And, therefore, may I gladly say,
"Surely the things he loved the best
    Are his to-day."

                  THEODOSIA GARRISON

CHANGES

Whom first we love, you know, we seldom wed.
    Time rules us all. And Life, indeed, is not
The thing we planned it out ere hope was dead,
    And then, we women cannot choose our lot.

Much must be borne which it is hard to bear:
    Much given away which it were sweet to keep.
God help us all! who need, indeed, His care,
    And yet, I know, the Shepherd loves His sheep.

My little boy begins to babble now
    Upon my knee his earliest infant prayer.
He has his father's eager eyes, I know,
    And they say, too, his mother's sunny hair.

But when he sleeps and smiles upon my knee,
    And I can feel his light breath come and go,
I think of one (Heaven help and pity me!)
    Who loved me, and whom I loved, long ago.

Who might have been . . . ah, what I dare not think!
    We all are changed. God judges for us best.
God help us do our duty, and not shrink,
    And trust in Heaven humbly for the rest.

But blame us women not, if some appear
    Too cold at times; and some too gay and light.
Some griefs gnaw deep. Some woes are hard to bear.
    Who knows the Past? and who can judge us right?

Ah, were we judged by what we might have been,
    And not by what we are, too apt to fall!
My little child—he sleeps and smiles between
    These thoughts and me. In heaven we shall know all.

                    ROBERT BULWER-LYTTON

THE OLD STOIC

Riches I hold in light esteem,
    And Love I laugh to scorn;
And lust of fame was but a dream
    That vanished with the morn:

And if I pray, the only prayer
    That moves my lips for me
Is, "Leave the heart that now I bear,
    And give me liberty!"

Yes, as my swift days near their goal,
    'Tis all that I implore;
Through life and death a chainless soul,
    With courage to endure.

                    EMILY BRONTË

QUIET THINGS

These I have loved with passion, loved them long:
The house that stands when the building hammers cease,

After wild syncopation, a sane song,
A tree that straightens after the winds' release,
The cool green stillness of an April wood,
A silver pool, unruffled by the breeze,
The clean expanse of a prairie's solitude,
And calm, unhurried hours—I love these.

I have been tangled in the nets too long;
I shall escape and find my way again
Back to the quiet place where I belong,
Far from the tinseled provinces of men.
These will be waiting after my release:
The sheltered ways, the quiet ways of peace.

GRACE NOLL CROWELL

LIFE'S A FUNNY PROPOSITION AFTER ALL

Did you ever sit and ponder, sit and wonder, sit and think,
    Why we're here and what this life is all about?
It's a problem that has driven many brainy men to drink,
    It's the weirdest thing they've tried to figure out;
About a thousand different theories, all the scientists can show,
    But never yet have proved a reason why.
With all we've thought, and all we're taught, why all we seem to
    know
Is, we're born and live a while, and then we die.

Life's a very funny proposition, after all;
Imagination, jealousy, hypocrisy and all;
Three meals a day, a whole lot to say;
When you haven't got the coin, you're always in the way.
Ev'rybody's fighting, as we wend our way along,
Ev'ry fellow claims the other fellow's in the wrong;
Hurried and worried, until we're buried and there's no curtain
    call;
Life's a very funny proposition, after all.

When all things are coming easy, and when luck is with a man,
    Why, then life to him is sunshine ev'rywhere;
Then the fates blow rather breezy and they quite upset a plan,
    Then he'll cry that life's a burden hard to bear.

Though today may be a day of smiles, tomorrow's still in doubt
  And, what brings me joy, may bring you care and woe.
We're born to die, but don't know why or what it's all about
  And, the more we try to learn, the less we know.

Life's a very funny proposition, you can bet,
And no one's ever solved the problem properly, as yet;
Young for a day, then old and gray,
Like the rose that buds and blooms, and fades and falls away.
Losing health, to gain our wealth, as through this dream we tour;
Ev'rything's a guess and nothing's absolutely sure.
Battles exciting, and fates we're fighting, until the curtain fall;
Life's a very funny proposition, after all.

GEORGE M. COHAN

THE MAN WHO THINKS HE CAN

If you think you are beaten, you are;
    If you think you dare not, you don't;
If you'd like to win, but think you can't,
    It's almost a cinch you won't.
If you think you'll lose, you're lost,
    For out in the world we find
Success begins with a fellow's will;
    It's all in the state of mind.

If you think you're outclassed, you are;
    You've got to think high to rise.
You've got to be sure of yourself before
    You can ever win a prize.
Life's battles don't always go
    To the stronger or faster man;
But soon or late the man who wins
    Is the man who thinks he can.

WALTER D. WINTLE

WHIST

Hour after hour the cards were fairly shuffled
    And fairly dealt, but still I got no hand;
The morning came, and with a mind unruffled
    I only said, "I do not understand."

Life is a game of whist. From unseen sources
    The cards are shuffled and the hands are dealt;
Blind are our efforts to control the forces
    That, though unseen, are no less strongly felt.

I do not like the way the cards are shuffled,
    But yet I like the game and want to play;
And through the long, long night will I, unruffled,
    Play what I get until the break of day.

                                    EUGENE FITCH WARE

MY CREED

I would be true, for there are those who trust me;
    I would be pure, for there are those who care;
I would be strong, for there is much to suffer;
    I would be brave, for there is much to dare.
I would be friend of all—the foe, the friendless;
    I would be giving, and forget the gift.
I would be humble, for I know my weakness;
    I would look up—and laugh—and love—and lift.

                                    HOWARD ARNOLD WALTER

TO BE HONEST, TO BE KIND

(from *A Christmas Sermon*)

To be honest, to be kind—to earn
a little and to spend a little less, to make
upon the whole a family happier for his
presence, to renounce when that shall be

necessary and not be embittered,
to keep a few friends, but these without
capitulation—above all, on the same
grim condition, to keep friends with himself—
here is a task for all that a man has of forti-
tude and delicacy.

ROBERT LOUIS STEVENSON

SCULPTURE

I took a piece of plastic clay
And idly fashioned it one day.
And as my fingers pressed it, still
It moved and yielded to my will.

I came again when days were past:
The bit of clay was hard at last.
The form I gave it still it bore,
But I could change that form no more!

I took a piece of living clay,
And gently pressed it day by day,
And molded with my power and art
A young child's soft and yielding heart.

I came again when years had gone:
It was a man I looked upon.
He still that early impress bore,
And I could fashion it no more!

UNKNOWN

THE MEASURE OF A MAN

Not—"How did he die?" But—"How did he live?"
Not—"What did he gain?" But—"What did he give?"
These are the units to measure the worth
Of a man as a man, regardless of birth.

Not—"What was his station?" But—"Had he a heart?"
And—"How did he play his God-given part?
    Was he ever ready with a word of good cheer,
    To bring back a smile, to banish a tear?"

Not—"What was his church?" Nor—"What was his creed?"
But—"Had he befriended those really in need?"
Not—"What did the sketch in the newspaper say?"
But—"How many were sorry when he passed away?"

UNKNOWN

SUN AND RAIN AND DEW FROM HEAVEN

(from *Ye Wearie Wayfarer*)

Sun and rain and dew from heaven,
    Light and shade and air,
Heat and moisture freely given,
    Thorns and thistles share.
Vegetation rank and rotten
    Feels the cheering ray;
Not uncared for, unforgotten,
    We, too, have our day.
Unforgotten! though we cumber
    Earth, we work His will.
Shall we sleep through night's long slumber,
    Unforgotten still?
Onward! onward! toiling ever,
    Weary steps and slow,
Doubting oft, despairing never,
    To the goal we go!

Hark! the bells on distant cattle
    Waft across the range,
Through the golden-tufted wattle,
    Music low and strange;
Like the marriage peal of fairies
    Comes the tinkling sound,
Or like chimes of sweet St. Mary's
    On far English ground.
How my courser champs the snaffle,
    And with nostrils spread,

Snorts and scarcely seems to ruffle
    Fern leaves with his tread;
Cool and pleasant on his haunches
    Blows an evening breeze,
Through the overhanging branches
    Of the wattle trees:
Onward! to the Southern Ocean,
    Glides the breath of Spring,
Onward, with a dreamy motion,
    I, too, glide and sing—
Forward! forward! still we wander—
    Tinted hills that lie
In the red horizon yonder—
    Is the goal so nigh?

Whisper, spring-wind, softly singing,
    Whisper in my ear;
Respite and nepenthe bringing,
    Can the goal be near?
Laden with the dew of vespers,
    From the fragrant sky,
In my ear the wind that whispers
    Seems to make reply—

"Question not, but live and labor
    Till yon goal be won,
Helping every feeble neighbor,
    Seeking help from none;
Life is mostly froth and bubble,
    Two things stand like stone—
KINDNESS in another's trouble,
    COURAGE in your own."

Courage, comrades, this is certain
    All is for the best—
There are lights behind the curtain—
    Gentles let us rest.
As the smoke-rack veers to seaward,
    From "the ancient clay,"
With its moral drifting leeward,
    Ends the wanderer's lay.

ADAM LINDSAY GORDON

THE WANTS OF MAN

"Man wants but little here below,
   Nor wants that little long."
'Tis not with *me* exactly so;
   But 'tis so in the song.
My wants are many and, if told,
   Would muster many a score;
And were each wish a mint of gold,
   I still should long for more.

What first I want is daily bread—
   And canvas-backs—and wine—
And all the realms of nature spread
   Before me, when I dine.
Four courses scarcely can provide
   My appetite to quell;
With four choice cooks from France beside,
   To dress my dinner well.

What next I want, at princely cost,
   Is elegant attire:
Black sable furs for winter's frost,
   And silks for summer's fire,
And Cashmere shawls, and Brussels lace
   My bosom's front to deck—
And diamond rings my hands to grace,
   And rubies for my neck.

I want (who does not want?) a wife—
   Affectionate and fair;
To solace all the woes of life,
And all its joys to share.
Of temper sweet, of yielding will,
   Of firm, yet placid mind—
With all my faults to love me still
   With sentiment refined.

And as Time's car incessant runs,
   And Fortune fills my store,

I want of daughters and of sons
  From eight to half a score.
I want (alas! can mortal dare
  Such bliss on earth to crave?)
That all the girls be chaste and fair,
  The boys all wise and brave.

I want a warm and faithful friend,
  To cheer the adverse hour;
Who ne'er to flatter will descend,
  Nor bend the knee to power—
A friend to chide me when I'm wrong,
  My inmost soul to see;
And that my friendship prove as strong
  For him as his for me.

I want the seals of power and place,
  The ensigns of command;
Charged by the People's unbought grace
  To rule my native land
Nor crown nor scepter would I ask
  But from my country's will,
By day, by night, to ply the task
  Her cup of bliss to fill.

I want the voice of honest praise
  To follow me behind,
And to be thought in future days
  The friend of human kind,
That after ages, as they rise,
  Exulting may proclaim
In choral union to the skies
  Their blessings on my name.

These are the Wants of mortal Man—
  I cannot want them long,
For life itself is but a span,
  And earthly bliss—a song.
My last great Want—absorbing all—
  Is, when beneath the sod,
And summoned to my final call,
  The Mercy of My God.
                    JOHN QUINCY ADAMS

THE ROAD NOT TAKEN

Two roads diverged in a yellow wood,
And sorry I could not travel both
And be one traveler, long I stood
And looked down one as far as I could
To where it bent in the undergrowth;

Then took the other, as just as fair,
And having perhaps the better claim,
Because it was grassy and wanted wear;
Though as for that the passing there
Had worn them really about the same,

And both that morning equally lay
In leaves no step had trodden black.
Oh, I kept the first for another day!
Yet knowing how way leads on to way,
I doubted if I should ever come back.

I shall be telling this with a sigh
Somewhere ages and ages hence:
Two roads diverged in a wood, and I—
I took the one less traveled by,
And that has made all the difference.

ROBERT FROST

X. Faith and Inspiration

O WORLD

O world, thou choosest not the better part!
It is not wisdom to be only wise,
And on the inward vision close the eyes,
But it is wisdom to believe the heart.
Columbus found a world, and had no chart,
Save one that faith deciphered in the skies;
To trust the soul's invincible surmise
Was all his science and his only art.
Our knowledge is a torch of smoky pine
That lights the pathway but one step ahead
Across a void of mystery and dread.
Bid, then, the tender light of faith to shine
By which alone the mortal heart is led
Unto the thinking of the thought divine.

GEORGE SANTAYANA

ON HIS BLINDNESS

When I consider how my light is spent
Ere half my days in this dark world and wide,
And that one talent, which is death to hide,
Lodged with me useless, though my soul more bent
To serve therewith my Maker, and present
My true account, lest He returning chide;
"Doth God exact day-labor, light denied?"
I fondly ask. But Patience, to prevent
That murmur, soon replies, "God doth not need
Either man's work or his own gifts; who best
Bear his mild yoke, they serve him best; his state
Is kingly; thousands at his bidding speed,
And post o'er land and ocean without rest;
They also serve who only stand and wait."

JOHN MILTON

THE FOOL'S PRAYER

The royal feast was done; the King
    Sought some new sport to banish care,
And to his jester cried: "Sir Fool,
    Kneel now, and make for us a prayer!"

The jester doffed his cap and bells,
    And stood the mocking court before;
They could not see the bitter smile
    Behind the painted grin he wore.

He bowed his head, and bent his knee
    Upon the monarch's silken stool;
His pleading voice arose: "O Lord,
    Be merciful to me, a fool!

"No pity, Lord, could change the heart
    From red with wrong to white as wool;
The rod must heal the sin: but Lord,
    Be merciful to me, a fool!

"'Tis not by guilt the onward sweep
    Of truth and right, O Lord, we stay;
'Tis by our follies that so long
    We hold the earth from heaven away.

"These clumsy feet, still in the mire,
    Go crushing blossoms without end;
These hard, well-meaning hands we thrust
    Among the heart-strings of a friend.

"The ill-timed truth we might have kept—
    Who knows how sharp it pierced and stung?
The word we had not sense to say—
    Who knows how grandly it had rung!

"Our faults no tenderness should ask,
    The chastening stripes must cleanse them all;
But for our blunders—oh, in shame
    Before the eyes of heaven we fall.

"Earth bears no balsam for mistakes;
  Men crown the knave, and scourge the tool
That did his will; but Thou, O Lord,
  Be merciful to me, a fool!"

The room was hushed; in silence rose
  The King, and sought his gardens cool,
And walked apart, and murmured low,
  "Be merciful to me, a fool!"

                 EDWARD ROWLAND SILL

UNAWARES

They said, "The Master is coming
  To honor the town today,
And none can tell at what house or home
  The Master will choose to stay."
And I thought while my heart beat wildly,
  What if He should come to mine,
How would I strive to entertain
  And honor the Guest Divine!

And straight I turned to toiling,
  To make my home more neat;
I swept, and polished and garnished,
  And decked it with blossoms sweet.
I was troubled for fear the Master
  Might come ere my work was done
And I hasted and worked the faster,
  And watched the hurrying sun.

But right in the midst of my duties
  A woman came to my door;
She had come to tell her sorrows
  And my comfort and aid to implore,
And I said, "I cannot listen,
  Nor help you any, today;
I have greater things to attend to."
  And the pleader turned away.

But soon there came another—
  A cripple, thin, pale and gray—
And said: "Oh, let me stop and rest
  A while in your house, I pray!
I have traveled far since morning,
  I am hungry and faint and weak;
My heart is full of misery,
  And comfort and help I seek."

And I cried, "I am grieved and sorry
  But I cannot help you today.
I look for a great and noble Guest,"
  And the cripple went away;
And the day wore onward swiftly—
  And my task was nearly done,
And a prayer was ever in my heart
  That the Master to me might come.

And I thought I would spring to meet Him,
  And serve Him with utmost care,
When a little child stood near me
  With a face so sweet and fair—
Sweet, but with marks of teardrops—
  And his clothes were tattered and old;
A finger was bruised and bleeding,
  And his little bare feet were cold.

And I said, "I'm sorry for you—
  You are sorely in need of care;
But I cannot stop to give it,
  You must hasten otherwhere."
And at the words, a shadow
  Swept o'er his blue-veined brow—
"Someone will feed and clothe you, dear,
  But I am too busy now."

At last the day was ended,
  And my toil was over and done;
My house was swept and garnished—
  And I watched in the dark—alone.
Watched—but no footfall sounded,
  No one paused at my gate;

No one entered my cottage door;
  I could only pray—and wait.

I waited till night had deepened,
  And the Master had not come.
"He has entered some other door," I said,
  "And gladdened some other home!"
My labor had been for nothing,
  And I bowed my head and I wept,
My heart was sore with longing—
  Yet—in spite of it all—I slept.

Then the Master stood before me,
  And his face was grave and fair;
"Three times today I came to your door,
  And I craved your pity and care;
Three times you sent me onward,
  Unhelped and uncomforted;
And the blessing you might have had was lost,
  And your chance to serve has fled."

"O Lord, dear Lord, forgive me!
  How could I know it was Thee?"
My very soul was shamed and bowed
  In the depths of humility,
And He said, "The sin is pardoned,
  But the blessing is lost to thee;
For, comforting not the least of Mine,
  You have failed to comfort Me."

EMMA A. LENT

JUDAS ISCARIOT

I think when Judas' mother heard
  His first faint cry the night
That he was born, that worship stirred
  Her at the sound and sight.
She thought his was as fair a frame
  As flesh and blood had worn;
I think she made this lovely name
  For him—"Star of my morn."

As any mother's son he grew
From spring to crimson spring;
I think his eyes were black, or blue,
His hair curled like a ring.
His mother's heart-strings were a lute
Whereon he all day played;
She listened rapt, abandoned, mute,
To every note he made.

I think he knew the growing Christ,
And played with Mary's son,
And where more mortal craft sufficed,
There Judas may have won.
Perhaps he little cared or knew,
So folly-wise is youth,
That He whose hand his hand clung to
Was flesh-embodied Truth;

Until one day he heard young Christ,
With far-off eyes agleam,
Tell of a mystic, solemn tryst
Between Him and a dream.
And Judas listened, wonder-eyed,
Until the Christ was through,
Then said, "And I, though good betide,
Or ill, will go with you."

And so he followed, heard Christ preach,
Saw how by miracle
The blind man saw, the dumb got speech,
The leper found him well.
And Judas in those holy hours
Loved Christ, and loved Him much,
And in his heart he sensed dead flowers
Bloom at the Master's touch.

And when Christ felt the death hour creep
With sullen, drunken lurch,
He said to Peter, "Feed my sheep,
And build my holy church."
He gave to each the special task
That should be his to do,

But reaching one, I hear him ask,
  "What shall I give to you?"

Then Judas in his hot desire
  Said, "Give me what you will."
Christ spoke to him with words of fire,
  "Then, Judas, you must kill
One whom you love, One who loves you
  As only God's son can:
This is the work for you to do
  To save the creature man."

"And men to come will curse your name,
  And hold you up to scorn;
In all the world will be no shame
  Like yours; this is love's thorn.
It takes strong will of heart and soul,
  But man is under ban.
Think, Judas, can you play this role
  In Heaven's mystic plan?"

So Judas took the sorry part,
  Went out and spoke the word,
And gave the kiss that broke his heart,
  But no one knew or heard.
And no one knew what poison ate
  Into his palm that day,
Where, bright and damned, the monstrous weight
  Of thirty white coins lay.

It was not death that Judas found
  Upon a kindly tree;
The man was dead long ere he bound
  His throat as final fee.
And who can say if on that day
  When gates of pearl swung wide,
Christ did not go His honored way
  With Judas by His side?

I think somewhere a table round
  Owns Jesus as its head,
And there the saintly twelve are found

Who followed where He led.
And Judas sits down with the rest,
  And none shrinks from His hand,
For there the worst is as the best,
  And there they understand.

And you may think of Judas, friend,
  As one who broke his word,
Whose neck came to a bitter end
  For giving up his Lord.
But I would rather think of him
  As the little Jewish lad
Who gave young Christ heart, soul, and limb,
  And all the love he had.

COUNTEE CULLEN

NEARER TO THEE

Nearer, my God, to Thee,
  Nearer to Thee!
E'en though it be a cross
  That raiseth me;
Still all my song shall be,
Nearer, my God, to Thee,
  Nearer to Thee!

Though like the wanderer,
  The sun gone down,
Darkness be over me,
  My rest a stone;
Yet in my dreams I'd be
Nearer, my God, to Thee,
  Nearer to Thee!

There let the way appear
  Steps unto heaven;
All that Thou send'st to me
  In mercy given;

Angels to beckon me
Nearer, my God, to Thee,
　　Nearer to Thee!

Then, with my waking thoughts
　　Bright with Thy praise,
Out of my stony griefs
　　Bethel I'll raise;
So by my woes to be
Nearer, my God, to Thee,
　　Nearer to Thee!

Or if on joyful wing
　　Cleaving the sky,
Sun, moon, and stars forgot,
　　Upward I fly,
Still all my song shall be,
Nearer, my God, to Thee,
　　Nearer to Thee!

SARAH FLOWER ADAMS

NOW AND AFTERWARDS

"Two hands upon the breast, and labor is past"—RUSSIAN PROVERB

Two hands upon the breast,
　　And labor's done;
Two pale feet crossed in rest,—
　　The race is won;
Two eyes with coin-weights shut,
　　And all tears cease,
Two lips where grief is mute,
　　Anger at peace;—
So pray we oftentimes, mourning our lot;
God in His kindness answereth not.

Two hands to work addressed
　　Aye for His praise;
Two feet that never rest
　　Walking His ways;
Two eyes that look above

Through all their tears;
Two lips still breathing love,
  Not wrath, nor fears;—
So pray we afterwards, low on our knees;
Pardon those erring prayers! Father, hear these!
DINAH MARIA MULOCK CRAIK

THE DONKEY

When fishes flew and forests walked
  And figs grew upon thorn,
Some moment when the moon was blood
  Then surely I was born;

With monstrous head and sickening cry
  And ears like errant wings,
The devil's walking parody
  On all four-footed things;

The tattered outlaw of the earth,
  Of ancient crooked will:
Starve, scourge, deride me: I am dumb,
  I keep my secret still.

Fools! For I also had my hour;
  One far fierce hour and sweet;
There was shout about my ears,
  And palms before my feet.
G. K. CHESTERTON

A PRAYER IN DARKNESS

This much, O heaven—if I should brood or rave,
  Pity me not; but let the world be fed,
  Yea, in my madness if I strike me dead,
Heed you the grass that grows upon my grave.

If I dare snarl between this sun and sod,
  Whimper and clamor, give me grace to own,

In sun and rain and fruit in season shown,
The shining silence of the scorn of God.

Thank God the stars are set beyond my power,
 If I must travail in a night of wrath;
  Thank God my tears will never vex a moth,
Nor any curse of mine cut down a flower.

Men say the sun was darkened: yet I had
 Thought it beat brightly, even on—Calvary;
  And He that hung upon the Torturing Tree
Heard all the crickets singing, and was glad.

G. K. CHESTERTON

HEAVEN

Think of—
Stepping on shore, and finding it Heaven!
Of taking hold of a hand, and finding it God's hand.
Of breathing a new air, and finding it celestial air.
Of feeling invigorated, and finding it immortality.
Of passing from storm to tempest to an unbroken calm.
Of waking up, and finding it Home.

UNKNOWN

I SEE HIS BLOOD UPON THE ROSE

I see His blood upon the rose
And in the stars the glory of His eyes,
His body gleams amid eternal snows,
His tears fall from the skies.

I see His face in every flower;
The thunder and the singing of the birds
Are but His voice—and carven by His power
Rocks are His written words.

All pathways by His feet are worn,
His strong heart stirs the ever beating sea,
His crown of thorns is twined with every thorn,
His cross is every tree.

JOSEPH MARY PLUNKETT

THE SACRAMENT OF SLEEP

Thank God for sleep!
And, when you cannot sleep,
Still thank Him that you live
To lie awake.

And pray Him, of His grace,
When He sees fit, sweet sleep to give,
That you may rise, with new-born eyes,
To look once more into His shining face.

In sleep—limbs all loose—laxed and slipt the chains—
We draw sweet-close to Him from whom our breath
Has life. In His sole hands we leave the reins,
In fullest faith trust Him for life or death.

This sleep in life close kinsman is to death;
And, as from sleep we wake to greet the day,
So, too, from death we shall with joy awake
To greet the glories of The Great Essay.

To His belov'd new life in sleep He gives,
And, unto all, awakening from sleep,
Each day is resurrection—a new birth
To nearer heaven and recreated earth—
To all Life's possibilities—of good
Or ill—with joys and woes endued—
Till that last, shortest sleep of all,
And that first great awakening from Life's thrall.

Thank God for sleep!
And when you cannot sleep,
Still thank Him for the grace
That lets you live
To feel the comfort of His soft embrace.

JOHN OXENHAM

HAMMER AND ANVIL

Look forth and tell me what they do
On Life's broad field. Oh still they fight,
The false forever with the true,
The wrong forever with the right.
And still God's faithful ones, as men
Who hold a fortress strong and high,
Cry out in confidence again,
And find a comfort in the cry:
"Hammer away, ye hostile hands,
Your hammers break, God's anvil stands."

Older than pyramids or sphinx,
Old as the stars themselves, the word
Whereby, when other courage sinks,
The courage born of Heaven is stirred.
For, when God made the world and knew
That good and evil could not blend,
He planned, however men might do,
What should be, would be in the end,
And, though as thick as ocean sands
They rain the blows, the anvil stands.

Oh, many a time has this vain world
Essayed to thwart the mighty plan;
Its fleets and armies have been hurled
Against the common rights of man.
But wrecked Armadas, Waterloos,
Empires abandoned to decay,
Proclaim the truth they did not choose—
What broken hammers strew the way!
Though all the world together bands
To smite it, still the anvil stands.

Thou knowest that thy cause is just?
Then rest in that; thy cause is sure.
Thy word is true; oh, then it must
In spite of slanderous tongues endure.
As toward the crag the billow rides,

Then falls back, shattered, to its place;
As fans the breeze, the mountain sides,
Nor moves the mountain from its base—
So, in all times and in all lands
Men's hammers break. God's anvil stands.

SAMUEL VALENTINE COLE

CONVERSION

Look God, I have never spoken to You.
But now I want to say: "How do You do?"
You see, God, they told me You didn't exist—
And like a fool I believed all this.
Last night from a shellhole I saw Your sky
And figured right then they told me a lie.
Had I taken time to see things You made,
I'd known they weren't calling a spade a spade.
I wonder, God, if You'd shake my hand.
Somehow I feel that You'll understand.
Funny I had to come to this hellish place
Before I had time to see Your face.
Well, I guess there isn't much more to say;
But I'm sure glad, God, I met You today.
I guess the zero hour will soon be here,
But I'm not afraid since I know You're here.
The signal! Well, God, I'll have to go—
I like you lots, this I want You to know.
Look now! This will be a horrible fight;
Who knows, I may come to Your House tonight.
Tho' I wasn't friendly with You before,
I wonder, God, if You'd wait at Your door?
Look, I'm crying—me shedding tears!
I wish I'd known You these many years.
Well, God, I have to go now—good-bye—
Strange, since I met You I'm not afraid to die.

FRANCES ANGERMAYER

THE DIVINE OFFICE OF THE KITCHEN

"God walks among the pots and pipkins"—ST. TERESA

Lord of the pots and pipkins, since I have no time to be
A saint by doing lovely things and vigiling with Thee,
By watching in the twilight dawn, and storming Heaven's gates,
Make me a saint by getting meals, and washing up the plates!

Lord of the pots and pipkins, please, I offer Thee my souls,
The tiresomeness of tea leaves, and the sticky porridge bowls!
Remind me of the things I need, not just to save the stairs,
But so that I may perfectly lay tables into prayers.

Accept my roughened hands because I made them so for Thee!
Pretend my dishmop is a bow, which heavenly harmony
Makes on a fiddle frying pan; it is so hard to clean,
And, ah, so horrid! Hear, dear Lord, the music that I mean!

Although I must have Martha hands, I have a Mary mind,
And when I black the boots, I try Thy sandals, Lord, to find.
I think of how they trod our earth, what time I scrub the floor.
Accept this meditation when I haven't time for more!

Vespers and Compline come to pass by washing supper things.
And, mostly I am very tired; and all the heart that sings
About the morning's work, is gone, before me into bed.
Lend me, dear Lord, Thy Tireless Heart to work in me instead!

My matins are said overnight to praise and bless Thy Name
Beforehand for tomorrow's work, which will be just the same;
So that it seems I go to bed still in my working dress.
Lord make Thy Cinderella soon a heavenly Princess.

Warm all the kitchen with Thy Love and light it with Thy Peace!
Forgive the worrying, and make the grumbling words to cease.
Lord, who laid Breakfast on the shore, forgive the world which saith
"Can any good thing come to God out of poor Nazareth?"

                                        CECILY HALLACK

GOD'S DARK

The Dark is kind and cozy,
   The Dark is soft and deep;
The Dark will pat my pillow
   And love me as I sleep.

The Dark is smooth as velvet,
   And gentle as the air,
And he is *good* to children
   And people everywhere.

The Dark can see and love me
   Without a bit of light.
He gives me dreams and resting,
   He brings the gentle Night.

God made the Dark, so Daytime
   Could close its tired eyes
And sleep awhile in comfort
   Beneath the starry skies.

The Daytime, just like children,
   Needs rest from work and play,
So it can give us children
   Another happy day.

God made the Dark for children
   And birdies in their nest.
All in the Dark, He watches
   And guards us while we rest.
               JOHN MARTIN

TURN AGAIN TO LIFE

If I should die and leave you here a while,
Be not like others, sore undone, who keep
Long vigil by the silent dust and weep.

For my sake turn again to life and smile,
Nerving thy heart and trembling hand to do
That which will comfort other souls than thine;
Complete these dear unfinished tasks of mine,
And I, perchance, may therein comfort you.

MARY LEE HALL

I MET THE MASTER

I had walked life's way with an easy tread,
Had followed where comfort and pleasures led.
Until one day in a quiet place
I met the Master face to face.

With station and rank and wealth for my goal,
Much thought for my body but none for my soul,
I had entered to win in life's mad race,
When I met the Master face to face.

I met Him, and knew Him and blushed to see
That His eyes full of sorrow were fixed on me;
And I faltered and fell at His feet that day,
While my castles melted and vanished away.

Melted and vanished and in their place
Naught else did I see but the Master's face.
And I cried aloud, "Oh, make me meet
To follow the steps of Thy wounded feet."

My thought is now for the souls of men,
I have lost my life to find it again,
E'er since one day in a quiet place
I met the Master face to face.

UNKNOWN

TO MY SON

I will not say to you, "This is the Way; walk in it."
For I do not know your way or where the Spirit may call you.
It may be to paths I have never trod or ships on the sea leading to
    unimagined lands afar,
Or haply, to a star!
Or yet again
Through dark and perilous places racked with pain and full of fear
Your road may lead you far away from me or near—
I cannot guess or guide, but only stand aside.
Just this I say:
I know for every truth there is a way for each to walk, a right for
    each to choose, a truth to use.
And though you wander far, your soul will know that true path when
    you find it.
Therefore, go!
I will fear nothing for you day or night!
I will not grieve at all because your light is called by some new name;
Truth is the same!
It matters nothing to call it star or sun—
All light is one.

UNKNOWN

DESTINY

Somewhere there waiteth in this world of ours
    For one lone soul another lonely soul—
Each chasing each through all the weary hours,
    And meeting strangely at one sudden goal;
Then blend they—like green leaves with golden flowers,
    Into one beautiful and perfect whole—
And life's long night is ended, and the way
    Lies open onward to eternal day.

EDWIN ARNOLD

LIFE'S LESSONS

I learn, as the years roll onward
  And leave the past behind,
That much I had counted sorrow
  But proves that God is kind;
That many a flower I had longed for
  Had hidden a thorn of pain,
And many a rugged bypath
  Led to fields of ripened grain.

The clouds that cover the sunshine
  They can not banish the sun;
And the earth shines out the brighter
  When the weary rain is done.
We must stand in the deepest shadow
  To see the clearest light;
And often through wrong's own darkness
  Comes the very strength of light.

The sweetest rest is at even,
  After a wearisome day,
When the heavy burden of labor
  Has borne from our hearts away;
And those who have never known sorrow
  Can not know the infinite peace
That falls on the troubled spirit
  When it sees at least release.

We must live through the dreary winter
  If we would value the spring;
And the woods must be cold and silent
  Before the robins sing.
The flowers must be buried in darkness
  Before they can bud and bloom,
And the sweetest, warmest sunshine
  Comes after the storm and gloom.

UNKNOWN

LITTLE AND GREAT

A traveler on a dusty road
   Strewed acorns on the lea;
And one took root and sprouted up,
   And grew into a tree.
Love sought its shade at evening-time,
   To breathe its early vows;
And Age was pleased, in heats of noon,
   To bask beneath its boughs.
The dormouse loved its dangling twigs,
   The birds sweet music bore—
It stood a glory in its place,
   A blessing evermore.

A little spring had lost its way
   Amid the grass and fern;
A passing stranger scooped a well
   Where weary men might turn;
He walled it in, and hung with care
   A ladle at the brink;
He thought not of the deed he did,
   But judged that Toil might drink.
He passed again; and lo! the well,
   By summer never dried,
Had cooled ten thousand parched tongues,
   And saved a life beside.

A dreamer dropped a random thought;
'Twas old, and yet 'twas new;
A simple fancy of the brain,
   But strong in being true.
It shone upon a genial mind,
   And, lo! its light became
A lamp of life, a beacon ray,
   A monitory flame:
The thought was small; its issue great;
   A watch-fire on the hill,
It sheds its radiance far adown,
   And cheers the valley still.

A nameless man, amid the crowd
  That thronged the daily mart,
Let fall a word of hope and love,
  Unstudied from the heart;—
A whisper on the tumult thrown,
  A transitory breath,—
It raised a brother from the dust,
  It saved a soul from death.
O germ! O fount! O word of love!
  O thought at random cast!
Ye were but little at the first,
  But mighty at the last.

CHARLES MACKAY

BALLAD OF THE TEMPEST

We were crowded in the cabin,
  Not a soul would dare to sleep,—
It was midnight on the waters,
  And a storm was on the deep.

'Tis a fearful thing in winter
  To be shattered by the blast,
And to hear the rattling trumpet
  Thunder, "Cut away the mast!"

So we shuddered there in silence,—
  For the stoutest held his breath,
While the hungry sea was roaring
  And the breakers talked with death.

As thus we sat in darkness,
  Each one busy with his prayers,
"We are lost!" the captain shouted,
  As he staggered down the stairs.

But his little daughter whispered,
  As she took his icy hand,
"Isn't God upon the ocean,
  Just the same as on the land?"

Then we kissed the little maiden,
  And we spake in better cheer,
And we anchored safe in harbor
  When the morn was shining clear.
                    JAMES THOMAS FIELDS

DISCIPLINE

Throw away Thy rod,
Throw away Thy wrath;
    O my God,
Take the gentle path!

For my heart's desire
Unto Thine is bent:
    I aspire
To a full consent.

Not a word or look
I affect to own,
    But by book,
And Thy Book alone.

Though I fail, I weep;
Though I halt in pace,
    Yet I creep
To the throne of grace.

Then let wrath remove;
Love will do the deed;
    For with love
Stony hearts will bleed.

Love is swift of foot;
Love's a man of war,
    And can shoot,
And can hit from far.

Who can 'scape his bow?
That which wrought on Thee,
    Brought Thee low,
Needs must work on me.

Throw away Thy rod;
Though man frailties hath,
    Thou art God:
Throw away Thy wrath.

GEORGE HERBERT

HIS LITANY TO THE HOLY SPIRIT

In the hour of my distress,
When temptations me oppress,
And when I my sins confess,
    Sweet Spirit, comfort me!

When I lie within my bed,
Sick in heart and sick in head,
And with doubts discomforted,
    Sweet Spirit, comfort me!

When the house doth sigh and weep,
And the world is drowned in sleep,
Yet mine eyes the watch do keep,
    Sweet Spirit, comfort me!

When the artless doctor sees
No one hope, but of his fees,
And his skill runs on the lees,
    Sweet Spirit, comfort me!

When his potion and his pill,
His, or none, or little skill,
Meet for nothing, but to kill,
    Sweet Spirit, comfort me!

When the passing-bell doth toll,
And the furies in a shoal
Come to fright a parting soul,
    Sweet Spirit, comfort me!

When the tapers now burn blue,
And the comforters are few,
And that number more than true,
    Sweet Spirit, comfort me!

When the priest his last hath prayed,
And I nod to what is said
'Cause my speech is now decayed,
    Sweet Spirit, comfort me!

When, God knows, I'm tossed about
Either with despair or doubt,
Yet, before the glass be out,
    Sweet Spirit, comfort me!

When the tempter me pursu'th
With the sins of all my youth,
And half damns me with untruth,
    Sweet Spirit, comfort me!

When the flames and hellish cries
Fright mine ears and fright mine eyes,
And all terrors me surprise,
    Sweet Spirit, comfort me!

When the Judgment is revealed,
And that opened which was sealed,
When to Thee I have appealed,
    Sweet Spirit, comfort me!

                                    ROBERT HERRICK

A BALLAD OF TREES AND THE MASTER

Into the woods my Master went,
Clean forspent, forspent.
Into the woods my Master came,
Forspent with love and shame.
But the olives they were not blind to Him;
The little gray leaves were kind to Him;
The thorn-tree had a mind to Him
When into the woods He came.

Out of the woods my Master went,
And He was well content.
Out of the woods my Master came,
Content with death and shame.
When Death and Shame would woo Him last,
From under the trees they drew Him last:
'Twas on a tree they slew Him—last
When out of the woods He came.

SIDNEY LANIER

CHARTLESS

I never saw a moor,
I never saw the sea;
Yet know I how the heather looks,
And what a wave must be.
I never spoke with God,
Nor visited in heaven;
Yet certain am I of the spot
As if the chart were given.

EMILY DICKINSON

THE LORD'S PRAYER

Our Father which art in heaven, Hallowed be thy name.
Thy kingdom come. Thy will be done in earth, as it is in heaven.
Give us this day our daily bread.

And forgive us our debts, as we forgive our debtors.

And lead us not into temptation, but deliver us from evil: For thine is the kingdom, and the power, and the glory, for ever. Amen.

ST. MATTHEW 6:9–13

THE LORD IS MY SHEPHERD

The LORD is my shepherd; I shall not want.

He maketh me to lie down in green pastures: he leadeth me beside the still waters.

He restoreth my soul: he leadeth me in the paths of righteousness for his name's sake.

Yea, though I walk through the valley of the shadow of death, I will fear no evil: for thou art with me; thy rod and thy staff they comfort me.

Thou preparest a table before me in the presence of mine enemies: thou anointest my head with oil; my cup runneth over.

Surely goodness and mercy shall follow me all the days of my life: and I will dwell in the house of the LORD forever.

PSALM 23

PRAYER OF ST. FRANCIS OF ASSISI FOR PEACE

Lord, make me an instrument of Your peace.
Where there is hatred, let me sow love;
where there is injury, pardon; where there
is doubt, faith; where there is despair, hope;
where there is darkness, light; and where there is sadness, joy.
O Divine Master, grant that I may not so much seek to be
consoled as to console; to be understood as to understand;
to be loved as to love; for it is in giving that we receive;
it is in pardoning that we are pardoned; and it is in dying
that we are born to eternal life.

ST. FRANCIS OF ASSISI

XI. Nature's People

A NARROW FELLOW IN THE GRASS

A narrow fellow in the grass
Occasionally rides;
You may have met him,—did you not?
His notice sudden is.

The grass divides as with a comb,
A spotted shaft is seen;
And then it closes at your feet
And opens further on.

He likes a boggy acre,
A floor too cool for corn.
Yet when a child, and barefoot,
I more than once, at morn,

Have passed, I thought, a whip-lash
Unbraiding in the sun,—
When, stooping to secure it,
It wrinkled, and was gone.

Several of nature's people
I know, and they know me;
I feel for them a transport
Of cordiality;

But never met this fellow,
Attended or alone,
Without a tighter breathing,
And zero at the bone.

EMILY DICKINSON

A BIRD CAME DOWN THE WALK

A bird came down the walk:
He did not know I saw;
He bit an angle-worm in halves
And ate the fellow, raw.

And then he drank a dew
From a convenient grass,
And then hopped sidewise to the wall
To let a beetle pass.

He glanced with rapid eyes
That hurried all abroad,—
They looked like frightened beads, I thought
He stirred his velvet head

Like one in danger; cautious,
I offered him a crumb,
And he unrolled his feathers
And rowed him softer home

Than oars divide the ocean,
Too silver for a seam,
Or butterflies, off banks of noon,
Leap, plashless, as they swim.

EMILY DICKINSON

ON THE DEATH OF A FAVORITE CAT, DROWNED IN A TUB OF GOLD FISHES

'Twas on a lofty vase's side,
Where China's gayest art had dyed
  The azure flowers that blow;
Demurest of the tabby kind,
The pensive Selima, reclined,
  Gazed on the lake below.

Her conscious tail her joy declared;
The fair round face, the snowy beard,
   The velvet of her paws,
Her coat, that with the tortoise vies,
Her ears of jet, and emerald eyes,
   She saw; and purred applause.

Still had she gazed, but 'midst the tide
Two angel forms were seen to glide,
   The Genii of the stream:
Their scaly armor's Tyrian hue
Through richest purple to the view
   Betrayed a golden gleam.

The hapless Nymph with wonder saw:
A whisker first and then a claw,
   With many an ardent wish,
She stretched, in vain, to reach the prize.
What female heart can gold despise?
   What Cat's averse to fish?

Presumptuous Maid! with looks intent
Again she stretched, again she bent,
   Nor knew the gulf between.
(Malignant Fate sat by, and smiled.)
The slippery verge her feet beguiled,
   She tumbled headlong in.

Eight times emerging from the flood
She mewed to every watery god,
   Some speedy aid to send.
No Dolphin came, no Nereid stirred:
Nor cruel Tom nor Susan heard,—
   A Favorite has no friend!

From hence, ye Beauties, undeceived,
Know, one false step is ne'er retrieved,
   And be with caution bold.
Not all that tempts your wandering eyes
And heedless hearts, is lawful prize;
   Nor all that glisters, gold.

                THOMAS GRAY

A CAT'S CONSCIENCE

A dog will often steal a bone,
But conscience lets him not alone,
And by his tail his guilt is known.

But cats consider theft a game,
And, howsoever you may blame,
Refuse the slightest sign of shame.

When food mysteriously goes,
The chances are that Pussy knows
More than she leads you to suppose.

And hence there is no need for you,
If Puss declines a meal or two,
To feel her pulse and make ado!

UNKNOWN

EPITAPH FOR A CAT

If in some far-off, future day,
A stranger's feet should pass this way,
And if his gaze should seek the ground,
Wondering what lies beneath the mound:
Know that a cat of humble birth
Claims this small portion of the earth.
But I thought not of pedigree,
When, like a child, he came to me,—
A lonely waif, whose piteous cries
Were mirrored in his frightened eyes.
And so I beg that you will not
Defame or desecrate this spot
By ruthless act or idle jeer,
Though but a cat lies buried here.

MARGARET E. BRUNER

TO THE CUCKOO

O blithe New-comer! I have heard,
  I hear thee and rejoice.
O Cuckoo! shall I call thee Bird,
  Or but a wandering Voice?

While I am lying on the grass
  Thy twofold shout I hear;
From hill to hill it seems to pass,
  At once far off, and near.

Though babbling only to the Vale
  Of sunshine and of flowers,
Thou bringest unto me a tale
  Of visionary hours.

Thrice welcome, darling of the Spring!
  Even yet thou art to me
No bird, but an invisible thing,
  A voice, a mystery;

The same whom in my school-boy days
  I listened to; that Cry
Which made me look a thousand ways,
  In bush, and tree, and sky.

To seek thee did I often rove
  Through woods and on the green;
And thou wert still a hope, a love;
  Still longed for, never seen

And I can listen to thee yet;
  Can lie upon the plain
And listen, till I do beget
  That golden time again.

O blessed Bird! the earth we pace
  Again appears to be
An unsubstantial, faery place;
  That is fit home for Thee!

               WILLIAM WORDSWORTH

THE CRICKET

Little inmate, full of mirth,
Chirping on my kitchen hearth,
Wheresoe'er be thine abode
Always harbinger of good,
Pay me for thy warm retreat
With a song more soft and sweet;
In return thou shalt receive
Such a strain as I can give.

Thus thy praise shall be expressed,
Inoffensive, welcome guest!
While the rat is on the scout,
And the mouse with curious snout,
With what vermin else infest
Every dish, and spoil the best;
Frisking thus before the fire,
Thou hast all thy heart's desire.

Though in voice and shape they be
Formed as if akin to thee,
Thou surpassest, happier far,
Happiest grasshoppers that are;
Theirs is but a summer's song,
Thine endures the winter long,
Unimpaired, and shrill, and clear,
Melody throughout the year.

Neither night nor dawn of day
Puts a period to thy play:
Sing then—and extend thy span
Far beyond the date of man;
Wretched man, whose years are spent
In repining discontent,
Lives not, aged though he be,
Half a span, compared with thee.

From the Latin of Vincent Bourne, by WILLIAM COWPER

THE HOUSEKEEPER

The frugal snail, with forecast of repose,
Carries his house with him where'er he goes;
Peeps out,—and if there comes a shower of rain,
Retreats to his small domicile amain.
Touch but a tip of him, a horn,—'tis well,—
He curls up in his sanctuary shell.
He's his own landlord, his own tenant; stay
Long as he will, he dreads no Quarter Day.
Himself he boards and lodges; both invites
And feasts himself; sleeps with himself o' nights.
He spares the upholsterer trouble to procure
Chattels; himself is his own furniture,
And his sole riches. Whereso'er he roam,—
Knock when you will,—he's sure to be at home.
From the Latin of Vincent Bourne, by CHARLES LAMB

TO A WATERFOWL

Whither, midst falling dew,
While glow the heavens with the last steps of day,
Far, through their rosy depth, dost thou pursue
Thy solitary way?

Vainly the fowler's eye
Might mark thy distant flight to do thee wrong,
As, darkly painted on the crimson sky,
Thy figure floats along.

Seek'st thou the plashy brink
Of weedy lake, or marge of river wide,
Or where the rocking billows rise and sink
On the chafed ocean-side?

There is a Power whose care
Teaches thy way along that pathless coast,—
The desert and illimitable air,—
Lone wandering, but not lost.

All day thy wings have fanned
At that far height, the cold, thin atmosphere,
Yet stoop not, weary, to the welcome land,
  Though the dark night is near.

And soon that toil shall end;
Soon shalt thou find a summer home, and rest,
And scream among thy fellows; reeds shall bend.
  Soon, o'er thy sheltered nest.

Thou'rt gone, the abyss of heaven
Hath swallowed up thy form; yet, on my heart
Deeply hath sunk the lesson thou hast given,
  And shall not soon depart.

He who, from zone to zone,
Guides through the boundless sky thy certain flight,
In the long way that I must tread alone,
  Will lead my steps aright.

                                WILLIAM CULLEN BRYANT

TO A SKYLARK

Hail to thee, blithe spirit!
  Bird thou never wert,
That from heaven, or near it,
  Pourest thy full heart
In profuse strains of unpremeditated art.

Higher still and higher,
  From the earth thou springest
Like a cloud of fire;
  The blue deep thou wingest,
And singing still dost soar, and soaring ever singest.

In the golden lightning
  Of the sunken sun,
O'er which clouds are bright'ning,
  Thou dost float and run;
Like an unbodied joy whose race is just begun.

The pale purple even
  Melts around thy flight;
Like a star of heaven
  In the broad daylight
Thou art unseen, but yet I hear thy shrill delight.

Keen as are the arrows
  Of that silver sphere,
Whose intense lamp narrows
  In the white dawn clear,
Until we hardly see, we feel that it is there.

All the earth and air
  With thy voice is loud,
As, when night is bare,
  From one lonely cloud
The moon rains out her beams, and heaven is overflowed.

What thou art we know not;
  What is most like thee?
From rainbow clouds there flow not
  Drops so bright to see
As from thy presence showers a rain of melody.

Like a poet hidden
  In the light of thought,
Singing hymns unbidden
  Till the world is wrought
To sympathy with hopes and fears it heeded not:

Like a high-born maiden
  In a palace tower,
Soothing her love-laden
  Soul in secret hour
With music sweet as love, which overflows her bower:

Like a glow-worm golden
  In a dell of dew,
Scattering unbeholden
  Its aerial hue
Among the flowers and grass, which screen it from the view:

Like a rose embowered
    In its own green leaves,
By warm winds deflowered,
    Till the scent it gives
Makes faint with too much sweet these heavy winged thieves:

Sound of vernal showers
    On the twinkling grass,
Rain-awakened flowers,
    All that ever was
Joyous, and clear, and fresh, thy music doth surpass.

Teach us, sprite or bird,
    What sweet thoughts are thine:
I have never heard
    Praise of love or wine
That panted forth a flood of rapture so divine.

Chorus hymeneal,
    Or triumphal chaunt,
Matched with thine would be all
    But an empty vaunt—
A thing wherein we feel there is some hidden want.

What objects are the fountains
    Of thy happy strain?
What fields, or waves, or mountains?
    What shapes of sky or plain?
What love of thine own kind? what ignorance of pain?

With thy clear keen joyance
    Languor cannot be:
Shadow of annoyance
    Never came near thee:
Thou lovest; but ne'er knew love's sad satiety.

Waking or asleep,
    Thou of death must deem
Things more true and deep
    Than we mortals dream,
Or how could thy notes flow in such a crystal stream?

We look before and after,
　　And pine for what is not:
Our sincerest laughter
　　With some pain is fraught;
Our sweetest songs are those that tell of saddest thought.

Yet if we could scorn
　　Hate, and pride, and fear;
If we were things born
　　Not to shed a tear,
I know not how thy joy we ever should come near.

Better than all measures
　　Of delightful sound,
Better than all treasures
　　That in books are found,
Thy skill to poet were, thou scorner of the ground!

Teach me half the gladness
　　That thy brain must know,
Such harmonious madness
　　From my lips would flow,
The world should listen then, as I am listening now.

PERCY BYSSHE SHELLEY

STRAY DOG

Your wistful eyes searched each one as he passed.
　　Stray dog—so lost, so starved and starkly thin,
And yet your gallant hope held to the last
　　That there would come a heart to take you in.

Some came who jeered at your bewilderment,
　　Some kicked you, shouted, threw things till you'd gone,
But, oh, more cruel was the one who bent
　　And petted you, and murmured—and went on.

CHARLOTTE MISH

THE LITTLE DOG UNDER THE WAGON

"Come, wife," said good old Farmer Gray;
"Put on your things, 'tis market day,
And we'll be off to the nearest town,
There and back ere the sun goes down.
Spot? No, we'll leave old Spot behind."
But Spot he barked, and Spot he whined,
And soon made up his doggish mind
    To follow under the wagon.

Away they went at a good round pace,
And joy came into the farmer's face.
"Poor Spot," said he, "did want to come,
But I'm awful glad he's left at home;
He'll guard the barn and guard the cot,
And keep the cattle out of the lot."
"I'm not so sure of that," thought Spot,
    The little dog under the wagon.

The farmer all his produce sold,
And got his pay in yellow gold.
Then started homeward after dark,
Home through the lonely forest. Hark!
A robber springs from behind a tree,
"Your money or else your life," says he.
The moon was up, but he didn't see
    The little dog under the wagon.

Spot ne'er barked and Spot ne'er whined,
But quickly caught the thief behind.
He dragged him down in the mire and dirt,
He tore his coat and tore his shirt,
Then held him fast on the miry ground.
The robber uttered not a sound
While his hands and feet the farmer bound
    And tumbled him into the wagon.

So Spot he saved the farmer's life,
The farmer's money, the farmer's wife,

And now a hero grand and gay
A silver collar he wears today.
Among his friends, among his foes,
And everywhere his master goes
He follows on his horny toes,
    The little dog under the wagon.

UNKNOWN

A LITTLE DOG-ANGEL

High up in the courts of heaven today
    A little dog-angel waits,
With the other angels he will not play,
    But he sits alone at the gates;
"For I know that my master will come," says he:
"And when he comes, he will call for me."

He sees the spirits that pass him by
    As they hasten toward the Throne,
And he watches them with a wistful eye
    As he sits at the gates alone;
"But I know if I just wait patiently
That some day my master will come," says he.

And his master far on the earth below,
    As he sits in his easy chair,
Forgets sometimes, and he whistles low
    For the dog that is not there;
And the little dog-angel cocks his ears,
And dreams that his master's call he hears.

And I know, when at length his master waits
    Outside in the dark and cold
For the hand of Death to open the gates
    That lead to those courts of gold,
The little dog-angel's eager bark
Will comfort his soul in the shivering dark.

NORAH M. HOLLAND

THE LITTLE BLACK DOG

I wonder if Christ had a little black dog,
    All curly and wooly like mine,
With two silk ears and a nose round and wet,
    And two eyes brown and tender that shine;
I'm sure if He had, that little black dog
    Knew right from the first He was God,
That he needed no proofs that Christ was divine,
    But just worshiped the ground He trod.
I'm afraid that He hadn't, because I have read
    How He prayed in the Garden alone,
When all of His friends and disciples had fled,
    Even Peter, that one called a stone.
And Oh, I am sure that little black dog
    With a true heart so tender and warm
Would never have left Him to suffer alone,
    But creeping right under His arm,
Would have licked those dear fingers in agony clasped,
    And counting all favors but loss,
When they led Him away, would have trotted behind
    And followed Him quite to the cross.

                   ELIZABETH GARDNER REYNOLDS

TO MY DOG "BLANCO"

My dear, dumb friend, low lying there,
A willing vassal at my feet,
Glad partner of my home and fare,
My shadow in the street,

I look into your great brown eyes,
Where love and loyal homage shine,
And wonder where the difference lies
Between your soul and mine!

For all of good that I have found
Within myself or human kind,

Hath royally informed and crowned
Your gentle heart and mind.

I scan the whole broad earth around
For that one heart which, leal and true,
Bears friendship without end or bound,
And find the prize in you.

I trust you as I trust the stars;
Nor cruel loss, nor scoff of pride,
Nor beggary, nor dungeon bars,
Can move you from my side!

As patient under injury
As any Christian saint of old,
As gentle as a lamb with me,
But with your brothers bold.

More playful than a frolic boy,
More watchful than a sentinel,
By day and night your constant joy
To guard and please me well,

I clasp your head upon my breast—
The while you whine and lick my hand—
And thus our friendship is confessed,
And thus we understand!

Ah, Blanco! did I worship God
As truly as you worship me,
Or follow where my Master trod
With your humility,

Did I sit fondly at His feet,
As you, dear Blanco, sit at mine,
And watch Him with a love as sweet,
My life would grow divine!

JOSIAH GILBERT HOLLAND

REST IN PEACE

Father, in Thy starry tent
I kneel, a humble suppliant . . .
A dog has died today on earth,
Of little worth
Yet very dear.
Gather him in Thine arms
If only
For a while.
I fear
He will be lonely . . .
Shield him with Thy smile.

DR. WILFRED J. FUNK

TO SCOTT

(A COLLIE, FOR NINE YEARS OUR FRIEND)

Old friend, your place is empty now. No more
Shall we obey the imperious deep-mouthed call
That begged the instant freedom of our hall.
We shall not trace your foot-fall on the floor
Nor hear your urgent paws upon the door.
The loud-thumped tail that welcomed one and all,
The volleyed bark that nightly would appal
Our tim'rous errand boys—these things are o'er.

But always yours shall be a household name,
And other dogs must list' your storied fame;
So gallant and so courteous, Scott, you were,
Mighty abroad, at home most debonair.
Now God who made you will not count it blame
That we commend your spirit to His care.

WINIFRED LETTS

THE COW IN APPLE TIME

Something inspires the only cow of late
To make no more of a wall than an open gate,
And think no more of wall-builders than fools.
Her face is flecked with pomace and she drools
A cider syrup. Having tasted fruit,
She scorns a pasture withering to the root.
She runs from tree to tree where lie and sweeten
The windfalls spiked with stubble and worm-eaten.
She leaves them bitten when she has to fly.
She bellows on a knoll against the sky.
Her udder shrivels and the milk goes dry.

ROBERT FROST

SAY THIS OF HORSES

Across the ages they come thundering
    On faithful hoofs, the horses man disowns.
Their velvet eyes are wide with wondering;
    They whinny down the wind in silver tones
Vibrant with all the bugles of old wars;
    Their nostrils quiver with the summer scent
Of grasses in deep fields lit by pale stars
    Hung in a wide and silent firmament,
And in their hearts they keep the dreams of earth
    Their patient plodding furrowed to the sun
Unnumbered springs before the engine's birth
    Doomed them to sadness and oblivion.
Across the swift new day I watch them go,
    Driven by wheel and gear and dynamo.

Say this of horses: engines leave behind
    No glorious legacy of waving manes
And wild, proud hearts, and heels before the wind,
    No heritage of ancient Arab strains
Blazes within a cylinder's cold spark;
    An engine labors with a sullen force,
Hoarding no dreams of acres sweet and dark:

No love for man has ever surged through wire
Along the farthest slopes I hear the rumble
Of these last hoofs—tomorrow they will be still;
Then shall the strength of countless horses crumble
The staunchest rock and level the highest hill;
A man who made machines to gain an hour
Shall lose himself before their ruthless power.

MINNIE HITE MOODY

THE TIGER

Tiger! Tiger! burning bright,
In the forests of the night,
What immortal hand or eye
Could frame thy fearful symmetry?

In what distant deeps or skies
Burnt the fire of thine eyes?
On what wings dare he aspire?
What the hand dare seize the fire?

And what shoulder, and what art,
Could twist the sinews of thy heart?
And when thy heart began to beat,
What dread hand and what dread feet?

What the hammer? what the chain?
In what furnace was thy brain?
What the anvil? what dread grasp
Dare its deadly terrors clasp?

When the stars threw down their spears,
And watered heaven with their tears,
Did He smile His work to see?
Did He who made the Lamb, make thee?

Tiger! Tiger! burning bright,
In the forests of the night,
What immortal hand or eye
Dare frame thy fearful symmetry?

WILLIAM BLAKE

TO A MOUSE

ON TURNING UP HER NEST WITH THE PLOW, NOVEMBER 1785

Wee, sleekit, cow'rin', tim'rous beastie,
O, what a panic's in thy breastie!
Thou need na start awa' sae hasty,
    Wi' bickering brattle!
I wad be laith to rin an' chase thee,
    Wi' murd'ring pattle!

I'm truly sorry man's dominion
Has broken Nature's social union,
An' justifies that ill opinion,
    Which makes thee startle
At me, thy poor, earth-born companion,
    An' fellow-mortal!

I doubt na, whiles, but thou may thieve;
What then? poor beastie, thou maun live!
A daimen icker in a thrave
    'S a sma' request;
I'll get a blessin' wi' the laive,
    And never miss't!

Thy wee bit housie, too, in ruin!
Its silly wa's the win's are strewin'!
An' naething, now, to big a new ane,
    O' foggage green!
An' bleak December's winds ensuin',
    Baith snell an' keen!

Thou saw the fields laid bare an' waste,
An' weary winter comin' fast,
An' cozie here, beneath the blast,
    Thou thought to dwell,—
Till, crash! the cruel coulter passed
    Out through thy cell.

That wee bit heap o' leaves an' stibble
Has cost thee mony a weary nibble!
Now thou's turned out, for a' thy trouble,
        But house or hald,
To thole the winter's sleety dribble,
        An' cranreuch cauld!

But, Mousie, thou art no thy lane,
In proving foresight may be vain:
The best-laid schemes o' mice an' men,
        Gang aft a-gley,
An' lea'e us naught but grief an' pain,
        For promised joy!

Still thou art blest, compared wi' me!
The present only toucheth thee:
But, och! I backward cast my e'e
        On prospects drear!
An' forward, though I canna see,
        I guess an' fear!

                              ROBERT BURNS

XII. The Seasons

LOVELIEST OF TREES

Loveliest of trees, the cherry now
Is hung with bloom along the bough,
And stands about the woodland ride
Wearing white for Eastertide.

Now, of my threescore years and ten,
Twenty will not come again,
And take from seventy springs a score,
It only leaves me fifty more.

And since to look at things in bloom
Fifty springs are little room,
About the woodlands I will go
To see the cherry hung with snow.

A. E. HOUSMAN

A SPRING SONG

Old Mother Earth woke up from her sleep,
    And found she was cold and bare;
The winter was over, the spring was near,
    And she had not a dress to wear.
"Alas!" she sighed, with great dismay,
    "Oh, where shall I get my clothes?
There's not a place to buy a suit,
    And a dressmaker no one knows."

"I'll make you a dress," said the springing grass,
    Just looking above the ground,
"A dress of green of the loveliest sheen,
    To cover you all around."
"And we," said the dandelions gay,
    "Will dot it with yellow bright."
"I'll make it a fringe," said forget-me-not,
    "Of blue, very soft and light."

"We'll embroider the front," said the violets,
  "With a lovely purple hue!"
"And we," said the roses, "will make you a crown
  Of red, jeweled over the dew."
"And we'll be your gems," said a voice from the shade,
  Where the ladies' eardrops live—
"Orange is the color for any queen
  And the best we have to give."

Old Mother Earth was thankful and glad,
  As she put on her dress so gay;
And that is the reason, my little ones,
  She is looking so lovely today.

                                     UNKNOWN

LINES WRITTEN IN EARLY SPRING

I heard a thousand blended notes,
While in a grove I sat reclined,
In that sweet mood when pleasant thoughts
Bring sad thoughts to the mind.

To her fair works did Nature link
The human soul that through me ran;
And much it grieved my heart to think
What Man has made of Man.

Through primrose tufts, in that sweet bower,
The periwinkle trailed its wreaths;
And 'tis my faith that every flower
Enjoys the air it breathes.

The birds around me hopped and played,
Their thoughts I cannot measure,—
But the least motion which they made
It seemed a thrill of pleasure.

The budding twigs spread out their fan
To catch the breezy air;
And I must think, do all I can,
That there was pleasure there.

If this belief from heaven be sent,
If such be Nature's holy plan,
Have I not reason to lament
What Man has made of Man?

WILLIAM WORDSWORTH

TO SPRING

O Thou with dewy locks, who lookest down
Through the clear windows of the morning, turn
Thine angel eyes upon our western isle,
Which in full choir hails thy approach, O Spring!

The hills tell one another, and the listening
Valleys hear; all our longing eyes are turned
Up to thy bright pavilions: issue forth
And let thy holy feet visit our clime!

Come o'er the eastern hills, and let our winds
Kiss thy perfumed garments; let us taste
Thy morn and evening breath; scatter thy pearls
Upon our lovesick land that mourns for thee.

O deck her forth with thy fair fingers; pour
Thy soft kisses on her bosom; and put
Thy golden crown upon her languished head,
Whose modest tresses are bound up for thee!

WILLIAM BLAKE

THE YELLOW VIOLET

When beechen buds begin to swell,
    And woods the blue-bird's warble know,
The yellow violet's modest bell
    Peeps from the last year's leaves below.

Ere russet fields their green resume,
    Sweet flower, I love, in forest bare,
To meet thee, when thy faint perfume
    Alone is in the virgin air.

Of all her train, the hands of Spring
  First plant thee in the watery mould,
And I have seen thee blossoming
  Beside the snow-bank's edges cold.

Thy parent sun, who bade thee view
  Pale skies, and chilling moisture sip,
Has bathed thee in his own bright hue,
  And streaked with jet thy glowing lip.

Yet slight thy form, and low thy seat,
  And earthward bent thy gentle eye,
Unapt the passing view to meet
  When loftier flowers are flaunting nigh.

Oft, in the sunless April day,
  Thy early smile has stayed my walk;
But midst the gorgeous blooms of May,
  I passed thee on thy humble stalk.

So they, who climb to wealth, forget
  The friends in darker fortunes tried.
I copied them—but I regret
  That I should ape the ways of pride.

And when again the genial hour
  Awakes the painted tribes of light,
I'll not o'erlook the modest flower
  That made the woods of April bright.

                        WILLIAM CULLEN BRYANT

TO A MOUNTAIN DAISY

ON TURNING ONE DOWN WITH THE PLOUGH, IN APRIL 1786

Wee, modest, crimson-tipped flower,
Thou's met me in an evil hour;
For I maun crush amang the stoure
    Thy slender stem:
To spare thee now is past my power,
    Thou bonny gem.

Alas! it's no thy neibor sweet,
The bonny lark, companion meet,
Bending thee 'mang the dewy weet,
    Wi' speckled breast,
When upward-springing, blithe, to greet
    The purpling east!

Cauld blew the bitter-biting north
Upon thy early, humble birth;
Yet cheerfully thou glinted forth
    Amid the storm,
Scarce reared above the parent earth
    Thy tender form.

The flaunting flowers our gardens yield
High sheltering woods and wa's maun shield;
But thou, beneath the random bield
    O' clod, or stane,
Adorns the histie stibble-field,
    Unseen, alane.

There, in thy scanty mantle clad,
Thy snawie bosom sunward spread,
Thou lifts thy unassuming head
    In humble guise;
But now the share uptears thy bed,
    And low thou lies!

Such is the fate of artless maid,
Sweet floweret of the rural shade!
By love's simplicity betrayed,
    And guileless trust,
Till she, like thee, all soiled, is laid
    Low i' the dust.

Such is the fate of simple bard,
On life's rough ocean luckless starred!
Unskillful he to note the card
    Of prudent lore,
Till billows rage, and gales blow hard,
    And whelm him o'er!

Such fate to suffering worth is given,
Who long with wants and woes has striven,
By human pride or cunning driven
    To misery's brink,
Till, wrenched of every stay but Heaven,
    He, ruined, sink!

Even thou who mourn'st the Daisy's fate,
That fate is thine—no distant date;
Stern Ruin's ploughshare drives, elate,
    Full on thy bloom,
Till crushed beneath the furrow's weight
    Shall be thy doom.

ROBERT BURNS

HOME THOUGHTS, FROM ABROAD

Oh, to be in England
Now that April's there,
And whoever wakes in England
Sees, some morning, unaware,
That the lowest boughs and the brushwood sheaf
Round the elm-tree bole are in tiny leaf,
While the chaffinch sings on the orchard bough
In England—now!

And after April, when May follows
And the white-throat builds, and all the swallows!
Hark, where my blossomed pear-tree in the hedge
Leans to the field and scatters on the clover
Blossoms and dewdrops—at the bent spray's edge—
That's the wise thrush: he sings each song twice over,

Lest you should think he never could recapture
The first fine careless rapture!
And though the fields look rough with hoary dew,
All will be gay when noontide wakes anew
The buttercups, the little children's dower
—Far brighter than this gaudy melon-flower!

ROBERT BROWNING

A WHITE IRIS

Tall and clothed in samite,
Chaste and pure,
In smooth armor—
Your head held high
In its helmet
Of silver:
Jeanne d'Arc riding
Among the sword blades!

Has Spring for you
Wrought visions,
As it did for her
In a garden?

PAULINE B. BARRINGTON

THE LAWYER'S INVOCATION TO SPRING

Whereas, on certain boughs and sprays
  Now divers birds are heard to sing,
And sundry flowers their heads upraise,
  Hail to the coming on of Spring!

The songs of those said birds arouse
  The memory of our youthful hours,
As green as those said sprays and boughs,
  As fresh and sweet as those said flowers.

The birds aforesaid—happy pairs—
  Love, 'mid the aforesaid boughs, inshrines
In freehold nests; themselves their heirs,
  Administrators, and assigns.

O busiest term of Cupid's Court,
  Where tender plaintiffs actions bring,—
Season of frolic and of sport,
  Hail, as aforesaid, coming Spring!

HENRY HOWARD BROWNELL

MEMORY

My mind lets go a thousand things,
Like dates of wars and deaths of kings,
And yet recalls the very hour—
'Twas noon by yonder village tower,
And on the last blue moon in May—
The wind came briskly up this way,
Crisping the brook beside the road;
Then, pausing here, set down its load
Of pine-scents, and shook listlessly
Two petals from that wild-rose tree.

THOMAS BAILEY ALDRICH

JUNE

(from the Prelude to *The Vision of Sir Launfal*)

Over his keys the musing organist,
  Beginning doubtfully and far away,
First lets his fingers wander as they list,
  And builds a bridge from Dreamland for his lay:
Then, as the touch of his loved instrument
  Gives hope and fervor, nearer draws his theme,
First guessed by faint auroral flushes sent
  Along the wavering vista of his dream.

  Not only around our infancy
  Doth heaven with all its splendors lie;
  Daily, with souls that cringe and plot,
  We Sinais climb and know it not.

Over our manhood bend the skies;
  Against our fallen and traitor lives
The great winds utter prophecies;
  With our faint hearts the mountain strives;
Its arms outstretched, the druid wood
  Waits with its benedicite;
And to our age's drowsy blood
  Still shouts the inspiring sea.

Earth gets its price for what Earth gives us;
   The beggar is taxed for a corner to die in,
The priest hath his fee who comes and shrives us,
   We bargain for the graves we live in;
At the devil's booth are all things sold,
Each ounce of dross costs its ounce of gold;
   For a cap and bells our lives we pay,
Bubbles we buy with a whole soul's tasking:
   'Tis heaven alone that is given away,
'Tis only God may be had for the asking;
No price is set on the lavish summer;
June may be had by the poorest comer.

And what is so rare as a day in June?
   Then, if ever, come perfect days;
Then Heaven tries earth if it be in tune,
   And over it softly her warm ear lays;
Whether we look, or whether we listen,
We hear life murmur, or see it glisten;
Every clod feels a stir of might,
   An instinct within it that reaches and towers,
And, groping blindly above it for light,
   Climbs to a soul in grass and flowers;
The flush of life may well be seen
   Thrilling back over hills and valleys;
The cowslip startles in meadows green,
   The buttercup catches the sun in its chalice,
And there's never a leaf nor a blade too mean
   To be some happy creature's palace;
The little bird sits at his door in the sun,
   Atilt like a blossom among the leaves,
And lets his illumined being o'errun
   With the deluge of summer it receives;
His mate feels the eggs beneath her wings,
And the heart in her dumb breast flutters and sings;
He sings to the wide world and she to her nest,—
In the nice ear of Nature which song is the best?

Now is the high-tide of the year,
   And whatever of life hath ebbed away
Comes flooding back with a ripply cheer,
   Into every bare inlet and creek and bay;

Now the heart is so full that a drop overfills it,
We are happy now because God wills it;
No matter how barren the past may have been,
'Tis enough for us now that the leaves are green;
We sit in the warm shade and feel right well
How the sap creeps up and the blossoms swell;
We may shut our eyes, but we cannot help knowing
That skies are clear and grass is growing;
The breeze comes whispering in our ear,
That dandelions are blossoming near,
That maize has sprouted, that streams are flowing,
That the river is bluer than the sky,
That the robin is plastering his house hard by;
And if the breeze kept the good news back,
For other couriers we should not lack;
    We could guess it all by yon heifer's lowing,
And hark! how clear bold chanticleer,
Warmed with the new wine of the year,
    Tells all in his lusty crowing!

                        JAMES RUSSELL LOWELL

MY GARDEN

    A garden is a lovesome thing, God wot!
        Rose plot,
          Fringed pool,
        Ferned grot—
          The veriest school
          Of peace; and yet the fool
    Contends that God is not—
    Not God! in gardens! when the eve is cool?
          Nay, but I have a sign:
          'Tis very sure God walks in mine.

                 THOMAS EDWARD BROWN

A CHARLESTON GARDEN

    I love old gardens best—
    tired old gardens
    that rest in the sun.

There the rusty tamarisk
and knotted fig trees
lean on the wall,
and paper-whites break rank
to wander carelessly
among tall grasses.
The yellow roses
slip from the trellis,
and the wistaria goes adventuring
to the neighboring trees.

The forgotten comfort
of the wilderness comes again.
The legend of the twisted walks
is broken,
and the marble seats are green
like woodland banks.

HENRY BELLAMANN

THE GARDEN

How vainly men themselves amaze
To win the palm, the oak, or bays,
And their uncessant labor see
Crowned from some single herb or tree,
Whose short and narrow verged shade
Does prudently their toils upbraid;
While all flowers and all trees do close
To weave the garlands of repose.

Fair quiet, have I found thee here,
And innocence, thy sister dear!
Mistaken long, I sought you then
In busy companies of men;
Your sacred plants, if here below,
Only among the plants will grow.
Society is all but rude,
To this delicious solitude.

No white nor red was ever seen
So am'rous as this lovely green.
Fond lovers, cruel as their flame,

Cut in these trees their mistress' name;
Little, alas, they know or heed
How far these beauties hers exceed!
Fair trees! wheres' e'er your barks I wound,
No name shall but your own be found.

When we have run our passion's heat,
Love hither makes his best retreat.
The gods that mortal beauty chase,
Still in a tree did end their race:
Apollo hunted Daphne so,
Only that she might laurel grow;
And Pan did after Syrinx speed,
Not as a nymph, but for a reed.

What wond'rous life in this I lead!
Ripe apples drop about my head;
The luscious clusters of the vine
Upon my mouth do crush their wine;
The nectarine and curious peach
Into my hands themselves do reach;
Stumbling on melons as I pass,
Ensnared with flowers, I fall on grass.

Meanwhile the mind from pleasure less
Withdraws into its happiness;
The mind, that ocean where each kind
Does straight its own resemblance find,
Yet it creates, transcending these,
Far other worlds and other seas,
Annihilating all that's made
To a green thought in a green shade.

Here at the fountain's sliding foot,
Or at some fruit tree's mossy root,
Casting the body's vest aside,
My soul into the boughs does glide;
There like a bird it sits and sings,
Then whets, then combs its silver wings;
And till prepared for longer flight,
Waves in its plumes the various light.

Such was that happy garden-state
While man there walked without a mate;
After a place so pure and sweet,
What other help could yet be meet!
But 'twas beyond a mortal's share
To wander solitary there;
Two paradises 'twere, in one,
To live in paradise alone.

How well the skillful gard'ner drew
Of flowers and herbs this dial new,
Where, from above, the milder sun
Does through a fragrant zodiac run;
And as it works, th' industrious bee
Computes its time as well as we.
How could such sweet and wholesome hours
Be reckoned but with herbs and flowers?

ANDREW MARVELL

THE WILD HONEYSUCKLE

Fair flower, that dost so comely grow,
  Hid in this silent, dull retreat,
Untouched thy honied blossoms blow,
  Unseen thy little branches greet:
    No roving foot shall crush thee here,
    No busy hand provoke a tear.

By Nature's self in white arrayed,
  She bade thee shun the vulgar eye,
And planted here the guardian shade,
  And sent soft waters murmuring by;
    Thus quietly thy summer goes,
    Thy days declining to repose.

Smit with those charms, that must decay,
  I grieve to see your future doom;
They died—nor were those flowers more gay,
  The flowers that did in Eden bloom;
    Unpitying frosts and Autumn's power
    Shall leave no vestige of this flower.

From morning suns and evening dews
  At first thy little being came;
If nothing once, you nothing lose,
  For when you die you are the same;
    The space between is but an hour,
    The frail duration of a flower.

PHILIP FRENEAU

EXEUNT

Piecemeal the summer dies;
  At the field's edge a daisy lives alone;
  A last shawl of burning lies
    On a gray field-stone.

All cries are thin and terse;
  The field has droned the summer's final mass;
  A cricket like a dwindled hearse
    Crawls from the dry grass.

RICHARD WILBUR

TO AUTUMN

Season of mists and mellow fruitfulness!
Close bosom-friend of the maturing sun;
Conspiring with him how to load and bless
With fruit the vines that round the thatch-eaves run;
To bend with apples the mossed cottage-trees,
And fill all fruit with ripeness to the core;
To swell the gourd, and plump the hazel shells
With a sweet kernel; to set budding more,
And still more, later flowers for the bees,
Until they think warm days will never cease,
For Summer has o'erbrimmed their clammy cells.

Who hath not seen thee oft amid thy store?
Sometimes whoever seeks abroad may find
Thee sitting careless on a granary floor,
Thy hair soft-lifted by the winnowing wind;
Or on a half-reaped furrow sound asleep,

Drowsed with the fume of poppies, while thy hook
Spares the next swath and all its twined flowers;
And sometimes like a gleaner thou dost keep
Steady thy laden head across a brook;
Or by a cider-press, with patient look,
Thou watchest the last oozings, hours by hours.

Where are the songs of Spring? Ay, where are they?
Think not of them, thou hast thy music too,
While barred clouds bloom the soft-dying day
And touch the stubble-plains with rosy hue;
Then in a wailful choir the small gnats mourn
Among the river shallows, borne aloft
Or sinking as the light wind lives or dies;
And full-grown lambs loud bleat from hilly bourn;
Hedge-crickets sing, and now with treble soft
The redbreast whistles from a garden-croft,
And gathering swallows twitter in the skies.

JOHN KEATS

SEPTEMBER

The golden-rod is yellow;
   The corn is turning brown;
The trees in apple orchards
   With fruit are bending down.

The gentian's bluest fringes
   Are curling in the sun;
In dusty pods the milkweed
   Its hidden silk has spun.

The sedges flaunt their harvest,
   In every meadow nook;
And asters by the brook-side
   Make asters in the brook,

From dewy lanes at morning
   The grapes' sweet odors rise;
At noon the roads all flutter
   With yellow butterflies.

By all these lovely tokens
  September days are here,
With summer's best of weather,
  And autumn's best of cheer.

But none of all this beauty
  Which floods the earth and air
Is unto me the secret
  Which makes September fair.

'Tis a thing which I remember;
  To name it thrills me yet:
One day of one September
  I never can forget.

HELEN HUNT JACKSON

OCTOBER'S PARTY

October gave a party;
  The leaves by hundreds came—
The Chestnuts, Oaks, and Maples,
  And leaves of every name.
The Sunshine spread a carpet,
  And everything was grand,
Miss Weather led the dancing,
  Professor Wind the band.

The Chestnuts came in yellow,
  The Oaks in crimson dressed;
The lovely Misses Maple
  In scarlet looked their best;
All balanced to their partners,
  And gaily fluttered by;
The sight was like a rainbow
  New fallen from the sky.

Then, in the rustic hollow,
  At hide-and-seek they played,
The party closed at sundown,
  And everybody stayed.

Professor Wind played louder;
    They flew along the ground;
And then the party ended
    In jolly "hands around."
GEORGE COOPER

WHEN THE FROST IS ON THE PUNKIN

When the frost is on the punkin and the fodder's in the shock,
And you hear the kyouck and gobble of the struttin' turkeycock,
And the clackin' of the guineys, and the cluckin' of the hens,
And the rooster's hallylooer as he tiptoes on the fence;
O, it's then's the times a feller is a-feelin' at his best,
With the risin' sun to greet him from a night of peaceful rest,
As he leaves the house, bareheaded, and goes out to feed the stock,
When the frost is on the punkin and the fodder's in the shock.

They's something kindo' harty-like about the atmusfere
When the heat of summer's over and the coolin' fall is here—
Of course we miss the flowers, and the blossoms on the trees,
And the mumble of the hummin'-birds and buzzin' of the bees;
But the air's so appetizin'; and the landscape through the haze
Of a crisp and sunny morning of the airly autumn days
Is a pictur' that no painter has the colorin' to mock—
When the frost is on the punkin and the fodder's in the shock.

The husky, rusty russel of the tossels of the corn,
And the raspin' of the tangled leaves, as golden as the morn;
The stubble in the furries—kindo' lonesome-like, but still
A-preachin' sermuns to us of the barns they growed to fill;
The strawstack in the medder, and the reaper in the shed;
The hosses in theyr stalls below—the clover overhead!—
O, it sets my hart a-clickin' like the tickin' of a clock,
When the frost is on the punkin and the fodder's in the shock.

Then your apples all is getherd, and the ones a feller keeps
Is poured around the celler-floor in red and yeller heaps;
And your cider-makin's over, and your wimmern-folks is through
With their mince and apple-butter, and theyr souse and saussage,
    too! . . .

I don't know how to tell it—but ef sich a thing could be
As the Angels wantin' boardin', and they'd call around on *me*—
I'd want to 'commodate 'em—all the whole-indurin' flock—
When the frost is on the punkin and the fodder's in the shock.

JAMES WHITCOMB RILEY

MY NOVEMBER GUEST

My Sorrow, when she's here with me,
    Thinks these dark days of autumn rain
Are beautiful as days can be;
She loves the bare, the withered tree;
    She walks the sodden pasture lane.

Her pleasure will not let me stay.
    She talks and I am fain to list:
She's glad the birds are gone away,
She's glad her simple worsted grey
    Is silver now with clinging mist.

The desolate, deserted trees,
    The faded earth, the heavy sky,
The beauties she so truly sees,
She thinks I have no eye for these,
    And vexes me for reason why.

Not yesterday I learned to know
    The love of bare November days
Before the coming of the snow,
But it were vain to tell her so,
    And they are better for her praise.

ROBERT FROST

THE SNOW-STORM

Announced by all the trumpets of the sky,
Arrives the snow, and, driving o'er the fields,
Seems nowhere to alight: the whited air
Hides hills and woods, the river, and the heaven,

And veils the farm-house at the garden's end.
The sled and traveller stopped, the courier's feet
Delayed, all friends shut out, the housemates sit
Around the radiant fireplace, enclosed
In a tumultuous privacy of storm.

Come see the north wind's masonry.
Out of an unseen quarry evermore
Furnished with tile, the fierce artificer
Curves his white bastions with projected roof
Round every windward stake, or tree, or door.
Speeding, the myriad-handed, his wild work
So fanciful, so savage, nought cares he
For number or proportion. Mockingly,
On coop or kennel he hangs Parian wreaths;
A swan-like form invests the hidden thorn;
Fills up the farmer's lane from wall to wall,

Maugre the farmer's sighs; and at the gate
A tapering turret overtops the work.
And when his hours are numbered, and the world
Is all his own, retiring, as he were not,
Leaves, when the sun appears, astonished Art
To mimic in slow structures, stone by stone,
Built in an age, the mad wind's night-work,
The frolic architecture of the snow.

RALPH WALDO EMERSON

I HEARD A BIRD SING

I heard a bird sing
    In the dark of December
A magical thing
    And sweet to remember.

"We are nearer to Spring
    Than we were in September,"
I heard a bird sing
    In the dark of December.

OLIVER HERFORD

ODE TO THE WEST WIND

I

O wild West Wind, thou breath of Autumn's being,
  Thou from whose unseen presence the leaves dead
Are driven, like ghosts from an enchanter fleeing,

  Yellow, and black, and pale, and hectic red,
Pestilence-stricken multitudes! O thou
  Who chariotest to their dark wintry bed

The winged seeds, where they lie cold and low,
  Each like a corpse within its grave, until
Thine azure sister of the Spring shall blow

  Her clarion o'er the dreaming earth, and fill
(Driving sweet buds like flocks to feed in air)
  With living hues and odors plain and hill;

Wild Spirit, which art moving everywhere;
Destroyer and preserver; hear, O hear!

II

Thou on whose stream, 'mid the steep sky's commotion,
  Loose clouds like earth's decaying leaves are shed,
Shook from the tangled boughs of heaven and ocean,

  Angels of rain and lightning! there are spread
On the blue surface of thine airy surge,
  Like the bright hair uplifted from the head

Of some fierce Maenad, even from the dim verge
  Of the horizon to the zenith's height,
The locks of the approaching storm. Thou dirge

Of the dying year, to which this closing night
Will be the dome of a vast sepulchre,
   Vaulted with all thy congregated might

Of vapors, from whose solid atmosphere
Black rain, and fire, and hail will burst: O hear!

III

Thou who didst waken from his summer dreams
   The blue Mediterranean, where he lay,
Lulled by the coil of his crystalline streams,

   Beside a pumice isle in Baiae's bay,
And saw in sleep old palaces and towers
   Quivering within the wave's intenser day,

All overgrown with azure moss, and flowers
   So sweet, the sense faints picturing them! Thou
For whose path the Atlantic's level powers

   Cleave themselves into chasms, while far below
The sea-blooms and the oozy woods which wear
   The sapless foliage of the ocean, know

Thy voice, and suddenly grow gray with fear,
And tremble and despoil themselves: O hear!

IV

If I were a dead leaf thou mightest bear;
   If I were a swift cloud to fly with thee;
A wave to pant beneath thy power, and share

   The impulse of thy strength, only less free
Than thou, O uncontrollable! If even
   I were as in my boyhood, and could be

The comrade of thy wanderings over heaven,
　　As then, when to outstrip thy skiey speed
Scarce seemed a vision—I would ne'er have striven

　　As thus with thee in prayer in my sore need.
O! lift me as a wave, a leaf, a cloud!
　　I fall upon the thorns of life! I bleed!

A heavy weight of hours has chained and bowed
One too like thee—tameless, and swift, and proud.

v

Make me thy lyre, even as the forest is:
　　What if my leaves are falling like its own?
The tumult of thy mighty harmonies

　　Will take from both a deep, autumnal tone,
Sweet though in sadness. Be thou, Spirit fierce,
　　My spirit! Be thou me, impetuous one!

Drive my dead thoughts over the universe,
　　Like withered leaves, to quicken a new birth;
And, by the incantation of this verse,

　　Scatter, as from an unextinguished hearth
Ashes and sparks, my words among mankind!
　　Be through my lips to unawakened earth

The trumpet of a prophecy! O Wind,
If Winter comes, can Spring be far behind?

PERCY BYSSHE SHELLEY

XIII. Dawn and Dusk

PRELUDE

(from *The New Day*)

The night was dark, though sometimes a faint star
A little while a little space made bright.
The night was dark and still the dawn seemed far,
When, o'er the muttering and invisible sea,
Slowly, within the East, there grew a light
Which half was starlight, and half seemed to be
The herald of a greater. The pale white
Turned slowly to pale rose, and up the height
Of heaven slowly climbed. The gray sea grew
Rose-colored like the sky. A white gull flew
Straight toward the utmost boundary of the East
Where slowly the rose gathered and increased.
There was light now, where all was black before:
It was as on the opening of a door
By one who in his hand a lamp doth hold
(Its flame being hidden by the garment's fold),—
The still air moves, the wide room is less dim.

   More bright the East became, the ocean turned
Dark and more dark against the brightening sky—
Sharper against the sky the long sea line.
The hollows of the breakers on the shore
Were green like leaves whereon no sun doth shine,
Though sunlight make the outer branches hoar.
From rose to red the level heaven burned;
Then sudden, as if a sword fell from on high,
A blade of gold flashed on the ocean's rim.

RICHARD WATSON GILDER

COMPOSED UPON WESTMINSTER BRIDGE, SEPTEMBER 3, 1802

Earth has not anything to show more fair:
Dull would he be of soul who could pass by
A sight so touching in its majesty:
This City now doth, like a garment, wear
The beauty of the morning; silent, bare,
Ships, towers, domes, theaters, and temples lie
Open unto the fields, and to the sky;
All bright and glittering in the smokeless air.
Never did sun more beautifully steep
In his first splendor, valley, rock, or hill;
Ne'er saw I, never felt, a calm so deep!
The river glideth at his own sweet will:
Dear God! the very houses seem asleep;
And all that mighty heart is lying still!

WILLIAM WORDSWORTH

DAYBREAK

A wind came up out of the sea,
And said, "O mists, make room for me!"

It hailed the ships, and cried, "Sail on,
Ye mariners, the night is gone!"

And hurried landward far away,
Crying, "Awake! it is the day!"

It said unto the forest, "Shout!
Hang all your leafy banners out!"

It touched the wood-bird's folded wing,
And said, "O bird, awake and sing!"

And o'er the farms, "O chanticleer,
Your clarion blow, the day is near!"

It whispered to the fields of corn,
"Bow down, and hail the coming morn!"

It shouted through the belfry-tower,
"Awake, O bell! proclaim the hour."

It crossed the churchyard with a sigh,
And said, "Not yet! in quiet lie."

HENRY WADSWORTH LONGFELLOW

THE SALUTATION OF THE DAWN

Listen to the Exhortation of the Dawn!
    Look to this Day!
For it is Life, the very Life of Life.
In its brief course lie all the
Verities and Realities of your Existence;
    The Bliss of Growth,
    The Glory of Action,
    The Splendor of Beauty;
For Yesterday is but a Dream,
And Tomorrow is only a Vision;
But Today well lived makes every
Yesterday a Dream of Happiness, and every
Tomorrow a Vision of Hope.
Look well therefore to this Day!
Such is the Salutation of the Dawn.

From the Sanskrit

DAWN

An angel, robed in spotless white,
Bent down and kissed the sleeping Night.
Night woke to blush; the sprite was gone.
Men saw the blush and called it Dawn.

PAUL LAURENCE DUNBAR

REVEILLE

(from A *Shropshire Lad*)

Wake! the silver dusk returning
  Up the beach of darkness brims,
And the ship of sunrise burning
  Strands upon the eastern rims.

Wake! the vaulted shadow shatters,
  Trampled to the door it spanned,
And the tent of night in tatters
  Straws the sky-pavilioned land.

Up, lad, up! 'Tis late for lying.
  Hear the drums of morning play;
Hark, the empty highways crying,
  "Who'll beyond the hills away?"

Towns and countries woo together,
  Forelands beacon, belfries call;
Never lad that trod on leather
  Lived to feast his heart with all.

Up, lad! Thews that lie and cumber
  Sunlit pallets never thrive;
Morns abed and daylight slumber
  Were not meant for man alive.

Clay lies still, but blood's a rover;
  Breath's a ware that will not keep.
Up, lad! When the journey's over
  There'll be time enough to sleep.
                  A. E. HOUSMAN

EARLY RISING

"God bless the man who first invented sleep!"
    So Sancho Panza said, and so say I:
And bless him, also, that he didn't keep
    His great discovery to himself; nor try
To make it—as the lucky fellow might—
A close monopoly by patent-right!

Yes; bless the man who first invented sleep
    (I really can't avoid the iteration);
But blast the man, with curses loud and deep,
    Whate'er the rascal's name, or age, or station,
Who first invented, and went round advising,
That artificial cut-off,—Early Rising!

"Rise with the lark, and with the lark to bed,"
    Observes some solemn, sentimental owl;
Maxims like these are very cheaply said:
    But, ere you make yourself a fool or fowl,
Pray, just inquire about his rise and fall,
And whether larks have any beds at all!

The time for honest folks to be abed
    Is in the morning, if I reason right;
And he who cannot keep his precious head
    Upon his pillow till it's fairly light,
And so enjoy his forty morning winks,
Is up to knavery, or else—he drinks!

Thomson, who sang about the "Seasons," said
    It was a glorious thing to *rise* in season;
But then he said it—lying—in his bed,
    At ten o'clock, A.M.,—the very reason
He wrote so charmingly. The simple fact is,
His preaching wasn't sanctioned by his practice.

'Tis, doubtless, well to be sometimes awake,—
    Awake to duty, and awake to truth,—
But when, alas! a nice review we take

Of our best deeds and days, we find, in sooth,
The hours that leave the slightest cause to weep
Are those we passed in childhood, or asleep!

'Tis beautiful to leave the world awhile
  For the soft visions of the gentle night;
And free, at last, from mortal care or guile,
  To live as only in the angels' sight,
In sleep's sweet realm so cozily shut in,
Where, at the worst, we only *dream* of sin!

So let us sleep and give the Maker praise.
  I like the lad who, when his father thought
To clip his morning nap by hackneyed phrase
  Of vagrant worm by early songster caught,
Cried, "Served him right!—it's not at all surprising;
The worm was punished, sir, for early rising!"

                              JOHN GODFREY SAXE

DAY THAT I HAVE LOVED

Tenderly, day that I have loved, I close your eyes,
  And smooth your quiet brow, and fold your thin dead hands.
The grey veils of the half-light deepen; colour dies.
  I bear you, a light burden, to the shrouded sands,

Where lies your waiting boat, by wreaths of the sea's making
  Mist-garlanded, with all grey weeds of the water crowned.
There you'll be laid, past fear of sleep or hope of waking;
  And over the unmoving sea, without a sound,

Faint hands will row you outward, out beyond our sight,
  Us with stretched arms and empty eyes on the far-gleaming
And marble sand . . .
    Beyond the shifting cold twilight,
  Further than laughter goes, or tears, further than dreaming,

There'll be no port, no dawn-lit islands! But the drear
  Waste darkening, and, at length, flame ultimate on the deep.
Oh, the last fire—and you, unkissed, unfriended there!
  Oh, the lone way's red ending, and we not there to weep!

(We found you pale and quiet, and strangely crowned with flowers,
  Lovely and secret as a child. You came with us,
Came happily, hand in hand with the young dancing hours,
  High on the downs at dawn!) Void now and tenebrous,

The grey sands curve before me . . .
    From the inland meadows,
  Fragrant of June and clover, floats the dark, and fills
The hollow sea's dead face with little creeping shadows,
  And the white silence brims the hollow of the hills.

Close in the nest is folded every weary wing,
  Hushed all the joyful voices; and we, who held you dear,
Eastward we turn, and homeward, alone, remembering . . .
  Day that I loved, day that I loved, the Night is here!

                                              RUPERT BROOKE

TO NIGHT

Swiftly walk o'er the western wave,
        Spirit of Night!
Out of the misty eastern cave
Where, all the long and lone daylight,
Thou wovest dreams of joy and fear,
Which make thee terrible and dear,
        Swift be thy flight!

Wrap thy form in a mantle gray,
        Star-inwrought!
Blind with thine hair the eyes of Day;
Kiss her until she be wearied out,
Then wander o'er city, and sea, and land,
Touching all with thine opiate wand—
        Come, long-sought!

When I arose and saw the dawn,
        I sighed for thee;
When light rode high, and the dew was gone,
And noon lay heavy on flower and tree,
And the weary Day turned to his rest,

Lingering like an unloved guest,
    I sighed for thee.

Thy brother Death came, and cried,
    "Would'st thou me?"
Thy sweet child Sleep, the filmy-eyed,
Murmured like a noontide bee,
  "Shall I nestle near thy side?
    Would'st thou me?"—And I replied,
      "No, not thee."

Death will come when thou art dead,
    Soon, too soon—
Sleep will come when thou art fled;
Of neither would I ask the boon
I ask of thee, beloved Night—
Swift be thine approaching flight,
    Come soon, soon!

                    PERCY BYSSHE SHELLEY

ACQUAINTED WITH THE NIGHT

I have been one acquainted with the night,
I have walked out in rain—and back in rain.
I have outwalked the furthest city light.

I have looked down the saddest city lane.
I have passed by the watchman on the beat
And dropped my eyes, unwilling to explain.

I have stood still and stopped the sound of feet
When far away an interrupted cry
Came over houses from another street.

But not to call me back or say good-bye;
And further still at an unearthly height,
One luminary clock against the sky

Proclaimed the time was neither wrong nor right
I have been one acquainted with the night.

                    ROBERT FROST

IT IS A BEAUTEOUS EVENING, CALM AND FREE

It is a beauteous evening, calm and free;
The holy time is quiet as a Nun
Breathless with adoration; the broad sun
Is sinking down in his tranquility;
The gentleness of heaven broods o'er the Sea;
Listen! the mighty Being is awake,
And doth with his eternal motion make
A sound like thunder—everlastingly.
Dear Child! dear Girl! that walkest with me here,
If thou appear untouched by solemn thought,
Thy nature is not therefore less divine:
Thou liest in Abraham's bosom all the year,
And worship'st at the Temple's inner shrine,
God being with thee when we know it not.

WILLIAM WORDSWORTH

TO THE EVENING STAR

Thou fair-hair'd angel of the evening,
Now, whilst the sun rests on the mountains, light
Thy bright torch of love; thy radiant crown
Put on, and smile upon our evening bed!
Smile on our loves, and, while thou drawest the
Blue curtains of the sky, scatter thy silver dew
On every flower that shuts its sweet eyes
In timely sleep. Let thy west wind sleep on
The lake; speak silence with thy glimmering eyes,
And wash the dusk with silver. Soon, full soon,
Dost thou withdraw; then the wolf rages wide,
And the lion glares thro' the dun forest:
The fleeces of our flocks are cover'd with
Thy sacred dew: protect them with thine influence.

WILLIAM BLAKE

NIGHT

The sun descending in the West,
The evening star does shine;
The birds are silent in their nest,
And I must seek for mine.
   The moon, like a flower
   In heaven's high bower,
   With silent delight
   Sits and smiles on the night.

Farewell, green fields and happy grove,
Where flocks have ta'en delight;
Where lambs have nibbled, silent move
The feet of angels bright:
   Unseen, they pour blessing,
   And joy without ceasing,
   On each bud and blossom,
   On each sleeping bosom.

They look in every thoughtless nest,
Where birds are covered warm;
They visit caves of every beast,
To keep them all from harm.
   If they see any weeping
   That should have been sleeping,
   They pour sleep on their head,
   And sit down by their bed.

When wolves and tigers howl for prey
They pitying stand and weep,
Seeking to drive their thirst away,
And keep them from the sheep.
   But, if they rush dreadful,
   The angels, most heedful,
   Receive each mild spirit
   New worlds to inherit.

And there the lion's ruddy eyes
Shall flow with tears of gold:
And pitying the tender cries,
And walking round the fold,
    Saying: "Wrath by His meekness,
    And by His health, sickness,
    Are driven away
    From our immortal day.

"And now beside thee, bleating lamb,
I can lie down and sleep.
Or think on Him who bore thy name,
Graze after thee, and weep.
    For, washed in life's river,
    My bright mane for ever
    Shall shine like the gold,
    As I guard o'er the fold."

WILLIAM BLAKE

WALKING AT NIGHT

My face is wet with rain
But my heart is warm to the core,
For I follow at will again
The road that I loved of yore,
And the dim trees beat the dark,
And the swelling ditches moan;
But my heart is a singing, soaring lark
I travel the road alone.

Alone in the living night
Away from the babble of tongues
Alone with the old delight
Of the night wind in my lungs,
And the wet air on my cheeks
And the warm blood in my veins
Alone with the joy he knows who seeks
The thresh of the young Spring rains,
With the smell of the pelted earth,
The tearful drip of the trees,

Making him dream of the sound of mirth
That comes with the clearing breeze.

'Tis a rare and wondrous sight
To walk in the wet a while,
And see the slow delight
Of the sun's first pallid smile,
And watch the meadows breathe again
And the far woods turn to green,
Drunk with the beauty of wind and rain
And the sun's warm smile between!

I have made me a vagrant song,
For my heart is warm to the core.
And I'm glad, Ah! glad that the night is long,
For I follow the road once more.
And the dim trees beat the dark,
And the swelling ditches moan;
With the joy of the singing, soaring lark
I travel the road, alone.

                                    AMARY HARE

XIV. Familiar and Varied Themes

HORSES AND MEN IN THE RAIN

Let us sit by the hissing steam radiator a winter's day, grey wind
    pattering frozen raindrops on the window,
And let us talk about milk wagon drivers and grocery delivery boys.

Let us keep our feet in wool slippers and mix hot punches—and
    talk about mail carriers and messenger boys slipping along the icy
    sidewalks.
Let us write of olden, golden days and hunters of the Holy Grail
    and men called 'knights' riding horses in the rain, in the cold
    frozen rain for ladies they loved.

A roustabout hunched on a coal wagon goes by, icicles drip on his
    hat rim, sheets of ice wrapping the hunks of coal, the caravanserai
    a grey blur in slant of rain.
Let us nudge the steam radiator with our wool slippers and write
    poems of Launcelot, the hero, and Roland, the hero, and all the
    olden golden men who rode horses in the rain.

                                      CARL SANDBURG

THREES

I was a boy when I heard three red words
a thousand Frenchmen died in the streets
for: Liberty, Equality, Fraternity—I asked
why men die for words.

I was older; men with moustaches, sideburns,
lilacs, told me the high golden words are:
Mother, Home, and Heaven—other older men with
face decorations said: God, Duty, Immortality—
they sang these threes slow from deep lungs.

Years ticked off their say-so on the great clocks
of doom and damnation, soup and nuts: meteors flashed

their say-so: and out of great Russia came three
dusky syllables workmen took guns and went out to die
for: Bread, Peace, Land.

And I met a marine of the U.S.A., a leatherneck
with a girl on his knee for a memory in ports circling
the earth and he said: Tell me how to say three things
and I always get by—gimme a plate of ham and eggs—
how much?—and—do you love me, kid?

CARL SANDBURG

THE ROAD TO VAGABONDIA

'E was sittin' on a door-step
  As I went strollin' by;
A lonely little beggar
  With a wistful 'omesick eye—
An' 'e weren't the kind you'd borrow,
  An' 'e weren't the kind you'd steal,
But I guessed 'is 'eart was breakin',
  So I w'istled 'im to 'eel.

They 'ad stoned 'im through the city streets, and naught the city
    cared,
But I was 'eadin' out'ard, and the roads are sweeter shared,
So I took 'im for a comrade, and I w'istled 'im away—
On the road to Vagabondia, that lies across the day!

Yellow dog 'e was; but bless you—
  'E was just the chap for me!
For I'd ruther 'ave an inch o' dog,
  Than miles o' pedigree.
So we stole away together,
  On the road that 'as no end,
With a new-coined day to fling away
  And all the stars to spend.

Oh, to walk the road at mornin', when the wind is blowin' clean,
And the yellow daisies fling their gold across a world o' green—
For the wind it 'eals the 'eartaches, an' the sun it dries the scars,
On the road to Vagabondia that lies beneath the stars.

'Twas the Wonder o' the Going
  Cast a spell about our feet—
An' we walked because the world was young,
  Because the way was sweet;
An' we slept in wild-rose meadows
  By the little wayside farms,
Till the Dawn came up the 'ighroad
  With the dead moon in 'er arms.

Oh, the Dawn it went before us through a shinin' lane o' skies,
And the Dream was at our 'eartstrings, an' the Light was in our eyes,
An' we made no boast o' glory an' we made no boast o' birth,
On the road to Vagabondia that lies across the earth!

DANA BURNET

TO A POST-OFFICE INKWELL

How many humble hearts have dipped
In you, and scrawled their manuscript!
Have shared their secrets, told their cares,
Their curious and quaint affairs!

Your pool of ink, your scratchy pen,
Have moved the lives of unborn men,
And watched young people, breathing hard,
Put Heaven on a postal card.

CHRISTOPHER MORLEY

OPPORTUNITY

Master of human destinies am I!
Fame, love, and fortune on my footsteps wait.
Cities and fields I walk; I penetrate
Deserts and seas remote, and passing by
Hovel and mart and palace—soon or late
I knock unbidden once at every gate!

If sleeping, wake—if feasting, rise before
I turn away. It is the hour of fate,
And they who follow me reach every state
Mortals desire, and conquer every foe

Save death; but those who doubt or hesitate,
Condemned to failure, penury, and woe,
Seek me in vain and uselessly implore.
I answer not, and I return no more!

JOHN JAMES INGALLS

INDIAN NAMES

Ye say, they all have passed away,
   That noble race and brave;
That their light canoes have vanished
   From off the crested wave;
That, 'mid the forests where they roamed,
   There rings no hunter's shout;
But their name is on your waters,
   Ye may not wash it out.

'Tis where Ontario's billow
   Like Ocean's surge is curled;
Where strong Niagara's thunders wake
   The echo of the world;
Where red Missouri bringeth
   Rich tribute from the West,
And Rappahannock sweetly sleeps
   On green Virginia's breast.

Ye say, their cone-like cabins,
   That clustered o'er the vale,
Have fled away, like withered leaves
   Before the Autumn gale;
But their memory liveth on your hills
   Their baptism on your shore,
Your everlasting rivers speak
   Their dialect of yore.

Old Massachusetts wears it
  Within her lordly crown,
And broad Ohio bears it
  Amid his young renown;
Connecticut hath wreathed it
  Where her quiet foliage waves,
And bold Kentucky breathes it hoarse
  Through all her ancient caves.

Wachuset hides its lingering voice
  Within its rocky heart.
And Alleghany graves its tone
  Throughout his lofty chart;
Monadnock, on his forehead hoar,
  Doth seal the sacred trust;
Your mountains build their monument,
  Though ye destroy their dust.

LYDIA HUNTLY SIGOURNEY

DOWN THE GLIMMERING STAIRCASE

(from *Vigils*)

Down the glimmering staircase, past the pensive clock,
Childhood creeps on tiptoe, fumbles at the lock
Out of night escaping, toward the arch of dawn,
What can childhood look for, over the wet lawn?

Standing in the strangeness of that garden air,
Ignorant adventure finds world wonder there:
Miles are more than distance when the cocks are crowing
And along the valley night's last goods-train going
Tells of earth untravelled and what lies beyond
Catching roach and gudgeon in the orchard pond.

SIEGFRIED SASSOON

A GOOD THANKSGIVING

Said Old Gentleman Gay, "On a Thanksgiving Day,
If you want a good time, then give something away."
So he sent a fat turkey to Shoemaker Price,
And the shoemaker said, "What a big bird! How nice!
And, since such a good dinner's before me, I ought
To give poor Widow Lee the small chicken I bought."

"This fine chicken, O see!" said the pleased Widow Lee,
"And the kindness that sent it, how precious to me!
I would like to make someone as happy as I—
I'll give Washerwoman Biddy my big pumpkin pie."
"And, O sure!" Biddy said, " 'tis the queen of all pies!
Just to look at its yellow face gladdens my eyes!
Now it's *my* turn, I think; and a sweet ginger-cake
For the motherless Finigan children I'll bake."

"A sweet-cake all our own! 'Tis too good to be true!"
Said the Finigan children, Rose, Denny and Hugh;
"It smells sweet of spice, and we'll carry a slice
To poor little lame Jake—who has nothing that's nice."
"O, I thank you, and thank you!" said little lame Jake:
"O what a bootiful, bootiful, bootiful cake!
And O, such a big slice! I will save all the crumbs,
And will give 'em to each little Sparrow that comes!"

And the sparrows, they twittered, as if they would say,
Like Old Gentleman Gay, "On a Thanksgiving Day,
If you want a good time, then give something away!"
ANNIE DOUGLAS GREEN ROBINSON

ON BEING A WOMAN

Why is it, when I am in Rome
I'd give an eye to be at home,
But when on native earth I be,
My soul is sick for Italy?

And why with you, my love, my lord,
Am I spectacularly bored,
Yet do you up and leave me—then
I scream to have you back again?

DOROTHY PARKER

MIS' SMITH

All day she hurried to get through
The same as lots of wimmin do;
Sometimes at night her husban' said,
"Ma, ain't you goin' to come to bed?"
And then she'd kinder give a hitch,
And pause half-way between a stitch,
And sorter sigh, and say that she
    Was ready as she'd ever be,
      She reckoned.

And so the years went one by one,
An' somehow she was never done;
An' when the angel said, as how
"Mis' Smith, it's time you rested now,"
She sorter raised her eyes to look
A second, as a stitch she took;
"All right, I'm comin' now," says she,
    "I'm ready as I'll ever be,
      I reckon."

ALBERT BIGELOW PAINE

THE LADIES' AID

We've put a fine addition on the good old church at home.
It's just the latest kilter, with a gallery and dome,
It seats a thousand people—finest church in all the town,
And when 'twas dedicated, why we planked ten thousand down;
That is, we paid five thousand—every deacon did his best—
And the Ladies' Aid Society, it promised all the rest.

We've got an organ in the church—very finest in the land,
It's got a thousand pipes or more, its melody is grand,
And when we sit on cushioned pews and hear the master play,

It carries us to realms of bliss unnumbered miles away,
It cost a cool three thousand, and it's stood the hardest test;
We'll pay a thousand on it—the Ladies' Aid the rest.

They'll give a hundred sociables, cantatas, too, and teas;
They'll bake a thousand angel cakes, and tons of cream they'll freeze
They'll beg and scrape and toil and sweat for seven years or more,
And then they'll start all o'er again, for a carpet for the floor.
No, it isn't just like digging out the money from your vest
When the Ladies' Aid gets busy and says: "We'll do the rest."

Of course we're proud of our big church from pulpit to spire;
It is the darling of our hearts, the crown of our desire,
But when I see the sisters work to raise the cash that lacks,
I somehow feel the church is built on women's tired backs.
And sometimes I can't help thinking when we reach the regions
    blest,
That men will get the toil and sweat, and the Ladies' Aid the Rest.

                                                    UNKNOWN

THE HEART OF A WOMAN

The heart of a woman goes forth with the dawn,
As a lone bird, soft winging, so restlessly on,
Afar o'er life's turrets and vales does it roam
In the wake of those echoes the heart calls home.

The heart of a woman falls back with the night,
And enters some alien cage in its plight,
And tries to forget it has dreamed of the stars,
While it breaks, breaks, breaks on the sheltering bars.

                              GEORGIA DOUGLAS JOHNSON

'A MAN'S WOMAN

I shall be capricious, I shall have a whim,
I shall build a tower of jade, and gaze far down at him—
A tower of green and gleaming jade within a misty field.
I shall be mysterious, with mystery for shield.
I shall never give to him, I'll make him give to me
All the hard-to-capture things of earth and sky and sea.

I was swift to do for him in every sort of way,
Thinking of his comfort, forgetting self each day;
I was loyal, faithful, devoted, kind and true
That is why I bored him—if women only knew!

I shall be capricious, I shall have a whim.
And neither earth nor sea nor sky shall rob me then of him.
MARY CAROLYN DAVIES

FIRST FIG

My candle burns at both ends;
    It will not last the night;
But, ah, my foes, and, oh, my friends—
    It gives a lovely light!
EDNA ST. VINCENT MILLAY

WHEN THE MINT IS IN THE LIQUOR

When the mint is in the liquor and its fragrance on the glass
It breathes a recollection that can never, never pass—
When the South was in the glory of a never-ending June,
The strings were on the banjo and the fiddle was in tune,
And we reveled in the plenty that we thought could never pass
And lingered at the julep in the ever-brimming glass.

There was mettle in the morning and adventure in the chase,
And Beauty sat the saddle with the poetry of grace;
And the singing of the darkies in the cotton and the corn
Was chorused with the echo of the old familiar horn.
There was splendor in the glamor of the canopy at noon,
And sweetness in the languor of the lazy afternoon,
And the breezes of the evening were the breathings of romance
That quickened into whispers in the rapture of the dance,
While the banjo in the cabin and the fiddle in the hall
With music filled the measure of the night's ecstatic thrall.

Oh, the beauty of the Southland in the splendor of its prime,
The fragrance and the plenty of a radiant summer time,

When we reveled in the glory that we thought could never pass,
And lingered at the julep in the ever-brimming glass.

CLARENCE OUSLEY

THE THREE FISHERS

Three fishers went sailing away to the West,
   Away to the West as the sun went down;
Each thought on the woman who loved him the best,
   And the children stood watching them out of the town;
For men must work, and women must weep,
And there's little to earn, and many to keep,
   Though the harbor bar be moaning.

Three wives sat up in the lighthouse tower
   And they trimmed the lamps as the sun went down;
They looked at the squall, and they looked at the shower,
   And the night-rack came rolling up ragged and brown.
But men must work, and women must weep,
Though storms be sudden, and waters deep,
   And the harbor bar be moaning.

Three corpses lay out on the shining sands
   In the morning gleam as the tide went down,
And the women are weeping and wringing their hands
   For those who will never come home to the town;
For men must work, and women must weep,
And the sooner it's over, the sooner to sleep;
   And good-bye to the bar and its moaning.

CHARLES KINGSLEY

WORDS

Boys flying kites haul in their white-winged birds,
You can't do that when you're flying words.
"Careful with fire," is good advice, we know,
"Careful with words," is ten times doubly so.
Thoughts unexpressed may sometimes fall back dead,
But God himself can't kill them when they're said!

UNKNOWN

OUT FISHIN'

A feller isn't thinkin' mean,
    Out fishin';
His thoughts are mostly good an' clean,
    Out fishin'.
He doesn't knock his fellow men,
Or harbor any grudges then;
A feller's at his finest when
    Out fishin'.

The rich are comrades to the poor,
    Out fishin';
All brothers of a common lure
    Out fishin'.
The urchin with the pin an' string
Can chum with millionaire and king;
Vain pride is a forgotten thing,
    Out fishin'.

A feller gits a chance to dream,
    Out fishin',
He learns the beauties of a stream,
    Out fishin';
An' he can wash his soul in air
That isn't foul with selfish care,
An' relish plain and simple fare,
    Out fishin'.

A feller has no time for hate,
    Out fishin';
He isn't eager to be great,
    Out fishin'.
He isn't thinkin' thoughts of pelf,
Or goods stacked high upon a shelf,
But he is always just himself,
    Out fishin'.

A feller's glad to be a friend,
    Out fishin';
A helpin' hand he'll always lend,
    Out fishin'.
The brotherhood of rod an' line
An' sky and stream is always fine;
Men come real close to God's design,
    Out fishin'.

A feller isn't plotting schemes,
    Out fishin';
He's only busy with his dreams,
    Out fishin'.
His livery is a coat of tan,
His creed—to do the best he can;
A feller's always mostly man,
    Out fishin'.   EDGAR A. GUEST

A NET TO SNARE THE MOONLIGHT

(*What the Man of Faith Said*)

The dew, the rain and moonlight
All prove our Father's mind.
The dew, the rain and moonlight
Descend to bless mankind.

Come, let us see that all men
Have land to catch the rain,
Have grass to snare the spheres of dew,
And fields spread for the grain.

Yea, we would give to each poor man
Ripe wheat and poppies red,—
A peaceful place at evening
With the stars just overhead:

A net to snare the moonlight,
A sod spread to the sun,
A place of toil by daytime,
Of dreams when toil is done.

VACHEL LINDSAY

THE GOLF LINKS LIE SO NEAR THE MILL

The golf links lie so near the mill
That almost every day
The laboring children can look out
And see the men at play.
SARAH N. CLEGHORN

THE FORGOTTEN MAN

Not on our golden fortunes builded high—
Not on our boasts that soar into the sky—
Not upon these is resting in this hour
The fate of the future; but upon the power
Of him who is forgotten—yes, on him
Rest all our hopes reaching from rim to rim.
In him we see all of earth's toiling bands,
With crooked backs, scarred faces, shattered hands.

He seeks no office and he asks no praise
For all the patient labor of his days.
He is the one supporting the huge weight;
He is the one guarding the country's gate.
He bears the burdens of these earthly ways:
We pile the debts, he is the one who pays.
He is the one who holds the solid power
To steady nations in their trembling hour.
Behold him as he silently goes by.
For it is at his word that nations die.

Shattered with loss and lack,
He is the one who holds upon his back
The continent and all its mighty loads—
This toiler makes possible the roads
On which the gilded thousands travel free—
Makes possible our feasts, our roaring boards,
Our pomps, our easy days, our golden hoards.
He gives stability to nations:
He makes possible our nation, sea to sea.

His strength makes possible our college walls—
Makes possible our legislative halls—
Makes possible our churches soaring high
With spires, the fingers pointing to the sky.

Shall then this man go hungry, here in lands
Blest by his honor, builded by his hands?
Do something for him: let him never be
Forgotten: let him have his daily bread:
He who has fed us, let him now be fed.
Let us remember all his tragic lot—
Remember, or else be ourselves forgot!
All honor to the one that in this hour
Cries to the world as from a lighted tower—
Cries for the Man Forgotten. Honor the one
Who asks for him a glad place in the sun.
He is a voice for the voiceless. Now, indeed,
We have a tongue that cries the mortal need.

                                        EDWIN MARKHAM

THE MAN FROM THE CROWD

Men seem as alike as the leaves on the trees,
As alike as the bees in a swarming of bees;
And we look at the millions that make up the state
All equally little and equally great,
      And the pride of our courage is cowed.
Then Fate calls for a man who is larger than men—
There's a surge in the crowd—there's a movement—and then
There arises a man that is larger than men—
      And the man comes up from the crowd.

The chasers of trifles run hither and yon,
And the little small days of small things go on,
And the world seems no better at sunset than dawn,
And the race still increases its plentiful spawn.
      And the voice of our wailing is loud.
Then the Great Deed calls out for the Great Men to come,
And the Crowd, unbelieving, sits sullen and dumb—
But the Great Deed is done, for the Great Man is come—
      Aye, the man comes up from the crowd.

There's a dead hum of voices, all say the same thing,
And our forefathers' songs are the songs that we sing,
And the deeds by our fathers and grandfathers done
Are done by the son of the son of the son,
    And our heads in contrition are bowed.
Lo, a call for a man who shall make all things new
Goes down through the throng! See! he rises in view!
Make room for the men who shall make all things new!—
    For the man who comes up from the crowd.

And where is the man who comes up from the throng
Who does the new deed and who sings the new song,
And makes the old world as a world that is new?
And who is the man? It is you! It is you!
    And our praise is exultant and proud.
We are waiting for you there—for you are the man!
Come up from the jostle as soon as you can;
Come up from the crowd there, for you are the man—
    The man who comes up from the crowd.

SAM WALTER FOSS

TO LABOR

Shall you complain who feed the world?
    Who clothe the world?
    Who house the world?
Shall you complain who are the world,
  Of what the world may do?
    As from this hour
    You use your power,
  The world must follow you!

The world's life hangs on your right hand!
    Your wrong right hand!
    Your skilled right hand!
You hold the whole world in your hand.
  See to it what you do!
    Or dark or light,
    Or strong or right,
  The world is made by you!

Then rise as you never rose before!
Nor hoped before!
Nor dared before!
And show as was never shown before,
The power that lies in you!
Stand all as one!
See justice done!
Believe, and Dare, and Do!
CHARLOTTE PERKINS STETSON GILMAN

HERE IS A TOAST THAT I WANT TO DRINK

Here is a toast that I want to drink
To a fellow I'll never know,
To the fellow who's going to take my place
When it's time for me to go,
I've wondered what kind of a chap he'll be
And I've wished I could take his hand,
Just to whisper, "I wish you well, Old Man,"
In a way that he'd understand.
I'd like to give him the cheering word
That I've longed at times to hear;
I'd like to give him the warm hand clasp
When never a friend seemed near.
I've earned my knowledge by sheer hard work
And I wish I could pass it on
To the fellow who'll come and take my place
Someday when I am gone.

Will he see the sad mistakes I've made
And note the battles lost?
Will he ever guess the tears they caused,
Or the headaches which they cost?
Will he gaze through failure and fruitless toil
To the underlying plan,
And catch a glimpse of the real interest,
And the heart of the vanished man?
I dare to hope he may pause someday,
As he toils where I have wrought;
And gain some strength for his weary task
From the battles which I have fought.

But I've only the task itself to leave
With the cares for him to face.
And never a cheering word may speak
To the fellow who'll take my place.

Then here's to your health, Old Chap, I drink
As a bridegroom to his bride;
I leave an unfinished task for you,
But God knows I have tried.
I've dreamed my dreams, as all men do;
Some of those dreams came true,
And my prayer today is that all these dreams
May be realized by you.
And we'll meet someday, in the Great Unknown,
Out of the realm of space.
You'll know my clasp, as I take your hand
And gaze in your tired face.
Then all our hopes will be realized
In the light of the new dawn,
So I'm drinking your health, and success, Old Chap,
Who takes my place when I'm gone.

DR. WALTER LATHROP

HOWDY, HONEY, HOWDY!

Do' a-stan'in' on a jar, fiah a-shinin' thoo,
Ol' folks drowsin' 'roun' de place, wide awake is Lou,
W'en I tap, she answeh, an' I see huh 'mence to grin,
"Howdy, honey, howdy, won't you step right in?"

Den I step erpon de log layin' at de do',
Bless de Lawd, huh mammy an' huh pap's done 'menced to sno',
Now's de time, ef evah, ef I's gwine to try an' win,
"Howdy, honey, howdy, won't you step right in?"

No use playin' on de aidge, trimblin' on de brink,
W'en a body love a gal, tell huh what he t'ink;
W'en huh hea't is open fu' de love you gwine to gin,
Pull yo'se'f togethah, suh, an' step right in.

Sweetes' imbitation dat a body evah hyeahed,
Sweetah den de music of a love-sick mockin' bird,
Comin' f'om de gal you loves bettah den yo' kin,
"Howdy, honey, howdy, won't you step right in?"

At de gate o' heaven w'en de storm o' life is pas',
'Spec' I'll be a-stan'in', 'twell de Mastah say at las',
"Hyeah he stan' all weary, but he winned his fight wid sin.
Howdy, honey, howdy, won't you step right in?"

PAUL LAURENCE DUNBAR

THE OLD CABIN

In de dead of night I sometimes
    Git to t'inkin' of de pas',
An' de days w'en slavery helt me
    In my mis'ry—ha'd an' fas'.
Dough de time was mighty tryin',
    In dese houahs somehow hit seem
Dat a brightah light come slippin'
    Thoo de kivahs of my dream.

An' my min' fu'gits de whuppins,
    Draps de feah o' block an' lash,
An' flies straight to somep'n' joyful
    In a secon's lightnin' flash.
Den hit seems I see a vision
    Of a dearah long ago
Of de childern tumblin' roun' me
    By my rough ol' cabin do'.

Talk about yo' go'geous mansions
    An' yo' big house great an' gran',
Des bring up de fines' palace
    Dat you know in all de lan'.
But dey's somep'n' dearah to me,
    Somep'n' faihah to my eyes
In dat cabin, less you bring me
    To you' mansion in de skies.

I kin see de light a-shinin'
    Thoo de chinks atween de logs,
I kin hyeah de way-off bayin'
    Of my mastah's huntin' dogs,
An' de neighin' of de hosses
    Stampin' on de ol' bahn flo',
But above dese soun's de laughin'
    At my deah ol' cabin do'.

We would gethah daih at evenin',
    All my frien's 'ud come erroun'
An' hit wan't no time, twell, bless you,
    You could hyeah de banjo's soun'.
You could see de dahkies dancin'
    Pigeon wing an' heel an' toe—
Joyous times I tell you people
    Roun' dat same ol' cabin do'.

But at times my t'oughts gits saddah,
    Ez I riccolec' de folks,
An' dey frolickin' an' talkin'
    Wid de laughin' an' dey jokes.
An' hit hu'ts me w'en I membahs
    Dat I'll nevah see no mo'
Dem ah faces gethered smilin'
    Roun' dat po' ol' cabin do'.

            PAUL LAURENCE DUNBAR

ACCOUNTABILITY

Folks ain't got no right to censuah othah folks about dey habits;
Him dat giv' de squir'ls de bushtails made de bobtails fu' de rabbits.
Him dat built de gread big mountains hollered out de little valleys,
Him dat made de streets an' driveways wasn't shamed to make de
    alleys.

We is all constructed diff'ent, d'ain't no two of us de same;
We cain't he'p ouah likes an' dislikes, ef we'se bad we ain't to blame.
Ef we'se good, we needn't show off, case you bet it ain't ouah doin'
We gits into su'ttain channels dat we jes' cain't he'p pu'suin'.

Poems That Live Forever

But we all fits into places dat no othah ones could fill,
An' we does the things we has to, big er little, good er ill.
John cain't tek de place o' Henry, Su an' Sally ain't alike;
Bass ain't nuthin' like a suckah, chub ain't nuthin' like a pike.

When you come to think about it, how it's all planned out it's
    splendid.
Nothin's done er evah happens, 'doubt hit's somefin' dat's in-
    tended;
Don't keer whut you does, you has to, an' hit sholy beats de
    dickens,—
Viney, go put on de kittle, I got one o' mastah's chickens.

PAUL LAURENCE DUNBAR

CROSS

My old man's a white old man
And my old mother's black.
If ever I cursed my white old man
I take my curses back.

If ever I cursed my black old mother
And wished she were in hell,
I'm sorry for that evil wish
And now I wish her well.

My old man died in a fine big house
My ma died in a shack.
I wonder where I'm gonna die,
Being neither white or black?

LANGSTON HUGHES

TIRED

I am tired of work; I am tired of building up somebody else's civiliza-
    tion.
Let us take a rest, M'Lissy Jane.
I will go down to the Last Chance Saloon, drink a gallon or two of
    gin, shoot a game or two of dice and sleep the rest of the night
    on one of Mike's barrels.

You will let the old shanty go to rot, the white people's clothes turn to dust, and the Calvary Baptist Church sink to the bottomless pit.

You will spend your days forgetting you married me and your nights hunting the warm gin Mike serves the ladies in the rear of the Last Chance Saloon.

Throw the children into the river; civilization has given us too many. It is better to die than to grow up and find that you are colored.

Pluck the stars out of the heavens. The stars mark our destiny. The stars marked my destiny.

I am tired of civilization.

FENTON JOHNSON

BEYOND THE CHAGRES

Beyond the Chagres River
    Are paths that lead to death—
To the fever's deadly breezes,
    To malaria's poisonous breath!
Beyond the tropic foliage,
    Where the alligator waits,
Are the mansions of the Devil—
    His original estates!

Beyond the Chagres River
    Are paths fore'er unknown,
With a spider 'neath each pebble,
    A scorpion 'neath each stone.
'Tis here the boa-constrictor
    His fatal banquet holds,
And to his slimy bosom
    His hapless guest enfolds!

Beyond the Chagres River
    Lurks the cougar in his lair,
And ten hundred thousand dangers
    Hide in the noxious air.
Behind the trembling leaflets
    Beneath the fallen reeds,
Are ever-present perils
    Of a million different breeds!

Beyond the Chagres River
  'Tis said—the story's old—
Are paths that lead to mountains
  Of purest virgin gold!
But 'tis my firm conviction
  Whatever tales they tell,
That beyond the Chagres River
  All paths lead straight to hell!

JAMES STANLEY GILBERT

GROWING SMILES

A smile is quite a funny thing,
It wrinkles up your face,
And when it's gone, you never find
Its secret hiding place.

But far more wonderful it is
To see what smiles can do;
You smile at one, he smiles at you,
And so one smile makes two.

He smiles at someone since you smiled,
And then that one smiles back;
And that one smiles, until in truth
You fail in keeping track.

Now since a smile can do great good
By cheering hearts of care,
Let's smile and smile, and not forget
That smiles go everywhere!

UNKNOWN

ZEPHYR

(*Fable No. 15*)

Once a Kansas zephyr strayed
Where a brass-eyed bird pup played,
And that foolish canine bayed
  At that zephyr, in a gay,

Semi-idiotic way.
Then that zephyr, in about
Half a jiffy, took that pup,
Tipped him over, wrong side up;
Then it turned him wrong side out.
And it calmly journeyed thence,
With a barn and string of fence.

MORAL

When communities turn loose
Social forces that produce
    The disorders of a gale,
And upon the well-known law:
Face the breeze, but close your jaw.
    It's a rule that will not fail:
If you bay it, in a gay,
Self-sufficient sort of way,
    It will land you, without doubt,
    Upside down and wrong side out.
        EUGENE FITCH WARE

THE DESTRUCTION OF SENNACHERIB

(710 B.C.)

The Assyrian came down like the wolf on the fold,
And his cohorts were gleaming in purple and gold;
And the sheen of their spears was like stars on the sea,
When the blue wave rolls nightly on deep Galilee.

Like the leaves of the forest when Summer is green,
That host with their banners at sunset were seen:
Like the leaves of the forest when Autumn hath blown,
That host on the morrow lay withered and strown.

For the Angel of Death spread his wings on the blast,
And breathed in the face of the foe as he passed;
And the eyes of the sleepers waxed deadly and chill,
And their hearts but once heaved, and for ever grew still!

And there lay the steed with his nostril all wide,
But through it there rolled not the breath of his pride:
And the foam of his gasping lay white on the turf,
And cold as the spray of the rock-beating surf.

And there lay the rider distorted and pale,
With the dew on his brow, and the rust on his mail;
And the tents were all silent, the banners alone,
The lances unlifted, the trumpet unblown.

And the widows of Ashur are loud in their wail,
And the idols are broke in the temple of Baal;
And the might of the Gentile, unsmote by the sword,
Hath melted like snow in the glance of the Lord!

GEORGE GORDON BYRON

FOR I DIPPED INTO THE FUTURE

(from *Locksley Hall*)

For I dipped into the future, far as human eye could see,
Saw the Vision of the world, and all the wonder that would be;

Saw the heavens fill with commerce, argosies of magic sails,
Pilots of the purple twilight, dropping down with costly bales;

Heard the heavens fill with shouting, and there rained a ghastly dew
From the nations' airy navies grappling in the central blue;

Far along the world-wide whisper of the south-wind rushing warm,
With the standards of the peoples plunging through the thunder-
storm;

Till the war-drum throbbed no longer, and the battle-flags were furled
In the Parliament of man, the Federation of the world.

ALFRED TENNYSON

THE ODYSSEY

As one that for a weary space has lain
   Lulled by the song of Circe and her wine
   In gardens near the pale of Proserpine,
Where that Ææan isle forgets the main,
And only the low lutes of love complain,
    And only shadows of wan lovers pine,
    As such an one were glad to know the brine
Salt on his lips, and the large air again,—
So gladly, from the songs of modern speech
    Men turn, and see the stars, and feel the free
      Shrill wind beyond the close of heavy flowers,
      And through the music of the languid hours,
They hear like ocean on a western beach
    The surge and thunder of the Odyssey.

ANDREW LANG

THE BELLS

I

Hear the sledges with the bells,
    Silver bells!
What a world of merriment their melody foretells!
How they tinkle, tinkle, tinkle,
   In the icy air of night!
While the stars that oversprinkle
All the heavens seem to twinkle
    With a crystalline delight;
   Keeping time, time, time,
   In a sort of Runic rhyme,
To the tintinabulation that so musically wells
   From the bells, bells, bells, bells,
    Bells, bells, bells—
From the jingling and the tinkling of the bells.

II

Hear the mellow wedding bells,
    Golden bells!
What a world of happiness their harmony foretells!
  Through the balmy air of night
  How they ring out their delight!
  From the molten-golden notes,
    And all in tune,
  What a liquid ditty floats
To the turtle-dove that listens, while she gloats
    On the moon!
  Oh, from out the sounding cells,
What a gush of euphony voluminously wells!
    How it swells!
    How it dwells
  On the future; how it tells
  Of the rapture that impels
To the swinging and the ringing
  Of the bells, bells, bells,
  Of the bells, bells, bells, bells,
    Bells, bells, bells—
To the rhyming and the chiming of the bells!

III

Hear the loud alarum bells—
    Brazen bells!
What a tale of terror, now, their turbulency tells
  In the startled ear of night
  How they scream out their affright!
    Too much horrified to speak,
    They can only shriek, shriek,
      Out of tune,
In a clamorous appealing to the mercy of the fire,
In a mad expostulation with the deaf and frantic fire.
  Leaping higher, higher, higher,
  With a desperate desire,
    And a resolute endeavor
    Now, now to sit, or never,

By the side of the pale-faced moon.
  Oh, the bells, bells, bells!
  What a tale their terror tells
    Of despair!
How they clang, and clash, and roar!
What a horror they outpour
On the bosom of the palpitating air!
  Yet the ear it fully knows,
    By the twanging,
    And the clanging,
  How the danger ebbs and flows;
  Yet the ear distinctly tells,
    In the jangling,
    And the wrangling,
  How the danger sinks and swells,
By the sinking or the swelling in the anger of the bells;
    Of the bells—
Of the bells, bells, bells, bells,
    Bells, bells, bells—
In the clamor and the clangor of the bells!

                    IV

  Hear the tolling of the bells,
      Iron bells!
What a world of solemn thought their melody compels!
    In the silence of the night,
    How we shiver with affright
At the melancholy menace of their tone!
    For every sound that floats
    From the rust within their throats,
      Is a groan.
  And the people—ah, the people,
  They that dwell up in the steeple,
      All alone.
  And who tolling, tolling, tolling,
    In that muffled monotone,
  Feel a glory in so rolling
    On the human heart a stone—
They are neither man nor woman,
They are neither brute nor human,
      They are ghouls:

And their king it is who tolls;
And he rolls, rolls, rolls,
    Rolls
A paean from the bells!
And his merry bosom swells
With the paean of the bells!
And he dances, and he yells;
  Keeping time, time, time,
  In a sort of Runic rhyme,
To the paean of the bells,
    Of the bells;
  Keeping time, time, time,
  In a sort of Runic rhyme,
To the throbbing of the bells;
Of the bells, bells, bells—
To the sobbing of the bells;
  Keeping time, time, time,
As he knells, knells, knells,
In a happy Runic rhyme,
To the rolling of the bells;
Of the bells, bells, bells—
To the tolling of the bells,
Of the bells, bells, bells, bells,
    Bells, bells, bells—
To the moaning and the groaning of the bells.

EDGAR ALLAN POE

OZYMANDIAS

I met a traveler from an antique land
Who said: Two vast and trunkless legs of stone
Stand in the desert. Near them, on the sand,
Half sunk, a shattered visage lies, whose frown
And wrinkled lip and sneer of cold command
Tell that its sculptor well those passions read
Which yet survive, stamped on these lifeless things,
The hand that mocked them and the heart that fed;
And on the pedestal these words appear:
"My name is Ozymandias, king of kings:
Look on my works, ye Mighty, and despair!"

Nothing beside remains. Round the decay
Of that colossal wreck, boundless and bare,
The lone and level sands stretch far away.

PERCY BYSSHE SHELLEY

BIRCHES

When I see birches bend to left and right
Across the lines of straighter darker trees,
I like to think some boy's been swinging them.
But swinging doesn't bend them down to stay.
Ice-storms do that. Often you must have seen them
Loaded with ice a sunny winter morning
After a rain. They click upon themselves
As the breeze rises, and turn many-colored
As the stir cracks and crazes their enamel.
Soon the sun's warmth makes them shed crystal shells
Shattering and avalanching on the snow-crust—
Such heaps of broken glass to sweep away
You'd think the inner dome of heaven had fallen.
They are dragged to the withered bracken by the load,
And they seem not to break; though once they are bowed
So low for long, they never right themselves:
You may see their trunks arching in the woods
Years afterwards, trailing their leaves on the ground
Like girls on hands and knees that throw their hair
Before them over their heads to dry in the sun.
But I was going to say when Truth broke in
With all her matter-of-fact about the ice-storm
I should prefer to have some boy bend them
As he went out and in to fetch the cows—
Some boy too far from town to learn baseball,
Whose only play was what he found himself,
Summer or winter, and could play alone.
One by one he subdued his father's trees
By riding them down over and over again
Until he took the stiffness out of them,
And not one but hung limp, not one was left
For him to conquer. He learned all there was
To learn about not launching out too soon
And so not carrying the tree away

Clear to the ground. He always kept his poise
To the top branches, climbing carefully
With the same pains you use to fill a cup
Up to the brim, and even above the brim.
Then he flung outward, feet first, with a swish,
Kicking his way down through the air to the ground.
So was I once myself a swinger of birches.
And so I dream of going back to be.
It's when I'm weary of considerations,
And life is too much like a pathless wood
Where your face burns and tickles with the cobwebs
Broken across it, and one eye is weeping
From a twig's having lashed across it open.
I'd like to get away from earth awhile
And then come back to it and begin over.
May no fate willfully misunderstand me
And half grant what I wish and snatch me away
Not to return. Earth's the right place for love:
I don't know where it's likely to go better.
I'd like to go by climbing a birch tree,
And climb black branches up a snow-white trunk
Toward heaven, till the tree could bear no more,
But dipped its top and set me down again.
That would be good both going and coming back.
One could do worse than be a swinger of birches.

ROBERT FROST

LOSE THIS DAY LOITERING

(from *Faust*)

Lose this day loitering—'twill be the same story
To-morrow—and the next more dilatory;
Each indecision brings its own delays,
And days are lost lamenting o'er lost days.
Are you in earnest? seize this very minute—
Boldness has genius, power and magic in it.
Only engage, and then the mind grows heated—
Begin it, and then the work will be completed!

JOHANN WOLFGANG VON GOETHE, *as translated by John Anster*

WORK: A SONG OF TRIUMPH

Work!
Thank God for the might of it,
The ardor, the urge, the delight of it—
Work that springs from the heart's desire,
Setting the brain and the soul on fire—
Oh, what is so good as the heat of it,
And what is so glad as the beat of it,
And what is so kind as the stern command,
Challenging brain and heart and hand?

Work!
Thank God for the pride of it,
For the beautiful, conquering tide of it.
Sweeping the life in its furious flood,
Thrilling the arteries, cleansing the blood,
Mastering stupor and dull despair,
Moving the dreamer to do and dare.
Oh, what is so good as the urge of it,
And what is so glad as the surge of it,
And what is so strong as the summons deep,
Rousing the torpid soul from sleep?

Work!
Thank God for the pace of it,
For the terrible, keen, swift race of it;
Fiery steeds in full control,
Nostrils a-quiver to meet the goal.
Work, the Power that drives behind,
Guiding the purposes, taming the mind,
Holding the runaway wishes back,
Reining the will to one steady track,
Speeding the energies faster, faster,
Triumphing over disaster.
Oh, what is so good as the pain of it,
And what is so great as the gain of it?
And what is so kind as the cruel goad,
Forcing us on through the rugged road?

Work!
Thank God for the swing of it,
For the clamoring, hammering ring of it,
Passion of labor daily hurled
On the mighty anvils of the world.
Oh, what is so fierce as the flame of it?
And what is so huge as the aim of it?
Thundering on through dearth and doubt,
Calling the plan of the Maker out.
Work, the Titan; Work, the friend,
Shaping the earth to a glorious end,
Draining the swamps and blasting the hills,
Doing whatever the Spirit wills—
Rending a continent apart,
To answer the dreams of the Master heart.
Thank God for a world where none may shirk—
Thank God for the splendor of work!

ANGELA MORGAN

SEA FEVER

I must go down to the seas again, to the lonely sea and the sky,
And all I ask is a tall ship and a star to steer her by;
And the wheel's kick and the wind's song and the white sail's shaking,
And a gray mist on the sea's face, and a gray dawn breaking.

I must go down to the seas again, for the call of the running tide
Is a wild call and a clear call that may not be denied;
And all I ask is a windy day with the white clouds flying,
And the flung spray and the blown spume, and the sea-gulls crying.

I must go down to the seas again, to the vagrant gipsy life,
To the gull's way and the whale's way where the wind's like a whetted
     knife;
And all I ask is a merry yarn from a laughing fellow-rover,
And quiet sleep and a sweet dream when the long trick's over.

JOHN MASEFIELD

INDEX OF AUTHORS AND TITLES

INDEX OF FIRST LINES

Index

INDEX OF TITLES